The Hebrew Scriptures
Called by the Father

Second Edition

Mary Kathleen Glavich, S.N.D.
Loretta Pastva, S.N.D.

General Editor: Loretta Pastva, S.N.D.

*Then God said: "Let there be light," and there was light.
God saw how good the light was. God then separated the
light from the darkness.*
—Genesis 1:3-4

Benziger Publishing Company
Woodland Hills, California

Consultant
The Reverend Ronald A. Pachence, Ph.D.
Associate Professor Practical Theology
Director, Institute for Christian
Ministries, University of San Diego.

Nihil Obstat
The Reverend Paul J. Sciarrotta, S.T.L.
Censor Deputatis

Imprimatur
The Most Reverend Anthony M. Pilla, D.D.,
M.A.
Bishop of Cleveland
Given at Cleveland, Ohio, on 9 July 1991

The Nihil Obstat and Imprimatur are official declarations that a book or pamphlet is free of doctrinal or moral error. No implication is contained therein that those who have granted the Nihil Obstat and Imprimatur agree with the contents, opinions, or statements expressed.

Scripture passages are taken from The New American Bible with Revised New Testament, copyright © 1988 by the Confraternity of Christian Doctrine, Washington, D.C. All rights reserved.

Revision Editor
Catherine Murphy, Ph.D. (candidate)

Printed in the United States of America.

Send all inquiries to:
BENZIGER PUBLISHING COMPANY
21600 Oxnard Street, Suite 500
Woodland Hills, California 91367

Second Edition

ISBN 0-02-655831-9 (Student's Edition)
ISBN 0-02-655832-7 (Teacher's Annotated Edition)

12 13 14 15 16 17   003   05 04

Cover Art: *The Creation of the Sun and the Moon*
by Michelangelo, (from the Sistine Chapel):
The Vatican Museums

Contents

Acknowledgments

The authors wish to thank Sister Mary Joell Overman, S.N.D., Superior General, Rome; Sister Rita Mary Harwood, S.N.D., Provincial Superior of the Sisters of Notre Dame, Chardon, Ohio; and Sister Margaret Mary McGovern, S.N.D., Assistant Superintendent, Education, Diocese of Cleveland, Eastern Region, who supported and encouraged the writing of the *Light of the World* series.

Humble gratitude is also due to all who in any way helped to create the *Light of the World* series: parents, teachers, co-workers, students, and friends. The following deserve special mention for their assistance in planning, organizing, testing, or critiquing the series: Notre Dame Sisters Mary Dolores Abood, Ann Baron, Karla Bognar, Mary Brady, Mary Catherine Caine, Virginia Marie Callen, Deborah Carlin, Naomi Cervenka, Reean Coyne, Mary Dowling, Patricia Mary Ferrara, Dorothy Fuchs, Kathleen Glavich, Margaret Mary Gorman, Jacquelyn Gusdane, Margaret Harig, Joanmarie Harks, Nathan Hess, Sally Huston, Christa Jacobs, Joanne Kepler, Owen Kleinhenz, Mary Jean Korejwo, Elizabeth Marie Kreager, Leanne Laney, William David Latiano, Aimee Levy, Ann McFadden, Inez McHugh, Louismarie Nudo, Donna Marie Paluf, Helen Mary Peter, Nancy Powell, Eileen Marie Quinlan, Patricia Rickard, Mark Daniel Roscoe, Kathleen Ruddy, Kathleen Scully, Dolores Stanko, Melannie Svoboda, Mary Louise Trivison, Donna Marie Wilhelm, Laura Wingert; Dr. Jean Alvarez, Ms. Mary Anderson; Ms. Meg Bracken; Sister Mary Kay Cmolik, O.F.M.; Mr. Robert Dilonardo, Rev. Mark DiNardo, Ms. Linda Ferrando, Mr. Michael Homza, Sister Kathleen King, H.H.M., Ms. Patricia Lange, Mr. James Marmion, Mr. Peter Meler, Rev. Herman P. Moman, Rev. Guy Noonan, T.O.R., Ms. Christine Smetana, and Ms. Karen Sorace.

The following high schools piloted materials: Bishop Ireton High School, Alexandria, Virginia; Clearwater Central Catholic High School, Clearwater, Florida; Elyria Catholic High School, Elyria, Ohio; Erieview Catholic High School, Cleveland, Ohio; John F. Kennedy High School, Warren, Ohio; Notre Dame Cathedral Latin High School, Chardon, Ohio; Regina High School, South Euclid, Ohio; St. Edward High School, Cleveland, Ohio; St. Matthias High School, Huntington Park, California.

The following parishes piloted the original Abridged Lessons: Corpus Christi, Cleveland, Ohio; St. Anselm, Chesterland, Ohio; St. John Nepomucene, Cleveland, Ohio; St. Thomas More, Paducah, Kentucky.

Special appreciation and thanks to Sister M. Dolores Stanko, S.N.D., for typing the final manuscripts of the series as well as for her many helpful suggestions and her insightful editorial assistance.

Deep appreciation to Mrs. Anita Johnson for research; to Sisters of Notre Dame Mary Regien Kingsbury, De Xavier Perusek, and Seton Schlather; to Robert Clair Smith for special services; and to typists Sisters Catherine Rennecker, S.N.D., Josetta Marie Livignano, S.N.D., and Ms. Charlaine Yomant.

Photo Credits

Hebrew Scriptures: Origins and Stories

OBJECTIVES

In this Chapter you will

- Discover the purpose and significance of the Bible.

- Focus on the Hebrew Scriptures.

- Learn how the Hebrew Scriptures record the history of the Israelites and confirm basic Jewish belief.

- Experience the two stories of creation as literary masterpieces.

- Recognize how sin came to divide people from God and from one another.

The whole created world eagerly awaits the revelation of the children of God...not without hope, because the world itself will be freed from its slavery to corruption and share in the glorious freedom of the children of God.
—Romans 8:19-21

The Hebrew Scriptures: Called by the Father

Sacred Scripture

What is the world's best-seller? What was the first book published in 1456 after Johann Gutenberg's invention of the printing press? What book covering two thousand years of history is among the oldest manuscripts in existence? The answer to all three questions is the Bible. In *The Brothers Karamazov,* the Russian author Fyodor Dostoyevski wrote: "What a book the Bible is, what a miracle, what strength is given with it to man. It is like a mould cast of the world and man and human nature, everything is there, and a law for everything for the ages."

Since the beginning of history, people have delighted in tales of courage, love, birth, and death. Maybe it is because stories mysteriously transform us, whereby we gain wisdom without going through the actual experience. The most important stories are those that center on the meaning of existence as it is revealed by God. Religious stories probe haunting human questions: Where did we come from? What is the meaning of life? Why do we have violence, wars, sickness, and death? What happens after we die?

Christians find the answers to these and other questions especially in the twenty-seven books of the New Testament, but the Christian Bible also contains the forty-six books of the Hebrew Scriptures. The Hebrew Scriptures trace the faith history of the Jewish people and are an essential part of the Christian's religious heritage.

Israel's Story and You

God is revealed to us in a special way through the Hebrew Scriptures. Although God's speaking through Jesus brought a new dimension to the ongoing process of revelation, Israel's stories form the foundation for understanding the teaching of Jesus. Jesus himself loved and taught the Jewish Scriptures as the Word of his Father. "Do not think that I have come to abolish the law or the prophets. I have come not to abolish but to fulfill" (Matthew 5:17).

Speaking for Yahweh, the prophet Hosea referred to Israel as God's favored son: "When Israel was a child I loved him, out of Egypt I called my son." In inviting the Jews to such a close relationship, God may seem to be playing favorites. Actually, however, God's gifts to the Chosen People were meant to benefit all nations.

You might think of the Hebrew Scriptures as a biography of God's "sons and daughters," the Jewish people. The folk tales of the patriarchs present the days of Israel's beginnings. Under Moses, Israel found its identity as a people. Gaining independence on its own land, the nation was united by King David who commanded the respect of the world powers. Israel made mistakes and, during the exile, was called to purification. Suffering enlightened God's Chosen People, and they gained new wisdom and hope, based not on politics but on the mercy of God. The hope of Israel was not misplaced; God continued to be present with them. In Israel's stories, God continues to speak with a fresh and vital voice. To get the most from these stories, it is helpful to briefly review the Bible's overall plan and then see how each part relates to it.

What the Bible Is

The Bible is many things to many people: It is a source of solace for those who grieve, a cause of joy for those who mourn, and a promise of hope for the future. The Bible can be so many things to so many people because it is the Word of God. Through the Bible, God communicates with humankind, and thus it is a sacred book. The Bible is revelation, God's self-disclosure. The message of the Bible is that God is a loving Creator who has entered into a pact, or covenant, with humankind in order to save us.

The Bible is our source of revelation. Through it, God reveals mysteries—truths that cannot be explained by

The message of the Bible is that God is a loving Creator who saves us.

human explanations—concerning salvation. Scripture and Tradition form the "Deposit of Faith," everything we need to know about salvation. Tradition is the sum of the teachings of the Catholic Church—dogmas, declarations, encyclicals, sermons, and writings. Revelation is presented in the Bible and is interpreted through Tradition.

The Purpose of the Bible

Human words inform, reassure, bind, heal, wound, build, and destroy. The words of God have the power to create, give life, and save. The Bible puts you into contact with God's words. "Bible" is from the Greek word *biblia,* which means "the books." The Bible can be compared to several objects:

- *The Bible is like a **picture** of a loved one. It reveals what God the Creator is like.*

- *The Bible is like a **mirror.** Looking into its pages, you can see yourself in the story of the Israelites, the story of Jesus, and the story of the early Church.*

- *The Bible is like a **road map.** It directs you to God. In revealing the meaning of history by showing you where you have come from, it gives meaning to life.*

- *The Bible is like a **letter.** God communicates to you through its words.*

- *The Bible is like a **library.** It is actually a collection of seventy-three books.*

> **Tradition:** when spelled with a capital "T," the sum of the teachings of the Catholic Church. When spelled with a lower case "t," it refers to the beliefs and customs handed down through generations.

The Bible is like a library. It is a collection of different types of religious literature.

Through the Bible, you can experience the Christ event, take on the mind and heart of Jesus, and respond to his invitation to a fuller life. You can see for yourself the mystery of God's creative and salvific love. When it is read in public or in private, the Bible makes God present to you through the Word. The Bible is an essential aspect of Catholic worship. The first part of the Mass (the Liturgy of the Word) is celebrated with readings from both the Hebrew and Christian Testaments.

Divisions of the Bible

The Bible is divided into the Hebrew Scriptures (known as the Old Testament) and the Christian Scriptures (known as the New Testament). Testament means agreement or covenant. Both sections combined make up the Christian Bible, and both sections are essential to the Christian faith.

The Hebrew Scriptures cover Jewish history from creation to about one hundred years before the birth of Jesus and were written between 1900 B.C.E. and 100 B.C.E. The

Hebrew Scriptures reveal God's working to prepare the world for the fulfillment of the covenant with them. The books are classified as follows:

- **Pentateuch** (or Law): Genesis, Exodus, Leviticus, Numbers, and Deuteronomy

- **Historical Books:** Joshua, Judges, Ruth, 1 and 2 Samuel, 1 and 2 Kings, 1 and 2 Chronicles, Ezra, Nehemiah, Tobit, Judith, Esther, 1 and 2 Maccabees

- **Writings:** Job, Psalms, Proverbs, Ecclesiastes, Song of Songs, Wisdom, Sirach

- **Prophets:** Isaiah, Jeremiah, Lamentations, Baruch, Ezekiel, Daniel, and the twelve minor prophets

The Christian Scriptures contain the life and teaching of Jesus Christ, the Messiah, and the beginnings of his Church. It covers the years 6 B.C.E. to C.E. 100 and tells of the new covenant established in Jesus Christ through the Holy Spirit. It includes the following:

- **The gospel accounts:** Matthew, Mark, Luke, and John

- **Acts of the Apostles:** The fifth book of the Christian Scriptures narrating the beginnings of the Church

- **Epistles:** Letters written by the Apostles or their representatives to individuals or Christian communities: Romans, 1 and 2 Corinthians, Galatians, Ephesians, Philippians; Colossians; 1 and 2 Thessalonians, 1 and 2 Timothy; Titus; Philemon; Hebrews; James; 1 and 2 Peter; 1, 2, and 3 John; Jude

- **The Book of Revelation:** The last book in the Christian Scriptures, written to exhort the early Christians who were being persecuted

The descriptive terms "Hebrew Scriptures" and "Christian Scriptures" are used to be sensitive to the faith of the Jewish people. The Hebrew Scriptures are not "old" in the sense of being out of date. They form the core of Jewish faith. The Christian Scriptures are not "new" in the sense of replacing what came before. Rather, they continue God's revelation through Jesus and the Holy Spirit in the early Christian community. This book will focus on the Hebrew Scriptures.

For Example

A device for remembering the order of the first fourteen epistles is using the first few letters of each name: RO-CO-CO/GAL-EPH-PHI/COL-THESS-THESS/TIM-TIM-TI/PHIL-HEB.

B.C.E.: Before the Common Era. This is commonly used by scholars in place of B.C. to identify the time prior to Jesus' birth.

C.E.: Common Era. Used by scholars in place of A.D. to identify the time after Jesus' birth.

Archaeology

The Hebrew Scriptures are a significant source of our knowledge of the history of Israel in ancient times. While all the events related in the Bible may not always be literally true, the entire text is not to be viewed as fictitious.

Until the eighteenth century, the Bible was accepted as historically accurate. In the nineteenth century, with the advent of the scientific theory of evolution, people began to doubt the absolute historical accuracy of biblical data. Today the pendulum is swinging back toward a recognition of the historical materials present in the Hebrew Scriptures. Much biblical data agrees with secular historical sources, and recent archaeological discoveries support the "history" recounted in the Hebrew texts.

The Bible Today

The Sacred Scriptures tell a story in which God is speaking all of the time—to Abraham, to Jacob, to Moses, to the prophets, to Jesus, and to the Apostles and disciples. God frees the oppressed, saves the righteous, and heals the sick. What do these miraculous acts of God have to do with common everyday life? What do the words of the Bible have to say to a society, to a world that often appears godless, violent, and consumed by greed? Is God silent now? People are living in oppressive conditions and need many kinds of healing—physical, emotional, and spiritual, to name a few. Does God no longer act in history?

These are difficult questions to answer. It is hard to understand the words of a text written many years ago. Reading Scripture is an act of faith. It should lead one to reread the story of human existence with the eyes of a believer. If you do so, you will find that God continues to speak to you today as God spoke to the patriarchs, the prophets, and the Apostles. God continues to act through the Scriptures.

Your first task is to understand the Bible in its own historical context. Having done so, you need to enter the world of the stories so that your perspectives can be enlarged and challenged. Only then can you take hold of the text and see how it applies to people living in the twentieth century.

---

1. *What images would you use to describe the Bible? Explain why you would use these images?*

2. *Look at the table of contents in your Bible. Look up each of the books listed. You might want to make tabs to help you find each book quickly.*

3. *In what ways do the stories of the Bible have meaning in the twentieth century?*

4. *How does God continue to act in human history?*

People have varying attitudes toward the Bible. Some think it is a collection of boring books written many years ago by people who are long dead. A person with a more positive view might consider the Bible as a love letter from God. As such, the Bible would be read repeatedly, in an effort to understand each unspoken message. The Bible would also be read with openness, faith, readiness, and with a sense of its being God's Holy Word.

Here is a way for you to get the most out of reading the Bible. As you read a particular text, note your spontaneous reactions: What do you like? What seems amazing to you? What questions do you have? Read the text more than once. On your second reading, note some of the following:

- **Language:** *Look for words that are repeated often or words that contrast with or correspond to one another.*

- **Characters** *(people) or things involved in the action: What happens to them? What do they say and do? Can you see changes in these people or things?*

- **Movement:** *Are certain geographical places connected with a person's name or with a particular idea? What happens between the beginning and the end of the particular text that you are reading?*

- **Context:** *The passage that you are reading is part of a larger whole. How does this text fit into the chapter where it is placed or into the entire book? What is the contribution of the story? When removed from its context and read in fragments, a story often does not make sense. Seen in its context, however, it takes on a more complete meaning.*

Finding references in the Bible can be difficult unless you know the methods for reading the Bible's codes. Throughout this text you will be asked to find specific references in your Bible and read what is there. What hope would you have of finding "1 Sm. 3:9-10," if you couldn't break the code? Here is a simple method that can help you find the proper reading quickly.

1. 1 Sm is an abbreviation for the first Book of Samuel. The title is often abbreviated in references

> **Theory of evolution:** the idea that complex organisms develop from simpler ones, suggesting that modern human species and apes have a common ancestry.

A Book of Books

Since the Bible is like a library, what types of books would you expect to find in it? Poetry? Fiction? Drama? History? Each type of writing has its own purpose. For example, your science teacher wouldn't have you study a science-fiction novel to get an accurate picture of reality, and you wouldn't read the editorial page of a newspaper to your little sister as a bedtime story.

Writing can be understood only when its forms, characteristics, and purposes are recognized. A historical book of the Bible should not be approached as a legend, nor should a legend in the Bible be read as a literal history. Since the Bible is ultimately a religious book rather than a scientific or historical book, it primarily conveys religious truths, not necessarily scientific or historical truths.

Because our focus is on the Hebrew Scriptures, we will explore some of the types of literature Israel used to talk about its relationship with God. These types of literature are often called "literary genres."

- **Stories:** *stories provide us with a history of our religious family.*

- **Epics:** *these accounts of the past arouse our enthusiasm and celebrate heroes. They may exaggerate the details.*

- **Laws:** *this literature gives organization to a people and allows a common life.*

- **Liturgy:** *what are the ritual celebrations that express the common life of a group? Religious actions show the bond between people and God.*

- **Poems:** *like canticles and psalms, this literature expresses the sentiments and faith of a people.*

- **Oracles:** *words from the prophets attributed to God, oracles call people back to true faith.*

(although in this text, the title is always spelled in total). A list of abbreviations is usually given in the front of the Bible. The digit before the name indicates which book is referenced.

2. The number "3" followed by a colon (:) indicates the proper chapter of the book. Chapter numbers are often found at the top of each page like the guide words of a dictionary.

3. The numbers "9-10" identify the verses to be read. In the case of 1 Samuel 3:9-10, you would read verses 9 and 10 from chapter 3 of the first Book of Samuel. The verse numbers are usually indicated in very small type.

With the help of this textbook, the notes in your Bible, and other aids, you will be able to answer questions that you have concerning the text. Reading the Bible will lead you to a deeper understanding of the relationship between God and human beings.

Each page of the Bible has many codes to help you find the right passage. How many codes do you see on this page?

Artists for many centuries have attempted to capture the writing of Scripture. Some show an apostle or Moses sitting in a cave in front of a candle. Writing with a quill pen, the author is never alone. With the author is an angel, a messenger of God. The angel is shown either speaking into the author's ear or directing the author's hand. In this way, the artist supports the Bible as being the true Word of God.

Scripture scholarship suggests that artists' renditions of revelation are most probably not true. Based on this

Artists attempt to show God's inspiration in the person of an angel. How was Scripture written?

The Hebrew Scriptures: Called by the Father

scholarship, it is accurate to say that the Bible passed through these three stages of development:

1. **Oral Stage:** The Israelites kept their history alive by repeating it throughout many generations.
2. **Written Stage:** Individuals or groups recorded the oral traditions of the Israelites.
3. **Edited Stage:** Editors combined traditions into an interpreted story of the dealings of God with humankind.

Although the stories contained in the Hebrew Scriptures may be thousands of years old, a majority of scholars believe that most of the books in the Hebrew Scriptures were actually written either during Solomon's reign (900 B.C.E.) or during the Exile (500 B.C.E.). The books were probably written on papyrus scrolls or clay tablets. None of the original manuscripts exist today.

---

5. *What is your favorite type of literature? Discuss what makes this type of special interest.*

6. *Why is it important to understand the different types of literature in Scripture? What difference does it make how Scripture came to be written?*

Summary

- Even though it was written many years ago, the Bible continues to bear witness to the human quest for God.

- The Hebrew Bible is a significant source of our knowledge of the history of Israel in ancient times.

- In order to understand the Bible, you must understand the context in which it was written.

- Within the different books of the Hebrew Scriptures, there are many types of literature. Among these are poetry, epic, law, story, oracle, and liturgy.

■ Review

1. What is the message of the Bible?

2. Into what two parts is the Bible divided?

3. Has the Bible always been accepted as historically accurate?

4. What kind of attitude should we have when reading the Bible?

5. When reading the Bible, what questions should you ask of the text?

6. Name and describe three types of literature in the Hebrew Scriptures.

7. Words to Know: Tradition, Hebrew Scriptures, Christian Scriptures, B.C.E., C.E., evolution, context, literary genre, epic, liturgy, oracle.

■ In Your World

1. What stories have been passed down for generations in your family? Ask a relative for such a story and write it down. Have details of this story been exaggerated or expanded? Why does this happen over time?

2. Browse through a daily newspaper from the front page to the last. How many types or kinds of literature can you find in it? Make a list of all the different types of writing that you can find in the newspaper.

■ Scripture Search

1. Familiarize yourself with the Bible that you are using for this class. Count the number of books in the Hebrew Scriptures. Christians refer to the first five books of the Hebrew Scriptures as the Pentateuch (Greek for "five books"). Jews call them the Torah (Hebrew for "law"). Name these first five books.

2. The Bible (both Hebrew and Christian Scriptures) has page numbers like other books, but information in the Bible is not looked up according to page numbers. Bible references are to be found according to this system: title, chapter, and verse. For practice, look up the following passages and copy them out: a) Genesis 24:67 b) Proverbs 12:19 c) 1 Samuel 17:49-51.

Two Stories of Creation

Through people, their traditions, and their customs, God's Word has been spoken throughout human history. Before writing was common, people told stories of God's goodness around camp fires. These stories would be passed faithfully from generation to generation. The stories made them a people. They also provided answers to difficult questions. The Bible is filled with stories that answer difficult questions. An example is found in the two creation stories at the beginning of the Book of Genesis. These stories also show various types of literary forms.

How Did It All Begin?

People did not know that the world is round until Columbus's voyage in 1492, that the earth revolves around the sun until Copernicus's discovery in 1563, or that humans as well as animals evolve until Darwin's *Origin of the Species* in 1859. There is much that we don't know about the world even today. Scientists are afraid that the world's rain forests will be destroyed before research can be conducted on the many animals and plants that live there, over two-thirds of the total number on earth, most of which are uncataloged.

The writers of the two stories of creation in Genesis, chapters 1 and 2, do not attempt to give a scientific account of creation. The writers were not interested in developing a scientific book. Even if they had been, such a "scientific" book would have been limited by their lack of knowledge. Although they would have been hampered in writing a scientific report, they were not constrained in writing a religious story. From their experience of God and creation, stories of God as Creator developed.

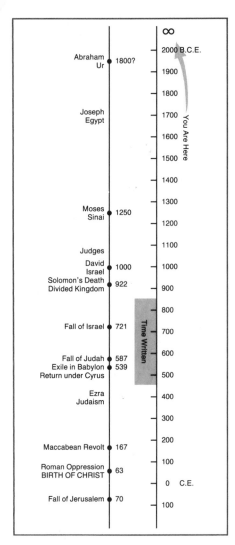

The Book of Genesis was written around 750 B.C.E., long after the time of creation.

For Example

If the last four billion years of the universe's existence were compressed into one year, human beings would arrive shortly before midnight on December 31st, and all of recorded history would occur in the last ninety seconds.

A person attempting to use the Bible as a science or history book misses the point. The Bible is a book of religious truths, and often these truths move beyond the scope of scientific fact and into the realm of faith and meaning. Science and religion both search for truth, but in different ways. We will see how this is true as we study the Genesis creation stories.

Two Traditions

The Bible is first and foremost a book to be read. As you attempt to understand the Bible, be aware that you will be reading the actual scriptural text along with this text. Begin now by finding the Book of Genesis and reading chapters 1-12.

Scientists today argue over the creation of the universe. Did it start with a "big bang" — an enormous explosion that sent energy and matter flying into space forming galaxies, suns, and planets? Or was there another means of creation? Scientists agree on the approximate age of the universe: the Milky Way is approximately 16 billion years old and the earth is about 4.6 billion years old. While human beings are tens of thousands of years old, written records have been kept for only the past five thousand years (less than one percent of humankind's existence).

Unconcerned about the age of the world or the age of humanity, the history of the Israelites from the beginning of time was recorded around 850 B.C.E. This was an awesome task. Remember that this historian was unconcerned about events other than how they affected the Hebrew people as God's Chosen People. The story of how they came to be the Chosen People is the story of the Hebrew Scriptures.

The anonymous writer, called the Yahwist because the word *Yahweh* was used for God's name, wrote an account of prehistoric times. This story is found in chapters 2-11 of Genesis, the first book of the Bible. The Yahwist worked with the same source material that other writers of epics used—the oral traditions of the people. Tales about the first human beings, a great flood, and the beginnings of different tribes were told as stories of the people's special relationship with God. As a nomadic people, the Israelites came into contact with other tribes and heard their stories. The tales of the Israelites about their beginnings took on the flavor of other creation stories. The stories recorded by the Yahwist are called the J tradition. The "J" is derived from the German word *Jahweh,* or Yahweh. These stories speak familiarly of God as though the Creator had a human body.

In about 750 B.C.E., another version of Israelite history was composed, known as the Elohist, or "E" tradition. This author used the Hebrew word *Elohim* for God. Both of these traditions, the Yahwist and the Elohist, contain much of the material in the early chapters of Genesis, along with the history of the Hebrew patriarchs that follows in Genesis 12-50. During the Exile, a group of editors, known today as the "P" (for Priestly) tradition, reshaped the Elohist account of creation and fashioned what we now have in Genesis 1:1-2:4. The "P" editors took the many accounts and developed the first five books of the Bible that we know today.

In the first eleven chapters of Genesis, the Yahwist's account dominates. As Israel's first theologian, the Yahwist made this account a confession of the one God, the Lord of the universe. For the Yahwist, the gods worshiped by other cultures were nothing compared to their God. It was Yahweh, the one true God of the Israelites, who was in control of the world and who wanted a relationship with this Chosen People.

The person attempting to use the Bible as a science or history book misses the point. The Bible is a book of religious truths.

Yahweh: the name for God given to Moses at the burning bush, meaning "I Am."

Prehistory: the time prior to written records or the memory of a people; usually captured in myth and legends.

Elohim: the plural form of the Hebrew word for God, meaning "the most high God."

Theologian: a believer who attempts to clarify the community's faith in God.

7. *The epics of the Israelites were similar to those of other Near Eastern cultures. Why do you think this is so?*

Creation: The Gift of a Good God

The Hubble telescope, even with a flawed mirror, sends back to Earth images of the universe from millions of light years away. The light from these stars was generated long before humankind began. Technological breakthroughs allow us to witness the conception and development of a human being. The more we discover about the universe, the more we stand in amazement and awe. What a mighty and wondrous God must have fashioned so glorious a cosmos!

The Hebrew people stood in awe of God and creation. The Israelites and their neighbors expressed this awe in

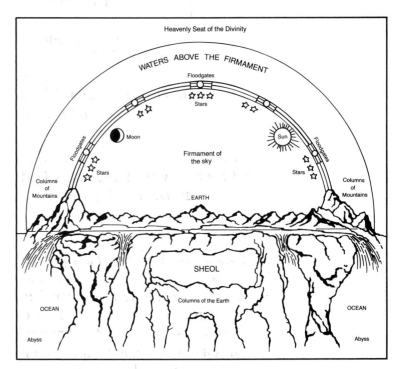

Ancient peoples explained rainfall by saying that God opened the floodgates of the heavens. This illustration provides an example of how they experienced the world.

The Hebrew Scriptures: Called by the Father

ways that made sense to them. To explain the wonderful gift of rain they reasoned that the world was covered by a solid bowl-shaped firmament—the sky—that held back the waters above the earth. The firmament had floodgates that opened periodically—at the command of God—to release the waters in the form of rain and snow. The sun, moon, and stars were set in the firmament to give light. The earth was supported from below by columns. Under the earth there was more water.

From this picture of the world, the Elohist composed what is still one of the most majestic, well-known, and best-loved descriptions of the origin of the universe. It is the story of creation as told in the beginning of the Book of Genesis (Genesis 1-2:4). Because of the poetic structure of the story, scholars believe that it was a liturgical song used by the Israelite community during worship to honor the power and goodness of God. Read Genesis 1-2:4 again slowly and note the poetic nature of the text.

Genesis 1-2:4 compares God, the architect of the universe, to a Jewish laborer who works for six days and then rests on the seventh day, the Sabbath. In the course of relating each day's activity, the writer uses the poetic devices of repetition and parallelism. The description of each day begins with a command by God who calls something into existence and ends with the refrain, "Evening came and morning followed, the _____ day." This resembles what composers do when they have a refrain that is repeated after each verse.

A beautiful balance is noted. On the first three days God prepared the world, and during the next three days God furnished it with the following elements: light; sky, water; land, plants; sun, moon, stars; birds, fish; animals, human beings.

This creation account poses problems when read as literal truth. It took billions of years for the universe to arrive at its present form, not just six days. Consider how there could be light on the first day if the sources of light were not created until the fourth day. Problems like this are not so pressing when you remember that the Bible is not meant to be a science book. It would have been natural to the Israelites to create light first. Who can work in the dark? Light is also symbolic of spirit, and the Spirit of God is seen as

---

Firmament: the vault or arch of the sky.

Genesis: means "beginnings." In Hebrew, the opening words of this biblical text are *Bereshith bara Elohim eth hashamayim weth haarets* which means "In the beginning, God created the heavens and the earth."

Parallelism: a poetic device of recurring similarities used for effect.

Visualizing Creation

Poetry suggests more than it says. Think of your favorite poem. How does it use images, symbols, or metaphors to describe something? As you read what follows, try to visualize creation in your mind.

First day (Genesis 1:1-5): In the midst of a vast, swirling darkness, a glow appears. It is an eerie light, like the early morning before sunrise.

Second day (Genesis 1:6-8): Surging tons of water are thrust in two by a solid, curved blue wall. With thunderous crashing sounds, the watery chaos splits.

Third day (Genesis 1:9-13): Rushing blue water drains off the land and settles into the ocean basins. Gigantic waves pound against the cliffs and break into spray. The dark earth takes on color as the first tiny green tendrils shoot forth, unfold, and then burst into bloom. Trees creak and groan as branches extend and push toward the sky. Lush forests cover the hills and fill in the valleys.

Fourth day (Genesis 1:14-19): The brilliant sun rises for the first time. It lends beauty to everything it touches, then sinks behind the mountains in a blaze of colors. Against the velvety blackness of the night, thousands of sparkling stars fill the firmament. The full moon, with its intense white light, hangs just above the horizon.

Fifth day (Genesis 1:20-23): The waters teem with millions of creatures. Immense whales silently glide through the seas; tiny fish dart around rocks in shallow streams. The air is filled with the chirps, calls, and songs of birds, punctuated by the sound of flapping wings.

Sixth day (Genesis 1:24-31): Herds of buffalo thunder across the plains, sleek panthers prowl the jungle, lions roar, snakes slither across the desert sands, lambs bleat. Finally, the first human beings, created male and female, survey all that their God has created.

permeating creation. The basic message that Genesis proclaims is that God is Creator. The Bible leaves the question of how God created as a puzzle for human beings to solve. The inspired biblical author made the point that God existed before the world by saying that all created things were brought forth by the Spirit and the Word of God.

One truth that cannot be missed is that God intended creation to be good. God appraised the divine handiwork seven times and saw how good it was. All things were meant to be part of God's plan of salvation. In creation, God saved all beings from nothingness and incorporated them into a magnificent scheme. Christians later pondered the Hebrew account of creation: "Eye has not seen, ear has not heard, nor has it so much as dawned upon man what God has prepared for those who love him" (1 Corinthians 2:9).

---

8. *How does the creation account in Genesis 1-2:4 agree with the principles of modern science? Discuss whether the creation account and science can be in agreement.*

The Second Creation Account

Genesis 1-2:4 is one account of creation. But one account of creation was not enough for the Hebrew people. The second account is found in Genesis 2:4-25. Read these passages and note the difference between the two stories.

Genesis 2:4-25 contains the Yahwist account of creation. Because it is a different form of literature, the structure and detail of the account are not the same as the liturgical song or poem found in Genesis 1 where human beings are created last, after the sky, earth, waters, sun, plants, fish and other animals. Genesis 1:27 states: "God created man in his image; in the divine image he created him; male and female he created them." In the first creation story, there is no subordination of female to male—they are created equally,

The second Creation story explains the relationship between men and women by having woman created from man.

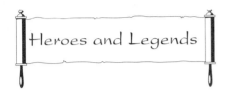

Heroes and Legends

The Genesis creation story has some parallels in other myths and legends that originated in Babylon, Egypt, and Canaan. The Babylonian creation epic, called the *Enuma Elish,* probably bears the greatest similarity to the structure of Genesis 1. According to this creation story, the universe was created after a fierce struggle between the forces of chaos (personified by the goddess Tiamat) and the god of the city of Babylon (Marduk). Marduk slew Tiamat and divided the body of the slain goddess into two parts, making a space between the watery chaos above and below. According to this Babylonian creation story, the god Marduk created the world out of the corpse of the slain Tiamat. Israel rejected the myth that creation was the product of divine battles. In Genesis, God has no rivals. Supreme creator, God brings forth the universe by the simple means of the Word.

at the same time. Human beings are presented as the climax of God's creative activity, and they are given dominion over all the earth. They are to care for, not exploit, the rest of creation.

In the Yahwist account, which uses a story form, this is not true. The male of the species is created first, with God in the role of a potter. The Israelites knew that people stopped breathing at death, and their bodies turned to dust. The process was reversed when God made the first man. God brought human beings into existence with a breath, the power of the Spirit.

After the first man was created out of the clay of the earth, God planted a garden in Eden and placed the man there. The man was to cultivate and care for the garden. He was allowed to eat from any of the trees in this beautiful garden, except for the tree of the knowledge of good and evil, which stands for the right to decide what is right or wrong. It is this power that allows for the possibility of evil.

God pondered the fact that Adam was alone and decided to make a partner for him. Before doing this, God created the other living things on the earth—birds and animals— and brought them to Adam so that Adam could give them names. In this Yahwist account, then, the order of creation is reversed. Man is created first, after the heavens and the earth, and then God creates the other animals. None of these creatures proved to be a suitable partner for the man, so God performed the first surgery—the removal of Adam's rib. In this symbolic story, a rib from Adam was removed to form the first female of the species. The woman is not named until later, in Genesis 3:20, where she is called Eve, mother of the living. Eve had the same nature as Adam because they shared the same body. There is a wordplay in Genesis 2:23, regarding the similar-sounding Hebrew words *ishsha* ("woman") and *ishah* ("her man" or "her husband").

The Israelites knew from experience that God is a saving, loving, forgiving God. Therefore, they wrote of a Creator who offered friendship and love to the creatures that had been made. Yahweh (the Yahwist's word for God) treated Adam and Eve as God's children and showered them with gifts: the beautiful garden of Eden, health, happiness, and a share in God's own life. The first people were totally preoccupied with God, joined with and overwhelmed by God's presence. In return, Yahweh asked that their love be shown by obedience.

Did people named Adam and Eve ever exist in a garden of Eden? Who knows? Clearly, that is not important to the authors of these accounts. Such questions ignore the literary way the biblical text yields the divine message. It is up to science to uncover exactly when, where, and how human beings populated the earth. The intention of the Bible is to explain human existence. It does this through the literary genre of story. Adam and Eve represent the original or primal human condition even as it exists today. Their names and the account of their origin as written in the Hebrew Scriptures are understood to be symbolic.

---

9. *What is the significance of the order of creation in Genesis 2?*

10. *Choose a literary genre to describe creation. Write your own creation account and share it with the class.*

Summary ▇▇▇▇▇▇▇▇▇▇▇▇▇▇▇

■ The Bible is a book of religious truths; it is not meant to be read as a science book.

■ The two most important traditions in the Book of Genesis are the Yahwist (850 B.C.E.) and the Elohist (750 B.C.E.). The Priestly tradition borrows from the "E" account to fashion the liturgical song about creation found in the first chapter of Genesis and, as an editor, brings all of the stories together to make a whole.

■ The creation account in Genesis 1 describes the creation of the universe in six days.

■ The Yahwist creation account differs in structure and detail from the first creation account.

Adam: the name given to the first man is derived from the Hebrew word *adamah*, which means earth or ground.

■ Review

1. What are the "J" and "E" traditions?

2. Who are the main characters in the Babylonian creation story?

3. What indications are there that the first account of creation in Genesis was once a liturgical song?

4. What literary genre is used in the second account of creation?

5. According to Genesis 1, in what order did God create? What order is suggested in the second account of creation?

6. Words to Know: Yahwist, Elohist, Marduk, Tiamat, *Enuma Elish,* firmament, Adam, Eve, Eden.

■ In Your World

1. At the end of the creation account in Genesis 1, God gave human beings dominion over all the earth. What does this mean in the twentieth century in terms of the environment, animal experimentation, and genetic engineering?

2. There is a saying that goes: "God made me; God doesn't make junk." Often we do not realize what precious gifts we possess. What can you do to cherish yourself? Make a list of what you consider to be your own personal gifts.

■ Scripture Search

1. Tell how these Scripture passages confirm the basic dignity of human beings: a) Deuteronomy 5:17, b) Matthew 6:26, c) Hebrews 2:16-17, and d) Ephesians 1:3-6.

2. Read Psalm 8. How does this psalm celebrate the dignity of being human?

A Gift of Creation: Free Will

You only have to look at today's newspaper to realize that we live in a troubled world. The crazy pattern of evil, suffering, and death that mars life is a mystery. This is not something new, however. The Israelites, too, read these signs in their lives. They saw in their own history the elements of sin and forgiveness, of promises made and broken. They did not, however, believe that the situation was hopeless. Instead they concluded that everything God had made was good, but that God had endowed human beings with a power that made them different from all other creatures: freedom of choice. Human beings are created with the power of decision. They can choose good or choose evil. The choice is in their hands, not dictated by some outside force.

This power of freedom enables us both to enhance our lives and our world or to mar the gift of a perfect universe, since we can refuse to choose good actions. We are free to choose to affirm goodness and life or to do evil and damage other people, things, and even ourselves. However, God's plan for us is not destroyed by our poor choices in this world. God offers forgiveness to us, a chance to make a fresh start. Yet, even though we are continually forgiven, we suffer the consequences of our evil choices. This is the story captured in Genesis 3:1-24. Read these verses before proceeding with this text.

Disobedience and Brokenness: The Onset of Sin

Have you ever done anything that you regretted or said something that you wish you could "take back"? Have you hurt someone with your anger or selfishness or given in to a bad habit even after fighting against temptation?

If you feel tension between what you would like to be and what you actually do, you are normal. Saint Paul wrote: "Even though I want to do what is right, a law that leads me to wrongdoing is always ready at hand. My inner self agrees with the law of God, but I see in my body's members another law at war with the law of my mind; this makes me the prisoner of the law of sin in my members" (Romans 7:21-24).

The plight of the human race from the Fall to the present day is a far cry from the paradise envisioned in the early chapters of Genesis. The first humans, as represented by Adam and Eve, made a fatal mistake that marked their descendants: they rejected God's love and sinned against their Creator. Their disobedience, presented symbolically in the text of Genesis 3, shattered the relationship between God and human beings. The bond between God and creation was broken, but not completely severed. To do good, we must struggle, like Saint Paul, against evil impulses to sin.

---

11. *Does there seem to be a great distance in your life between the person that you want to be and the person that you are now? What can you do now to bridge that gap?*

The Fall: A Refusal to Love

The story of the Fall of humanity, as told in Genesis 3:1-24, has intrigued scholars and fascinated readers of the Bible for centuries. The story presents vivid images of basic relationships between God and humans, humans and the natural world, and women and men. Interpretations of this story affect the way people view their lives today.

This is how the author explained the entrance of sin into the world. Not content with God's love and grace and gifts, Adam and Eve wanted more. The serpent (who is made to symbolize evil) appealed to the pride of the first humans by telling them that they would be like God if they listened to

Praying the Hebrew Scriptures

The following is an excerpt from the Jewish prayer book. It is a prayer that is read during the weekday synagogue service.

"Praised be the Lord our God, Ruler of the Universe, who makes light and creates darkness, who ordains peace and fashions all things.

"With compassion he gives light to the earth and all who dwell there; with goodness he renews the work of creation continually, day by day.

"...Let us all bless you, O Lord our God, for the excellence of your handiwork, and for the glowing stars that you have made: let them glorify you forever. Blessed is the Lord, the Maker of light."

it instead of the commands of their Creator. The serpent challenged the authority of God, and Adam and Eve chose to follow the serpent's reasoning instead of cooperating with God. Their real sin was that of disobedience, of wanting to be like God.

Where did the notion develop that Adam and Eve's sin was eating an apple? In Latin, the word for apple and the word for evil, *malum,* are identical. It is for this reason that a legend has grown since the Middle Ages that the Tree of the Knowledge of Good and Evil in the Garden of Eden was an apple tree. In artistic depictions of the Fall, Eve is usually shown with an apple in her hand, even though apples are not indigenous to the Near East, and there is no specific fruit mentioned in Genesis 3:3 or 3:6.

Clearly, the author of this account was not an eyewitness to this story. Rather, the author was relaying basic truths about human nature through the medium of folk history. The drama of the first people's refusal to cooperate with their loving Creator is told simply but vividly. It is a psychological study of sin that is valid today.

Read the account of the Fall of humanity in Genesis 3:1-24 again and analyze it in light of the psychological pattern of any sin, as expressed in "The Seven Steps to Sin and Sadness" presented below:

1. Allurement of the senses;
2. Questioning the command;
3. Toying with the idea in the imagination;
4. Concentration on the benefits of the sinful act;
5. The free and responsible choice to sin;
6. Shame;
7. Alienation from God.

---

12. *How does the story of the Fall fit into this pattern of sin and sadness?*

13. *List the reasons the author of Genesis gives for human sinfulness. What other reasons do you think account for sin?*

The effects of sin are dramatically portrayed in Genesis 3:8-24. Alone, Adam and Eve become broken people. Their rebellion left their intellect and wills injured. They were drawn toward evil and would more easily succumb to temptation. They became ashamed of their nakedness, and they acted in conflict, each accusing the other. Adam blamed Eve and Eve blamed the serpent. Neither the man nor the woman was willing to take responsibility for his or her own mistake. Eve could have said no to the serpent; Adam could have said no to Eve's offer of the fruit from the tree.

Even the world turned against them. Although they were originally destined to live forever, Adam and Eve had to accept mortality as a result of their disobedience against God. Adam, Eve, and the serpent each suffered specific negative consequences for their actions (see Genesis 3:14-19).

The effects of Adam and Eve's sin as presented in the biblical account are many. Sin pervades the world. Countries are ravaged by natural tragedies like earthquakes, mudslides, fires, and plagues, as well as tragedies caused by or allowed by human beings: war, violence, hunger, fraud. The author of the story of Adam and Eve in Genesis realized that most discord in the world is rooted in the misuse of freedom by human beings. In theological terms, the human inclination toward sin is called *concupiscence*. In order to do good, we must struggle against those impulses within us that pull us toward evil actions.

The term "original sin," then, has several meanings. It refers to the first sin or the root of sin. It also stands for the atmosphere of sin and evil in the world. Sin is a universal condition, and human beings are responsible for it.

How can natural disasters be considered the effect of original sin?

14. *In the story of Adam and Eve, on which person does the story place responsibility for sin? Who do you think bears the responsibility?*

15. *Read Genesis 3:14-19. What specific consequences were suffered by the serpent? By the woman? By the man?*

The Hebrew Scriptures: Called by the Father

These stories of the effects of sin on humanity are told in Genesis 4:1-22, 25, 26; 6:5-9, 18; 11:1-9. Once they were separated from God, people repeatedly sinned. The original sin started a chain reaction of wickedness and rebellion that spread through all of the human race like a contagious disease. Sin divided people from God, and it also divided them from one another. Three stories in Genesis record the progress of sin as the great separator. In the tale of Cain and Abel (Genesis 4:1-16), jealousy and pride split apart the first family. In the story of Noah and the flood (Genesis 6:5-9:17), sin reached such immense proportions that God almost erased all humanity from the face of the earth. Finally, in the account of the Tower of Babel (Genesis 11:1-9), sin divided all human beings from one another as portrayed through people speaking different languages.

The pattern in these three stories is the same. People sin and suffer the effects of their sin. Then God demonstrates forgiveness. Read each of these three stories, and see if you can identify (1) the sin, (2) the motive or temptation, (3) the consequences of sin, and (4) the sign of forgiveness.

Cain and Abel

Cain was a farmer like the Canaanites, Israel's enemy. Abel was a shepherd. This story may have more to do with showing the differences between the nomadic Hebrews and the sedentary, agriculturally-based people than it does with a struggle between two brothers for God's approval. Many scholars believe that the story of Cain and Abel reveals the tension between the Hebrews and the Canaanites.

Cain was unable to overcome the power of sin. His question, "Am I my brother's keeper?" (Genesis 4:10), has echoed through history as a representation of the selfishness of human beings and their inhumanity toward one another. The mark placed on Cain by God in forgiveness is mysterious; it may represent a tattoo or tribal mark that would protect Cain's life. Note that another son, Seth, was born to Adam and Eve after Abel's death to ease their pain.

Noah and the Flood

The reference to the sons of God having intercourse with the daughters of man (Genesis 6:4) might seem obscure, unless you know something about ancient religions. The ancient Canaanites worshiped the god Baal. Since the Canaanites were farmers, they prayed to their god to bring rain so that their crops would grow. One way of praying was to have intercourse with a temple prostitute, believing this would entice Baal to send rain. The Chosen People were tempted to worship Baal and to participate in this custom because they needed to grow crops in order to live. They did not have sufficient trust in God.

Lack of trust resulted in consequences. God brought the world back to the watery chaos that existed before creation because of humanity's sinfulness. The flood story might be based on a historical flood that covered much of the world as the people of that time knew it (that is, the ancient Near East). A worldwide flood occurs in a number of tales from many different ancient civilizations, like Sumeria and Babylonia. Although the Israelite account is very similar, it differs from other ancient flood stories in that it relates the story to sin and divine punishment.

The long lists of ancestors before and after Noah are called genealogies. Their purpose is to show the passage of time and explain the origin of the different peoples of the world.

The story of Noah and the flood speaks about the consequences of sin. Flood stories like Noah's are a legend in most mid-Eastern countries.

The Hebrew Scriptures: Called by the Father

The Gilgamesh Epic

Archaeologists have found other flood stories similar to the one in the Bible. One such story forms part of the "Epic of Gilgamesh," thought by many experts to be the oldest recorded story.

Gilgamesh, the young king of Uruk, is saddened when his closest friend, Enkidu, dies. The sadness stems not only from the loss but also from the realization that he too must die some day. Learning of an ancestor who lives in the "land of the immortals" who alone of all people has cheated death, Gilgamesh sets out to find his relative. But the land lies beyond the Bitter River—outside the limits of the human world.

After unbelievable ordeals, the youth reaches the Bitter River and crosses it into the land of the immortals. There he finds his relative and announces, "I am Gilgamesh; you are my ancestor. I have come far to seek your help. I am told that you know the secret of life and death." The old ancestor then tells how he survived a great flood that covered the earth. Because he survived, the gods granted him immortality.

The ancestor tells Gilgamesh of a magic plant that grows at the bottom of the Bitter River. If a person could ever find it and eat it, he or she would never die. The youth starts back across the river. Reaching midstream, he strips and dives into the deep waters. When he surfaces, he holds the magic plant in his hand. On the long journey home, a snake steals the magic plant. Deeply saddened, Gilgamesh resumes his journey.

Gilgamesh sets off on another journey, this time to try to discover where Enkidu resides in death. He is guided to the hidden "gate to the underworld," inside which the youth finds his friend and learns the fate of the dead. Afraid, Gilgamesh starts to run away, then stops. Considering his situation, Gilgamesh walks over to his friend, lies down beside him, and dies.

The tower of Babel mentioned in Genesis 12 probably refers to mid-Eastern prayer towers known as Ziggurats.

The Tower of Babel

The tower the people endeavored to build was probably a *ziggurat,* or sacred tower, like those the Babylonians used for worship. It was meant to stand for the first mound of creation that appeared out of the chaos at the beginning of time. The story provides a reason for the many languages in the world: God confused the language of the whole earth and scattered the people into many lands because of their pride. The sign of forgiveness is not found in the story itself but is implied at the beginning of the next section of Genesis, where God promises to give Abraham many descendants and promises to bless all nations through him (Genesis 12:3).

---

16. *How can you be your brother's keeper?*

17. *In the story of Noah, the flood resulted from the wickedness of humans. Bring newspaper or magazine stories to class showing how human beings continue to be cruel toward one another.*

18. *Give an example of a time in your life when you lacked trust in God. What were the circumstances? What was the outcome?*

Ziggurat: from a word meaning "to build high." A ziggurat was a temple tower of the ancient Assyrians and Babylonians that had the form of a terraced pyramid with steps leading to the temple on top.

Summary

- The first humans, represented by Adam and Eve, misused their free will and sinned by disobeying God and rejecting God's love.

- Adam and Eve, along with the serpent, suffered the consequences of their sin.

- The many effects of sin are present in today's world.

- The stories about Cain and Abel, Noah and the Flood, and the Tower of Babel record the progress of sin in the world after the Fall.

The Hebrew Scriptures: Called by the Father

■ Review

1. What power makes human beings different from the rest of creation?

2. What was the sin of the first human beings?

3. What was the sign of forgiveness in the story of Noah and the Flood?

4. How is the Gilgamesh epic similar to the stories both of Adam and Eve and of Noah?

5. Words to Know: free will, the Fall, concupiscence, Cain, Abel, Seth, Noah, original sin, Tower of Babel, ziggurat.

■ In Your World

1. When you throw a stone into water, waves ripple out from around the spot where the stone hit the water. In the same way, an evil act can have a ripple effect, spreading out and affecting the people around you until the evil becomes greater and greater. An act of goodness has the same effect. Provide an example of a sinful act that exhibits this "ripple effect." Then give an example of a good act that has the same effect.

2. Research the current status of the debate on the teaching of evolution vs. creationism in the United States.

■ Scripture Search

1. Anthropomorphism is speaking of God as if God were a human being and had a body. God's walking in the garden in the cool of the evening (Gen. 3:8) is one example of anthropomorphism. Find three more examples from chapters 3-11 of the Book of Genesis.

2. Write a modern version of the story of Cain and Abel in Genesis 4.

1 Review

■ Study

1. Why is understanding the context of a biblical story so important?

2. Is the Bible historically trustworthy?

3. What are the different types of literature in the Hebrew Scriptures?

4. Who were the Yahwist and the Elohist?

5. List the events of the six days of creation.

6. How does the account of creation in Genesis 2 differ from the account in Genesis 1?

7. Who do Adam and Eve represent?

8. What is the *Enuma Elish*? What is the Gilgamesh Epic?

9. What tree's fruit was forbidden to Adam and Eve?

10. How was the relationship between God and creation broken?

11. What are some modern-day sins?

12. Why is sin considered "the great separator"?

■ Action

1. Represent the work of the six days of creation in any art medium (collage, photo essay, drawing, and the like).

2. A popular saying is "What I am is God's gift to me; what I become is my gift to God." To create a better world, you have to begin with yourself to develop the gifts you have been given. Consider your strengths, weaknesses, abilities, and opportunities. What goals can you set for the coming year? For five years from now? For life? What immediate steps can you take to achieve those goals?

3. Find out more about the scientific theories for the origins of the universe (for example, the "Big Bang" theory). Do these conflict with the concept of a world created by God? Why or why not?

■ Prayer

The Psalms contain many songs of praise to God as the Creator of the universe. Many of these "Creation Psalms" were sung as a part of the Israelite's worship of Yahweh. Take some quiet time to read the following psalms: Psalm 8; Psalm 19; Psalm 33; and Psalm 104:1-4; 24-30. Then write your own Hymn of Praise to the Creator. You may want to use your "Hymn of Praise" as part of your daily prayer.

CHAPTER

2

OBJECTIVES

In this Chapter you will

- Discover Abraham's unique role in salvation history as the first patriarch.

- Learn to distinguish the one God of Abraham from the many gods of other ancient cultures.

- Look at the significance of God's promises to Abraham.

- See Abraham as a model of faith.

Abraham and Isaac: Pioneers of Faith

For the Church of Christ acknowledges that...the beginnings of her faith and election are already found among the patriarchs, Moses and the prophets. The Church, therefore, cannot forget that she received the revelation of the Old Testament through the people with whom God in his inexpressible mercy deigned to establish the Ancient Covenant.
—"Declaration on the Relationship of the Church to Non-Christian Religions"

The Hebrew Scriptures: Called by the Father

God's Call

You probably can trace your ancestors back as far as your parents, grandparents, and great-grandparents. These are the people who have made your life possible. What do you know about them? Were they born in the United States, or did they emigrate here from another country? What kinds of choices did they make in their lives that affect you now? Besides a name, you have also inherited a personal history from your family, including perhaps the religious faith that you profess today. But where did that faith start? Who was the first person in your family to believe in the one true God that you worship? What are your religious roots?

If you are a Muslim, a Jew, or a Christian, the faith you profess began with Abraham, the great father of believers. The history of his family is part of our heritage as a people of faith because Abraham was the one who heard and responded to the call of God. He is considered the father of biblical faith.

As you read the Book of Genesis throughout this chapter, remember that it is not a history book. Rather, it is a story expressing the religious traditions of the Hebrew people based on their oral legends. The events that take place here occurred around 1800 B.C.E., but were not written down until almost nine hundred years later.

The First Patriarch

A picture of Abram (this was Abraham's name before he entered into a covenant with God) and the patriarchs who followed him can be pieced together from information provided by the biblical accounts, ancient history, and modern excavations of sites in Mesopotamia and Canaan.

For Example

Originally the Hebrews, like their ancestors, lived as nomads or seminomads. When they settled down as a nation, they retained some of the characteristics of that way of life. The tribal organization of the Hebrews as depicted in the biblical texts bears great similarity to the life of nomadic Arabs today, who by race and country are closely related to the Israelites.

The real nomad, or Bedouin, is a breeder of camels, living in land areas that are strictly desert. This "people of the desert" travels great distances with herds in search of grazing land. Other nomadic people, however, breed sheep and goats and live in a half-desert region where the distances between one grazing ground and another are short. A nomad with sheep and goats still travels considerably.

Neither the Israelites nor their ancestors were ever true Bedouins. At the time of the patriarchs, the Hebrews were already settling. However, the patriarchs would always remember when their ancestors lived nomadic lives in the desert.

Abram was the head, or patriarch, of a clan of Semitic seminomads who roamed the Fertile Crescent between 2000 and 1700 B.C.E. These peoples lived on the outskirts of established communities in southwestern Asia, moving from time to time to find better pastures for their herds.

Read Genesis 11:27-31. Notice that Abram's father, Terah, took his family from Ur in Mesopotamia to Haran, six hundred miles northwest. Archaeologists have uncovered state records from this time period that refer to *Hapiru* or *Habiru,* names that suggest the Hebrews, Abram's descendants. Scholars also suggest that the name "Arab" comes from *Habiru* as well. It was in Haran that Abram encountered the mysterious reality that we now call God.

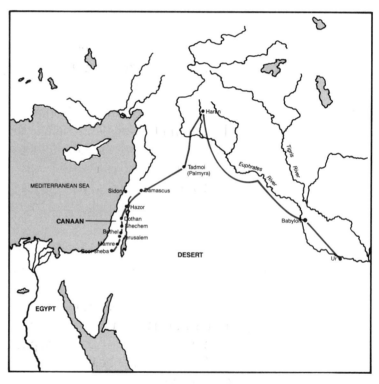

This map shows the journey of Abram from his ancestral home in Ur to the land of Canaan.

The Hebrew Scriptures: Called by the Father

Every so often, a person is born who changes the world: Columbus with his daring voyages, Edison with the light bulb, and Einstein with the theory of relativity are but a few examples. With Abram, the human race experienced a breakthrough in religious thought.

Before Abram, Semites were polytheistic. They believed in many different gods who controlled the forces of nature and granted prosperity or disaster according to whim. The people prayed to their gods for long life, good health, favorable weather conditions, and plentiful harvests. To curry favor or to ward off the anger of the gods, people sacrificed the best of their crops, their animals, and sometimes even their children. They also believed that their gods were limited to specific sacred places—the sky, a mountain, a particular tree or rock. Different cities even had their own "local" god, but whenever a city fell, its god surrendered to the god of the conquering people. Abram grew up in this system of belief where the people's changing fortunes shaped the lives of their gods.

Most likely, Abram worshiped the moon god, Nanna Sin, who was venerated in Ur and had a temple in Haran. The names of some of Abram's family reflect the significance of this god. Terah means "lunar month" and Sarai means "queen consort to the moon god." While he was in Haran, Abram learned of the existence of El Shaddai, the "mountain god" or "most high god."

In his struggle to understand the mysterious reality of the many gods, he realized that this one God was above all other gods, and yet unlike them since the God of Abram was a spiritual being not confined to a specific place and intent on protecting, not destroying the people. Instead of being shaped by the people, the God of Abram shaped a people by the bond of faith. To this day, believers continue to grow in the knowledge of Abram's God.

The story of Abram illustrates the transition from polytheism to henotheism, the belief that other gods exist, but one's own God is superior. Later, the Hebrews would move to a monotheistic position, believing in only one God.

Semite: the name given to descendants of Noah's son Shem, applied to people living in the Middle-East.

Fertile Crescent: the land between the Tigris and Euphrates rivers in what is now Iraq; one of the birthplaces of civilization.

Polytheism: the belief in more than one god.

Carved idols were used to worship the many different gods of the Mid-East.

The journey of the patriarchs was spiritual as well as geographical, for in finding their God they found their identity. They were spiritual models for us. God's fatherly call and care brought the Chosen People to birth with Abram. Despite pressures to adopt the local worship of Canaan, Abram's descendants remained faithful. Through them, the true God is known and honored by half the world's population today. Nothing remains of the moon god Nanna Sin or of any of the Canaanite gods, but the God of Abram lives on.

1. *Why do you think primitive peoples feared their gods? Are you afraid of God? Why?*

2. *How did you first learn about God? How has your understanding of God's identity changed as you've grown older?*

The Hebrew Scriptures: Called by the Father

Exploring for Yourself

Read Genesis 11:27-12:10, 13:1-8, and 14:11-24. The following suggestions may help you read the Bible more effectively: (1) Read one text at a time, silently or aloud to a partner. (2) Ask yourself questions similar to the ones below that relate to the verses. (3) Write the key words of the answer. (4) Discuss your answers with classmates. (5) If your answer is incorrect, reread the Genesis passage to find whatever you overlooked.

1. The Call 12:1-10
   a. What was Abram called to do?
   b. What promises did God make to Abram?
   c. How did Abram respond to this vague call?
   d. How did Abram worship?
2. The Quarrel 13:1-18
   a. Why did Lot's and Abram's herdsmen quarrel? How was the quarrel settled?
   b. What was Abram's reward for his generosity?
3. The Thanksgiving Sacrifice 14:11-24
   a. What happened to part of the Abramite tribe as a result of the war?
   b. What offer did the king of Sodom make Abram for his victory?
   c. What offering did Abram make to Melchizedek?

After answering these questions, reflect on the following:

1. What qualities did Abram need to be faithful to God's call? How can you develop similar qualities?
2. How is your experience like Abram's? What practical things might make your journey easier?
3. How does the Word of God come to you personally?

Think of three good friends. How long have you known them? How have you grown to know them better? Do you know any of them perfectly? When was the last time they did something to surprise you?

No matter how long you have known your friends, there will always be something about them that surprises you, and your closest friends will never understand you perfectly, either. If human beings are a mystery, God is even more of one. For centuries, ancient peoples recognized divine powers in nature. Although they had a sense of God, their knowledge of God was impersonal and vague. God was revealed more directly and personally to someone who believed. The Bible records this revelation in the story of Abram's call. Read the story of Abram's call and journey in Genesis 11:27-12:9, 13:1-18, and 14:11-24.

In the Scriptures, God used many ways to communicate: dreams, events, visions, direct words, and angels as messengers of God. Abram was a person who was receptive to the messages of God. God stepped into his life as someone who was genuinely interested in the welfare of human beings and someone who directed people through the simple, everyday events of their lives. Abram was the first in a long line of people called by God to a specific task or mission—one that was to be revealed to him gradually over time. What was required of Abram was trust and obedience.

God commanded Abram to leave his relatively secure life and "Go forth from the land of your kinsfolk and from your father's house to a land that I will show you. I will make of you a great nation" (Genesis 12:1-2a). Contained in these words were two important promises: land and descendants.

God told Abram to leave Haran for a new land. The command was full of mystery: it didn't say which land, and it didn't specify how the new land would be acquired, or when. Nor did it spell out what the journey would cost Abram. God expected Abram simply to follow. Abram was promised that his descendants would become a great nation and that the earth would be blessed through him. Abram believed that God would strengthen and support him as he took the great risks of a journey into unknown territory.

The Hebrew Scriptures: Called by the Father

The life of nomads today provides an idea of the migration of Abram and Lot to Canaan.

Because of his strong faith, Abram, his wife Sarai, and his nephew Lot responded to God's call. They placed their destiny in God's hands and migrated to Canaan, the Land of Promise. Their first stop was Shechem, where Abram built an altar to God.

The Quarrel

As Abram and Lot migrated through Canaan, they amassed a large herd of animals, herders to tend the animals, and other material possessions. Soon the land on which their flocks were grazing could not support the great numbers of livestock. The herders began to fight among themselves for pasture use. Often, individuals from the same tribe quarreled about migration routes, grazing lands, and watering places.

In his desire to keep the peace, Abram suggested that the only way to end the strife would be for him to move (Genesis 13:9). The large nomadic group was divided into two smaller groups and lived independently of each other.

Chapter 2   Abraham and Isaac: Pioneers of Faith

Abram was gracious and gave his nephew the first choice of the land. Lot pitched his tents eastward, near Sodom, in a land well-watered by the Jordan River. Abram chose to stay in Canaan. Because of Abram's generosity, God again promised him much land and numerous descendants.

The Rescue of Lot

Some time after Abram had settled in Canaan, he learned that his nephew Lot had been taken prisoner and that all of his possessions had been seized during an attack on the city of Sodom. Lot was captured in a battle between five rebel Canaanite kings and an invading coalition of Mesopotamian kings.

Upon hearing this news, Abram armed his household (which by this time had grown to 318 men) and pursued the invaders. He caught up with them, attacked them by night, and defeated them in a battle near Damascus. Lot and the other captives were freed, and the property was recovered. When Abram returned, he was greeted with gratitude by the Canaanite kings of Sodom and Salem. Melchizedek, king of Salem and a priest of El Elyon (chief god of the Canaanites), brought out bread and wine and blessed the victor. In turn, Abram gave one-tenth of the spoils of the battle as a tithe to Melchizedek.

3. *Imagine how Abram felt the night before he left Haran. Think of a time in your life when you took a risk. How did you feel when you made that decision?*

4. *How is your faith in God like your faith in your parents? Your friends? Yourself? How is it different?*

5. *When Abram and Lot part, Abram shows himself to be generous. By contrast, Lot seems self-centered. When have you acted like Abram? When have you acted selfishly, like Lot?*

6. *Read Genesis 14:21-24. What offer did the king of Sodom make Abram for his victory over the Mesopotamian kings? What was Abram's response?*

Archaeology

In Abram's time, as in ours, a place was considered "sacred" because that was where the worshiper could meet God. As Abram traveled from Haran to Canaan, he worshiped God in each new place where he stopped, establishing a sanctuary there out of homage to his God. Abram built altars at Shechem, Bethel, Mamre, and Beersheba. These sanctuaries were erected where nature manifested the presence of Abram's God—near a tree, or on a natural height, or close to a water source. These were the places where God appeared (called a *theophany*) and spoke to Abram.

In saying that "Lot pitched his tent," Scripture is reporting that Lot claimed ownership of the land.

Summary

- Abram, the first patriarch, revolutionized religion by recognizing the "most high God" as superior to all others.

- Many ancient peoples were polytheistic; they believed in many different gods whose actions were unpredictable.

- Abram followed the command of his God and migrated with his family from the security of Haran to an unknown future in Canaan.

- While in Canaan, Abram had to act both as a peacemaker and a warrior.

Tithe: ten percent of one's income given as a voluntary contribution or gift.

■ Review

1. Before Abram, what did people believe about the nature of the gods? How did Abram's belief differ?

2. What promises did the "most high God" make to Abram before he left Haran?

3. What were the Israelite sanctuaries?

4. Why did Lot's and Abram's herders quarrel?

5. What happened to Lot as a result of the war between the Canaanite rulers and the Mesopotamian kings? What did Abram do to counteract this situation?

6. Words to Know: Abram, Sarai, patriarch, Mesopotamia, Canaan, Semite, Fertile Crescent, Terah, Ur, Hapiru/Habiru/Hebrews, Haran, Lot, polytheism, henotheism, Nanna Sin, El Shaddai, Shechem, sanctuary, theophany, Sodom, Melchizedek, nomadism, Bedouin, tribe, tithe.

■ In Your World

1. Make a list of your ancestors. You can include family "heroes" as well as national or ethnic ones. Write an essay on how these people have influenced you and shaped your life.

2. Jews, Muslims, and Christians sometimes refer to themselves as "pilgrim people." In what ways is everyone's experience like Abram's? When are you most likely to feel uncertain of the road, like a pilgrim on the march? What practical things might make your journey smoother at these times?

■ Scripture Search

1. Read Genesis 12:10-20 and Genesis 20:1-18. What is the point of these two very similar stories?

2. Read Genesis 11:10-26. Trace the ancestral line from Noah's son Shem to Abram.

From Call to Covenant

Abram's call was more than an invitation to lead his family into Canaan. It was an invitation to a deeper spiritual understanding. While in Canaan, Abram became increasingly aware of God's plans for him and his descendants.

The Covenant with Abram

Earlier in Genesis you read that God promised land and descendants to Abram (Genesis 12:1-3). These promises were renewed and made more specific through a covenant, or formal agreement, between God and Abram. Genesis 15 and 17:1-4 describe God's agreements with Abram.

In ancient times treaties, contracts, and even agreements between two friends were called covenants. These agreements had standard elements: (1) review of the benefits bestowed by the superior party on the lesser one, (2) a response of trust and loyalty by the lesser party, and (3) the statement of the promise by the superior party. Although not in this specific order, these three parts were included in the covenant between Abram and God.

The covenant ceremony began with God's promise: "Fear not, Abram! I am your shield; I will make your reward very great" (Genesis 15:1). After Abram's questioning response of acceptance—"How am I to know that I shall possess it?"—God commanded him to split several animals in two and place each half opposite the other (Genesis 15:8). This signified that if either person violated the pact, that person would suffer the same fate as the animals. This ritual gesture was an ancient form of "shaking hands" on a deal. By staying with the carcasses, Abram kept the birds of prey away from the meat. Abram's faith would serve to

A covenant is a form of an agreement. What are some of the basic agreements you form daily?

keep anything from destroying the covenant that he had made with God (Genesis 15:9-12).

Finally, God reviewed the past benefits bestowed on Abram: the call out of Ur to Canaan, protection on the journey, and settlement on the land (Genesis 15:13-16). The last benefit mentioned would not be fully realized until the Israelites gained possession of Canaan during the reign of King David. The stark images of a setting sun, a trance or very deep sleep, and a terrifying darkness were efforts on the part of the biblical writer to convey the wonder of God. At the conclusion of the rite, a smoking brazier and a flaming torch passed between the split animals (Genesis 15:17-21). In most ancient covenants, both parties passed between the carcasses to symbolize their mutual cooperation. In this case, however, it appears that only God passed between the animal carcasses. This may symbolize that God took full responsibility for this covenant.

In Search of an Heir

Throughout his life, Abram sought God's will. However, as he grew older, he and his wife Sarai remained childless. Doubt crept into his mind as to how God's promise of descendants as numerous as the stars was to be realized (Genesis 15:5). Abram had put his faith in God's promises, although at times the future was shrouded in mystery.

In the time of the patriarchs, only sons had rights to inheritance. There was no such thing as a written will or testament. Before dying, a father would give verbal instructions about the distribution of his property. Abram's anguished plea to God, "O Lord God, what good will your gifts be, if I keep on being childless and have as my heir the steward of my house, Eliezer?", shows how the estate would be divided without an heir (Genesis 15:2). By law, a wife who could bear no children was under an obligation to provide a concubine for her husband from among her servants.

A marriage document found by archaeologists in the archives of the Mesopotamian city of Nuzi reads: "If Gilimninu bears children, Shennima shall not take another wife. But if Gilimninu fails to bear children, Gilimninu shall get for Shennima a slave girl as concubine. In that case,

The Hebrew Scriptures: Called by the Father

Gilimninu herself shall have authority over the offspring." The sons of a slave-woman concubine had no share in the inheritance unless their father legally adopted them.

Monogamy, or the taking of only one wife, is the biblical ideal and the standard practice today. The customs in ancient times of taking concubines and of practicing polygamy were applied to assure survival of the tribe (Genesis 16).

Jealousy and Promise

Sarai (like Gilimninu mentioned above) gave her Egyptian maidservant, Hagar, as a concubine to Abram, and Hagar became pregnant. Hagar also developed a superior attitude that infuriated her mistress. When Sarai complained to Abram about Hagar, Abram told her to do as she pleased with the girl. Sarai had carried out her obligation to Abram, but this did not prevent her from treating her maidservant harshly.

Hagar fled into the wilderness to escape Sarai's abuse. A messenger of God appeared to her there and announced that she was to bear a son from whom would come a multitude of descendants. Hagar returned and submitted to Sarai, but she was strengthened by God's promise that her son would be strong and free. Hagar gave birth to a son, and Abram named him Ishmael, which in Hebrew means "God has heard." Tradition considers Ishmael to be the father of the Arab peoples.

---

7. *You make many agreements with your parents, arrangements with your friends, and truces with your enemies. How do you measure the importance of each agreement? Are some contracts more one-sided than others?*

8. *What is the importance of the story of Hagar? What does it mean to have an Egyptian held oppressed and expelled from the family of promise? Why would the Israelites record God's revelation to Hagar?*

Concubine: a part of a man's household who would bear his children but is not a legal wife.

Polygamy: taking more than one wife or husband at a time.

The story of Hagar in the desert is a story of God's caring for the least fortunate. How can you care for those who are abandoned today?

Sign of the Covenant

Some years after the first covenant with Abram, God made another covenant with him. Read Genesis 17:1-14. How is this covenant different from the one in Genesis 15?

Revealed as "El Shaddai," God told Abram to "walk in my presence and be blameless. Between you and me I will establish my covenant, and I will multiply you exceedingly" (Genesis 17:1b-2). If Abram and his descendants were to act this way, God promised to remain with them always. Unlike the first covenant, keeping this covenant was the responsibility of both parties.

As a sign of the covenant, God changed Abram's name to Abraham and Sarai's name to Sarah. This name-changing often occurs in the biblical text. It indicates a person's realization of a new mission and purpose in life. God added further responsibility to Abraham's maintenance of the covenant: "Circumcise the flesh of your foreskin, and that shall be the mark of the covenant between you and me....Thus my covenant shall be in your flesh as an everlasting pact" (Genesis 17:11-13).

To seal the covenant relationship, circumcision was performed on Abraham, whereby the loose skin tissue surrounding the tip of the penis was cut off. Then Abraham performed this ceremony on Ishmael and all of his male servants in order to include them in the covenant relationship with God. Many ancient cultures performed this rite of circumcision as an initiation into manhood, but with Abraham, this ritual acquired additional religious purpose and significance.

---

9. *Baptism has replaced circumcision as the sign of the new covenant through Jesus (although circumcision is still practiced for medical reasons). How are the two actions related? How are they different?*

The Law of Hospitality

Think of your closest friend. What is it about this person that attracts you to him or her? People are usually attracted to friends because of characteristics they admire in them. Which two of the following qualities would you most want in a friend: generosity, humor, honesty, neatness, compassion, loyalty, intelligence, responsibility?

The patriarchs, like your friends, also had admirable qualities. Hospitality topped the list. This was an important characteristic to have if you lived in the ancient Middle East. In the desert, people who became separated from their own group or tribe depended on being welcomed by any other group through which they passed. Since anyone may have needed this help, each group was expected to offer it. This was the basis of the law of hospitality.

In nomadic society, it was inconceivable that an individual could live alone, unattached to any tribe. As a result, providing for a guest or a stranger in one's midst was highly esteemed. Hospitality was a necessity of life in the desert. The head of a household was expected to assume complete responsibility for the safety and well-being of all guests. The positive and negative aspects of hospitality will be seen as you read the stories of Abraham's visitors in Genesis 18:1-15 and the destruction of Sodom and Gomorrah in Genesis 19:1-29.

The law of hospitality was essential to living in the desert. What are ways that your family shows hospitality?

Abraham's Visitors

In Genesis 18:1-15, God appeared to Abraham, not as a flaming torch as in the covenant ritual but in the form of a person.

Once, Abraham was visited by three people. According to the law of hospitality, Abraham offered the men water for bathing, a place to rest, and food—essentially, the things they needed to stay alive. Sarah overheard the conversation between the visitors and her husband and laughed aloud when she heard one of the visitors say that in a year she would have a son. By this time both Abraham and Sarah were very old, and Sarah was well past child-bearing age. This story of Abraham's visitors repeats God's promise to Abraham that one day he would have many descendants and be the father of a great nation. Is it any surprise that Sarah laughed at this prediction?

Destruction of Sodom and Gomorrah

It appears that the original destination of Abraham's three visitors was Sodom, the city where Lot made his home. Sodom and the nearby city of Gomorrah, both now thought to lie under water in the Dead Sea, were places of great beauty and wealth that were corrupted by the sinfulness of their inhabitants. Read Genesis 19:1-29 to understand how the Bible presents the story.

God tells Abraham that the cities of Sodom and Gomorrah were to be destroyed because of the immorality of their inhabitants. As a good and compassionate person, Abraham bargained with the Lord in order to save his nephew and the other innocent people in those cities. He argued that a few good people far outweighed the many who were evil. Abraham prayed for his family in Sodom and was not afraid to bargain with God for Lot's safety.

Abraham's two other visitors arrived in Sodom, where Lot welcomed them into his home. His hospitality was similar to Abraham's, although the scene in Sodom has a very different ending. Later that evening, the men of the town gathered outside Lot's house and demanded that Lot bring out his guests so that they could be intimate with them. Here we get a glimpse into the negative aspect of

Angels

The word *angel* is usually used to represent either a messenger from God or a celestial, spiritual being. In the portions of the Bible that were written earliest, these two types of usage are well distinguished. Every divine messenger is regarded as a spiritual being, but not every spiritual being is a divine messenger.

In the patriarchal narratives, angels appear primarily as God's messengers. Their chief functions are

- *to convey the mandates of God to human beings;*
- *to foretell special events;*
- *to protect the Israelites, individually and collectively;*
- *to punish the adversaries of God's faithful people; and*
- *to serve as instruments of God's punishments against sinners within Israel itself.*

In the biblical text, angels often appear in human form. An angel foretold the birth of Ishmael (Genesis 16:11). Abraham showed hospitality to three of them without being aware of their true identity (Genesis 18:1-10). Lot protected two angels from an inhospitable crowd in Sodom (Genesis 19:1-29). Because of this act, he and his family were delivered from the judgment that these angels executed upon that city. The biblical authors continually stress that God works through these messengers, and their appearance in a story clearly indicates God's presence.

◆

Angels appear in human form in the Scriptures. Angels are generally understood to be messengers from God.

hospitality, since in order to follow the law of hospitality and protect the two strangers under his roof, Lot was ready to sacrifice the honor of his daughters.

The "sins" of Sodom included a lack of hospitality and sexual immorality. Because the evils of the city were so great, it was destroyed. With the help of the two angels, Lot and his family, except for his wife, escaped. Archaeologists propose that the destruction of Sodom was brought about by a great fire caused by the ignition of petroleum seepages and accompanying gas. The blaze may have been initiated either by an earthquake or by a stroke of lightning, interpreted by the biblical authors as originating from "the Lord out of heaven" (Genesis 19:24).

Although this story focuses on sexual immorality as the primary sin of the inhabitants of Sodom, this type of sin was not their only evildoing. Israelite tradition varied in regard to the nature of the wickedness of these people. The prophet Isaiah believed that their sinfulness was based on a lack of

Heroes and Legends

When Lot, his wife, and their family fled from Sodom, their rescuers told them not to look back or stop anywhere along the way. Legend has it that Lot's wife was unable to resist the temptation to look back at the burning city, and her punishment for this disobedience was that she turned immediately into a pillar of salt (Genesis 19:26).

The Dead Sea area in Israel has a very high saline content. Sometimes the salt forms into small pillars that line the shore, appearing from a distance like soldiers standing guard. This account about Lot's wife is probably a story used to explain these natural rock-salt formations in the area where Sodom once stood.

The cities of Sodom and Gomorrah are thought to be under the Dead Sea.

The Hebrew Scriptures: Called by the Father

social justice, whereas Jeremiah accused the residents of Sodom of general immorality, adultery, and living in lies. Ezekiel condemned the Sodomites because they were vain, greedy, and disregarded the poor.

---

10. *Are there other qualities that you value in a friend besides the ones listed above? Why are those qualities important to you?*

11. *What is the basis of the law of hospitality?*

12. *Why do you think that Sarah laughed when the visitor predicted that within a year she would give birth to a child?*

13. *How are natural disasters—such as earthquakes, tornadoes, and volcano eruptions—acts of God? Discuss whether natural disasters are punishments from God.*

Summary

■ God continued to favor Abram by renewing his promises, by making them more specific, and by entering into a formal agreement, or covenant, with him.

■ Worried that he would die childless and that God's promise would not be fulfilled, Abram took Sarai's maid, Hagar, as a concubine and had a child, Ishmael, with her.

■ Abraham circumcised himself and the male members of his household as an external sign of their covenant relationship with God.

■ The positive and negative aspects of the ancient law of hospitality are illustrated in the stories about Abraham's visitors and the destruction of Sodom and Gomorrah.

SECTION 2
Checkpoint!

Review

1. What is a covenant? List the steps of the covenant ritual depicted in Genesis 15. Explain the meaning of the animals, the birds of prey, and the flaming torch.

2. Why was the covenant depicted in Genesis 17 different from the earlier covenant? What external sign showed that the tribe of Abraham was covenanted to God?

3. Why was the practice of taking a concubine sometimes considered a necessity in Abraham's time?

4. What is the meaning of the name Ishmael?

5. What hospitality did Abraham show his visitors? How was his gracious hospitality rewarded?

6. Why did Abraham bargain with God to save the innocent people of Sodom?

7. Why was the city of Sodom destroyed?

8. Words to Know: covenant, Hagar, Ishmael, concubine, monogamy, polygamy, circumcision, law of hospitality, angel, Sodom.

In Your World

List one person in each of the following categories and describe a "contract" that you have with that person: a) parent, b) teacher, c) closest friend, d) girlfriend or boyfriend, e) acquaintance. Are all of these agreements equally important, or do you consider one or two of them to be more special than the others? Explain your answer.

Scripture Search

1. Read Judges 19:16-24. How does this story, like the one in Genesis 19, show the negative aspects of hospitality?

2. Look up the following Scripture passages: Isaiah 1:9-16, Jeremiah 23:14, Ezekiel 16:46-51. What do these prophets list as the crimes of the people of Sodom?

The Hebrew Scriptures: Called by the Father

Abraham's Supreme Trial

The connection between God's covenant promises and their fulfillment is the focus of this section. Abraham's long wait for an heir through his legal wife Sarah ended with the birth of Isaac, the miraculous event predicted in Genesis 18 by one of Abraham's visitors. If, however, God's promise of descendants for Abraham was to be continued through the line of Isaac, where did that leave Ishmael? Finally, how does Abraham remain faithful to God in the midst of trial?

Isaac's Birth and Ishmael's Expulsion

Abraham was nearly one hundred years old when Sarah gave birth to a son. They named the boy Isaac, which in Hebrew means "he laughs." Although God had blessed her greatly, Sarah was still jealous of Ishmael, Hagar's son. According to the Mesopotamian code of law, Sarah had legal authority over Ishmael. Although it was cruel, Sarah had the right to set her maidservant and her maidservant's son free and in so doing remove their claim to the inheritance of Abraham. Read Genesis 21:1-21 to understand Abraham's joy with the birth of Isaac and also his distress and reluctant compliance with Sarah's wishes.

Hagar and Ishmael were driven away from Abraham and his clan. Out in the desert, separated from the protective circle of the clan, they faced grave danger. Ishmael, exposed to the harshness of the wilderness, came close to death. Although seeming to defend Sarah's action, God cared tenderly for Hagar and Ishmael in the desert. God provided water and promised to make Ishmael the father of

Tracking Your Journey

In this chapter, we have been tracking Abraham's journey so that we can gain insight into the meaning of his life. Here is one way to "track" your life's journey.

Stepping-Stones. Close your eyes and reflect on some of the important events in your life. Concentrate on letting your thoughts flow freely; don't make judgments on the value of these memories. Think of the homes you lived in, significant people in your life, and your favorite books, movies, clothes, or other possessions. Recall your first friendship, and times that you have felt extremely sad, angry, or joyful. Note key phrases as they enter your mind. When you have collected a fair number, select the five most outstanding events and place them in chronological order. Label your list "Stepping-stones of My Life."

Digging More Deeply. Consider the five key stepping-stones that you have chosen and ask yourself these questions:

- *What was going on in my life at this time? What circumstances added to the meaning of the event?*

- *Who was important to me then (living, dead, or in books or movies)?*

- *How did I change as a result of it? Did I become stronger or weaker? What did I learn about myself and others?*

The Road Ahead. Look over your stepping-stones and try to find a pattern in them. Are they random moments in your life, or does some thread of meaning connect them? Do these events make sense to you? Do they still affect you now? Glance into the future and reflect on where you are going in your life compared to where you want to be going. Is there a big gap between the person that you are today and the person that you want to be? What will be your next stepping-stone? What obstacles stand in your way? (Adapted from "How to Track Your Journey" Walden Howard. *Faith at Work Jan/Feb 1980, pp. 14-15.*)

Abraham was willing to sacrifice everything for God. What do you learn from this story?

a great nation. Many Arab tribes consider Ishmael to be their father. This incident illustrates God's love for all peoples (not just the Hebrews), and also focuses attention back onto Isaac as the rightful inheritor of God's promises to Abraham.

---

14. *However cruel, how did Ishmael's expulsion bring about the fulfillment of salvation history?*

The Sacrifice of Isaac

The story of the sacrifice of Isaac is considered to be one of the most artistic and moving stories in the Hebrew Scriptures (Genesis 22:1-19). As painful as it was for Abraham to send Ishmael away, his most excruciating trial was yet to come. In an apparent paradox, Isaac, the reward of Abraham's faith, became the test of that same faith. Read this story of Abraham's obedience and consider how you would respond to such a test.

God called Abraham and said to him, "Take your son Isaac, your only one, whom you love, and go to the land of Moriah. There you shall offer him up as a holocaust on a height that I will point out to you" (Genesis 22:2). Abraham must have been bewildered by this request from God. His whole life up to this point had been one of obedience, based on the improbable hope of the birth—through Sarah—of a son who would carry on the tribal lineage and receive Abraham's patrimony. With Ishmael gone, Abraham's only heir was the beloved Isaac, and now God was demanding the sacrifice of this child. What kind of God would demand this? What kind of father would obey such a command?

Abraham's Journey

The story does not depict the outrage of Abraham; rather, we find him to be obedient and silent. With Isaac and two servants, Abraham traveled to the place about which God

Paradox: a true statement that is seemingly contradictory or opposed to common sense.

Holocaust: a sacrifice entirely consumed by fire.

Patrimony: an estate inherited from one's father or ancestor.

Praying the Hebrew Scriptures

The following prayer is used in synagogues on weekdays and on the Sabbath. It shows the importance of the covenant established between God and Abraham:

"Blessed is the Lord our God and God of all generations, God of Abraham, God of Isaac, and God of Jacob, great, mighty, and exalted. He bestows love and kindness on all His children. He remembers the devotion of ages past. In His love, He brings redemption to their descendants for the sake of His name. He is our Ruler and Helper, our Savior and Protector. Blessed is the Eternal God, the Shield of Abraham." (Taken from the *Siddur,* the Jewish Book of Prayer.)

had told him. Leaving the servants behind, Abraham and Isaac headed up the mountain carrying the wood, fire, and knife. Isaac must have been somewhat suspicious, since the passage shows him asking, "Father...where is the sheep for the holocaust?" (Genesis 22:7). Abraham replies, "God himself will provide the sheep for the holocaust" (Genesis 22:8).

At the appointed place, Abraham built an altar, laid the wood on it, and then tied Isaac down and put him on top of the wood. As he was about to kill Isaac, an angel stopped him and said, "Do not lay your hand on the boy ... I know now how devoted you are to God, since you did not withhold from me your own beloved son" (Genesis 22:12). Abraham then unbound Isaac and replaced him with a ram that he found caught in a nearby thicket.

The Meaning of Genesis 22

This powerful story operates on many levels. On the one hand, it may be an attempt to show a transition in Canaan from child sacrifice to animal sacrifice. Some of the Semites living in Canaan believed that the firstborn child could be offered in sacrifice in dramatic cases such as invasion or drought. This practice was rare, and the Semites from the East (Mesopotamia), like Abraham, knew nothing of this rite. Israel rejected this kind of sacrifice. The firstborn, instead, was redeemed, and an animal was offered in his place.

On the other hand, in the context of patriarchal history, Abraham's faith is the focus of the account. Through this story we discover how biblical faith not only calls for loving trust but also demands personal risk. When God commanded Abraham to sacrifice Isaac, the son in whom God's promises were centered, Abraham was put to a test. With Abraham's faithful obedience, God showed mercy toward Isaac and renewed the promise of descendants with a special solemnity: "I swear by myself...that because you acted as you did in not withholding from me your beloved son, I will bless you abundantly and make your descendants as countless as the stars of the sky and the sands of the seashore" (Genesis 22:16-17a).

15. *Can you think of a situation in your own life in which your faith and obedience to God's Word were severely tested? Describe what happened.*

16. *Abraham's faith was rewarded by a renewal of God's promises. What are the rewards of your faith?*

The Story Continues

After the rescue of Isaac, Abraham's story continues through the death of his wife Sarah and the need to find an appropriate wife for his son Isaac. Examine Genesis 23 and 24.

The Death of Sarah

When Sarah died, Abraham purchased a burial plot for her in Hebron. There were no cemeteries as we know them today. Instead, tombs were placed on property that already belonged to the family, or on a piece of land bought specifically as a burial place. Since Abraham and his household were resident aliens in Canaan, they did not own the land on which they lived. The field at Machpelah was bought specifically for Sarah's tomb.

The mother of the Chosen People, Sarah was laid to rest in Canaan. The purchase of this plot of land from the Hittites was very significant since it marked the first permanent occupancy of Abraham and his descendants in the land promised to them by God. Later chapters in Genesis note that other patriarchs and matriarchs were buried in the same cave.

Sarah is honored by the Church today for her role in our faith history.

A Wife for Isaac

Although Ishmael married a woman from a neighboring tribe, Abraham had to assure himself before he died that Isaac would not marry into a Canaanite family, since that would endanger the inheritance that God had promised. It

Hittites: a non-Semitic people who lived near present-day Ankara, Turkey.

was customary in tribal life to take a wife from among one's own kin. Marriages between persons of different families or marriages with foreign men and women were uncommon, but marriages between first cousins were not unusual. So Abraham sent his servant to find Isaac a wife from among his own family in Mesopotamia.

The story of Isaac and Rebekah is told beautifully in Genesis 24. It is composed of a series of dialogues between Abraham and his servant (vv. 1-9), the servant and God (vv. 10-14), the servant and Rebekah (vv. 15-27), the servant and Laban (vv. 28-49), and the servant and Rebekah's family (vv. 50-57). Reread these verses and note these divisions.

Under God's guidance, a wife fit to transmit the promises of the covenant was chosen. The future of the Chosen People is seen through the stories about Abraham and the continuation of the history of the patriarchs through the offspring of Isaac and Rebekah.

17. *Although Rebekah was promised to Isaac in Mesopotamia, the marriage took place only when she joined him in Canaan. What is the significance of this?*

Summary

■ God's promise of descendants is fulfilled with the birth of Isaac.

■ God tested Abraham's faith by demanding the sacrifice of Isaac. This story shows Abraham to be a model of faith, and it also depicts the rejection of child sacrifice.

■ Sarah's burial site at Machpelah marked the first permanent occupancy of the Hebrews in Canaan.

■ Isaac grows to adulthood and marries Rebekah.

The Hebrew Scriptures: Called by the Father

■ Review

1. Why was Ishmael banished? What good came from this cruel exile?

2. What is paradoxical about God's demand that Isaac be sacrificed?

3. List the two meanings of the sacrifice of Isaac.

4. What is significant about the purchase of a burial plot for Sarah in Canaan?

5. Why did Abraham want Isaac's wife to be chosen from among their kin?

6. Words to Know: Isaac, paradox, holocaust, patrimony, sacrifice, Machpelah, Hittites, Rebekah, Laban.

■ In Your World

1. God's guidance in helping Isaac choose a wife was very important. When you are making important decisions in your life, how does God provide you with guidance?

2. Select incidents from the life of Abraham that illustrate the following themes: a) Faith is God being so real to you that you entrust your whole person to God; b) You believe God's word simply because it comes from God; c) A sincere relationship with God must be expressed by both an internal conviction and some visible action.

■ Scripture Search

1. The Letter to the Hebrews (11:17-19) provides a Christian interpretation to Abraham's hope in offering his only son. In these verses, what did the return of Isaac to Abraham symbolize?

2. Read Genesis 25:9-10; 49:29-32; and 50:13. Who else is buried in the cave of Machpelah?

3. Examine the following Scripture passages: Hebrews 11:8-12, Galatians 3:6-9, Romans 4:1-25. How do these passages depict Abraham's faith as a model for Christians?

2 Review

■ Study

1. How did God show a continuing preference for Abram?

2. What are the differences between polytheism, henotheism, and monotheism?

3. Name some of the characteristics of nomadic life.

4. What did the covenant between God and Abram entail?

5. Why do Jewish people circumcise their sons?

6. Why were the names of Abram and Sarai changed to Abraham and Sarah?

7. Name two of the chief functions of angels.

8. What roles do Hagar and Ishmael play in Abraham's life?

9. Using this text and Genesis 22:1-19, list the main steps in the story of Isaac's sacrifice.

■ Action

1. Abraham is considered a model of faith, yet even he experienced moments of doubt. Can you think of a situation in your life when you doubted the word of a parent or a good friend? Can you think of a time when you doubted yourself? Write a paragraph or two about your personal experience of doubt.

2. Abraham faced many difficulties in his lifetime, yet he never lost his faith in God. What causes people to lose faith in God? Discuss these reasons in class.

3. *Hesed* is a Hebrew word meaning the special family loyalty, love, and faithfulness that nomadic people, who had no protection other than their own clan, owed one another. This word appears in the Bible about 250 times. In the following passages, how is *hesed* shown and what words are used to express it? Genesis 21:22-24; 24:27; 24:49; 47:29. Describe an example of *hesed* in your life.

4. Research the life of Bedouins in the Middle East today. How does their life differ from that of their ancestors from biblical times?

5. Imagine what might have gone through Abraham's and Isaac's minds as Abraham tied Isaac to the wood. Write a script and share it with a partner.

■ Prayer

Prayer is a response to God, an awareness of God's presence in our lives. How did Abraham respond to the presence of God in his life? When do you feel the presence of God in your life? Are you aware of God in moments of joy and celebration, or only in times of sadness and confusion? Take a few minutes to think about the times in your life when you truly felt close to God. Write a paragraph or two about this experience, expressing your gratitude to God.

God's Chosen Ones

OBJECTIVES

In this Chapter you will

- See how God works through human beings.

- Follow the biblical narrative as it details the lives of the patriarchs Jacob and Joseph.

- Learn how Jacob encountered God through dreams and visions and how Joseph's life was saved by his gift for interpreting dreams.

- Discover why the tribes of Israel came to be in Egypt.

Like Abraham and Isaac, Jacob was chosen by God. But God did not draw him close. It was Jacob who, of his own volition, sought to come close to God.
—Elie Wiesel

Even though you meant harm to me, God meant it for good, to achieve his present end, the survival of many people.
—Genesis 50:20

God's Imperfect Instruments

Athletes, entertainers, and public figures work diligently to keep their reputations clean because they realize that the wrong image can promptly ruin a career. Historians from ancient times knew the importance of image often hiding the faults of their heroes. The Hebrews, however, were not afraid to tell the truth. They realized that human weaknesses did not hinder God's plan, but actually revealed the depth of God's mercy and goodness in dealing with the Chosen People. The moral character of Jacob, the younger of Isaac and Rebekah's twin sons, left much to be desired. Yet it was to Jacob—the wild one—and not to Esau—his older brother—that the plan of God was revealed.

As you read these stories in Genesis, remember once again that these events occurred many years prior to their being written. They are part of the oral history of Israel and are meant to reveal the action of God working in the lives of the Chosen People.

Jacob and Esau: Early Struggles

The birth of Jacob and Esau is vividly depicted in Genesis 25:19-34. The details of their birth foretells the struggles these twin brothers would encounter later in their lives.

Rebekah, like Sarah before her, was initially barren. Isaac prayed to God on Rebekah's behalf, and God intervened to allow her to conceive. The two babies within her womb jostled and struggled so much that Rebekah wondered if . she would survive the pregnancy. She consulted with God

Esau and Jacob were twins. Speak with any twins you may know and discuss how they get along with each other. How is their relationship like Esau's and Jacob's?

about this, and received an oracle which told her that "two nations are in your womb, two peoples are quarreling while still within you; but one shall surpass the other, and the older shall serve the younger" (Genesis 25:23). Genesis proceeds to tell how this prediction came true.

In ancient times, the firstborn son received a double portion of his father's inheritance. This was the right of primogeniture, or birthright. In the case of the birth of twin sons, the first child out of the mother's womb received this right of inheritance.

When Rebekah's time of delivery came, the firstborn son was named Esau. The next son came out of the womb gripping the heel of his older brother. This son was named

The Hebrew Scriptures: Called by the Father

Jacob. Even in the womb, Scripture tells us, Jacob tried to gain an advantage as he would do later in life.

The birth of sons ensured Isaac that the promise of land and descendants given to Abraham and passed on to him would be fulfilled. However, the promise of God to the patriarchs was threatened by the conflicts between Jacob and Esau and the partiality of their parents.

1. *Read Deuteronomy 21:15-17. What does this passage tell you about the right of the firstborn son?*

2. *What are some of the legendary tales of the founders of the United States? How are the stories of Jacob and Esau similar or different from these stories?*

Esau Loses His Birthright

Have you ever noticed that gas stations located near superhighways always charge a bit more for their gasoline than stations on local roads? Why do you suppose this is so? If you owned a business, would you charge more for an item because you knew that your customers urgently needed it? We will see how the great patriarch Jacob was not above taking advantage of another person's needs when he tricked his brother Esau out of his inheritance.

Esau, skilled at hunting and a strong man of the fields, was Isaac's favorite son. Jacob, on the other hand, was a "simple man who kept to his tents" (Genesis 25:27). Jacob was Rebekah's favorite, not only because of his personality but also because of the oracle given to Rebekah before the birth of her sons. Rebekah wanted to maneuver her youngest son into the role of heir to Isaac's inheritance in order to fulfill the oracle (Genesis 25:23).

One day Jacob was cooking pottage, a thick stew made of red lentils. Esau came in from a day of hunting, tired and hungry. He begged Jacob to give him some of the food he was preparing. Taking advantage of Esau's moment of

Esau traded his future for an immediate need—hunger. How are you tempted by immediate needs?

Oracle: a prophecy that is usually given by means of a mysterious sign or saying. An oracle is usually received at a shrine. The person who gives the prophecy is also called an oracle.

Chapter 3   God's Chosen Ones

weakness, Jacob agreed to give Esau some of the stew in exchange for Esau's birthright. Esau thought only of his immediate state of hunger and, unable to see beyond the moment, he willingly sold his birthright to Jacob under oath in exchange for some of the pottage.

Although Jacob's behavior was not commendable in this situation, he did not deceive Esau. Jacob recognized a weakness in Esau's character and capitalized on it. Esau gave his birthright to Jacob simply because he wanted instant gratification. Esau refused to deny himself a small pleasure for the long-range good of tribal leadership that would come to him later on.

3.   *In this story, Esau is caught up "in the moment." Can you think of a time in your life when you, like Esau, made a foolish promise that came back to haunt you?*

Archaeology

Some historians see the purpose of the story of the loss of Esau's birthright as an attempt to explain some sociological truths about the Israelites. Esau the hunter is defeated, in a sense, by Jacob the farmer. On one level, the story is about how the oracle given to Rebekah regarding her children came a step nearer to fulfillment through Jacob's cleverness. On another level, the story explains how the Israelites abandoned their nomadic ways for an agricultural life-style. The frequently tense relationship between nomadic hunters and sedentary farmers is illustrated in this tale. Esau, who returned to the hunt, lost God's blessings. Jacob, who stayed with the tribe and settled on the land, prospered.

Jacob's Deception

Genesis 27:1-45 shows how Esau, who had previously given his birthright to Jacob, also lost Isaac's deathbed patriarchal blessing. Isaac was blind and near death. It was customary for a dying man to bless the family member who was to be in charge after his death. This special blessing of the firstborn was probably given to indicate the right of inheritance. Through the formal act of a blessing delivered orally, the power and status of the patriarch were to be passed on to the firstborn son.

Such a blessing was not simply a prediction of the future but consisted of words spoken that could not be taken back. In ancient societies where written language was not used by most of the people, the spoken word was more binding than any contemporary legal contract. Once uttered, words could never be revoked. This was especially true of curses and blessings.

Isaac asked Esau to hunt and prepare a meal for him as was Esau's habit. Isaac intended to give Esau his blessing

The Hebrew Scriptures: Called by the Father

after the meal. Rebekah overheard the conversation between her older son and his father and plotted the means by which her favorite son, Jacob, might deceive Isaac and secure his binding, patriarchal blessing.

In Esau's absence, Rebekah dressed Jacob in Esau's clothes and draped goatskin over Jacob's hands and neck so that Jacob would feel like Esau, "a hairy man," to his blind father Isaac. Rebekah also prepared some meat in a style that Isaac loved.

Pretending to be Esau, Jacob went to his father. Because of his blindness, Isaac was unsure of who had come to see him. Isaac said, "Although the voice is Jacob's, the hands are Esau's." Isaac ate the meal that had been prepared and then drew Jacob close to him so that he might kiss him and bless him. When Jacob came close to his father again, Isaac smelled Esau's clothes and believed that it was really his son Esau before him. Deceived by his youngest son and his wife, Isaac gave Jacob his deathbed blessing.

Today, land and other property is passed on through a legal document known as a will. How is a will like Jacob's final blessing?

The God of the Patriarchs

Just as your knowledge of God has developed during your life, the Israelites grew to know God better through the patriarchs, Moses, and the prophets. Who is this one called Yahweh? Originally the Israelites thought of Yahweh as the God of Abraham's family and their descendants. God was seen as being present to Isaac, Jacob, and Jacob's twelve sons.

Over time, the Israelites came to believe in *one* God, not a god of good, a god of evil, a god for *every* nation, and a god for *every* aspect of nature as believed by their neighbors. Their God was the God of everyone and everything.

The God of Israel is living—alert, attentive, and responsive. Without beginning or end, God is eternal. Invisible, the God of Israel does not take up space or have weight like man-made gods; instead, God is spirit.

Unlike the Mesopotamian gods who inspired fear with their unpredictable angry or destructive behavior, Yahweh is faithful, unchangeable (immutable), and loving. To the Israelites, God is all-powerful (omnipotent), all-knowing (omniscient), all-good, all-just, and all-wise.

The marvel of the God of Abraham, Isaac, and Jacob is that even though God is great, God still communicates with the Chosen Ones. God is more than a force; God is a Person. God is revealed as a friend, helper, and protector—one who is willing to forgive and save the people.

4. *Rebekah and Jacob act selfishly in this story, but in the end the will of God is carried out because of their actions. Why is this so?*

The Hebrew Scriptures: Called by the Father

Shortly after Jacob received the blessing, Esau returned from his hunt. He prepared the meat as his father had requested and went to see his father, unaware of the fact that the blessing had already been given to Jacob.

When Isaac realized that he had been deceived, he trembled uncontrollably. Esau pleaded with his father: "Haven't you saved a blessing for me?" But Isaac had spoken the words of blessing to Jacob, and those words could not be taken back. Thus Esau lost his father's blessing because of the deception of his mother and brother. Esau, understandably angry, vowed to kill his brother. Rebekah, knowing Esau's intentions, sent Jacob away to her brother Laban in Haran. She reasoned that Jacob would be safe there until Esau's anger subsided.

In the end, everyone lost: Esau was defrauded, Isaac was deceived, Rebekah would never see her favorite son again, and Jacob was forced to flee for his life, far away from his closest kin. Still, God loved all of these people, even though they were often imperfect.

---

5. *Put yourself in Esau's shoes. How would you feel about a brother, sister, or friend who had deceived you and stolen something that was rightfully yours? How would you respond?*

6. *What message is conveyed about deception, fraud, and lying through this story? Why do you think this message is included in the Book of Genesis?*

Summary

- The character flaws of the patriarchs are not hidden in Scripture: Jacob's faults are readily apparent.

- Through his own weakness and Jacob's shrewdness, Esau gave over his birthright for a bowl of lentil stew.

- Rebekah and Jacob deceived Isaac and tricked him into giving his deathbed blessing to Jacob instead of Esau.

Checkpoint!

■ Review

1. What oracle did Rebekah receive concerning her unborn children?

2. How did Jacob capitalize on his brother's weakness in obtaining Esau's birthright?

3. In ancient times, why was the spoken word so binding?

4. How and why did Rebekah and Jacob deceive Isaac? Are their actions excused or justified in Scripture?

5. Why did Jacob flee from his home? Where did he go?

6. Words to Know: oracle, birthright, patriarchal blessing, pottage, omnipotent, omniscient, Laban.

■ In Your World

1. The ancient Hebrews did not whitewash the faults of their heroes. Instead, they showed them to be imperfect human beings who sometimes made bad choices along with good ones. Name and discuss a contemporary person (politician, sports figure, actor) who is considered a hero but who has also shown a weaker side of his or her character.

2. The Israelites had a particular concept of God—that is, they believed certain things about God's character. Discuss what the Israelites believed about God's character. Then consider how your image of God is similar to or different from Israel's.

■ Scripture Search

1. Read Genesis 27:41-45 and then 27:46-28:9. How do these two stories differ in terms of the reasons given for Jacob's flight to his uncle Laban? What are some reasons for these differences?

2. Read Genesis 26:1-33. What was the cause of the controversy between Isaac and Abimelech?

Jacob's Dream Visions

Jacob fled from his brother's anger into the wilderness, where he faced himself and God. In the dream in which Jacob encountered God at Bethel, God renewed the covenant with Abraham. In a later dream, Jacob wrestled with a mysterious figure and emerged from this experience with renewed strength and a new name which indicated the important role that he would play in the history of the people of Israel. In both of these encounters with the Lord, Jacob grew in self-knowledge and in the understanding of his and his people's vocation.

Jacob's Dream at Bethel

Jacob was on his way to stay with his Uncle Laban in Haran. He stopped near a shrine at Bethel to spend the night. Bethel, mentioned as a sacred shrine earlier in Genesis 12:8 (when Abraham stopped there), takes on deeper significance with its connection to Jacob. Read Genesis 28:10-22 to understand the story.

Alone, Jacob received a transforming revelation. To emphasize the experience of Jacob at Bethel, the story repeats the idea that this vision occurred at a particular "shrine" or "spot." The revelatory vision that Jacob had was of a *sullam,* Hebrew for "stairway." This dream is often referred to as "Jacob's ladder." The imagery in Jacob's dream is derived from the Babylonian ziggurat, an image similar to the Tower of Babel described in Genesis 11.

Vocation: the special function of an individual or group.

Bethel: In Hebrew, *"Beth"* means "house of," and *"El"* means "god."

Through a dream, God made Jacob aware of his role in Salvation history.

In his dream, Jacob saw a ziggurat on which angels were going up and down, signifying a divine revelation. God stood near Jacob and repeated the covenant promises made to Jacob's ancestors, Abraham and Isaac. The role of Jacob's descendants in blessing the world was stressed in this dream.

Jacob suddenly saw the true purpose of his journey east: to marry and to have children. His descendants were to be chosen instruments of God's plan for creation. When Jacob awoke, he repeated, as if still in wonderment, "Truly, the Lord is in this spot, although I did not know it!...This is nothing else but an abode of God, and that is the gateway to heaven!" (Genesis 28:16). Jacob set up a stone to mark the spot, anointed it, and renamed the place Bethel, which in Hebrew means "House of God."

The dream left Jacob with a new understanding. His eyes were opened to the mercy of God in choosing him to lead God's people. But Jacob remained something of an opportunist. He bargained with God: if God would do something for him, then he would worship and give God a cut of his profit. But at least Jacob was no longer out for himself entirely. He offered to return a tenth of what he owned for God's purposes.

7. *What was the cost of Jacob's bargain with the Lord?*

Jacob Struggles with an Angel

As you read Genesis 32:23-33, you see that this biblical passage relates to a second dream of Jacob's. This is another important piece of Israel's folk history. Years after the vision at Bethel, when Jacob had acquired much wealth and a large family, he stopped at the Jabbok River to spend the night. He was alone at the time, apart from his family and all of his possessions.

A stranger appeared and wrestled all night with Jacob. At daybreak, when the stranger saw that he had not gotten the

The Hebrew Scriptures: Called by the Father

Jacob is seen wrestling with God before receiving his new name. What are some of the things you must wrestle with before you reach maturity and adulthood?

best of Jacob, he wrenched Jacob's hip out of joint, leaving him with a limp. Jacob struggled on and would not release the unknown attacker until he received a blessing. The visitor renamed Jacob "Israel" because Jacob had contended with divine beings and won. Jacob, in turn, named the place of the struggle Peniel, which means "the face of God." The implication here was that Jacob had seen the face of God through his struggle, yet he survived. Without learning the stranger's name or seeing him in the light of day, Jacob and his descendants gained a blessing.

This is a difficult story to interpret. Scholars believe that the story symbolizes Jacob's (and our own) struggle with God in the darkness of faith, a dangerous meeting that left him wounded but also graced him. Jacob's determination is evident throughout this passage. His struggle for blessing is profound. After the experience Jacob built an altar, not to the "God of our Fathers" but to the "God of Israel." The very human, imperfect man Jacob had become God's chosen patriarch, the father of the tribes of Israel.

Opportunist: someone who takes advantage of circumstances with little regard for principles or consequences.

8. *What did the wrestling at the ford of the Jabbok River symbolize? How does it correspond with events in your life?*

9. *Why do you think Jacob was left with a limp after his encounter with God?*

10. *What is the significance of Jacob building an altar to the "God of Israel"?*

Jacob the Family Man

Let's backtrack a bit, to the time in Jacob's life after Bethel but before Peniel. During this time Jacob arrived in Haran, met Laban, married two of Laban's daughters, and fathered thirteen children. These years in Jacob's life require a little explanation.

Laban Dupes Jacob

Thomas saw the ad when he picked up the newspaper. The stereo that he had been saving his money for months to buy was on sale. Getting his parents' permission, he rode to the store and attempted to purchase the equipment. Unfortunately, the salesclerk said that they had sold out of the one brand but were substituting another model in its place. Although Thomas had his heart set on the advertised stereo, he bought the replacement instead. After all, he reasoned, who knew when the other stereo would come on sale again?

Thomas had fallen victim to an illegal scheme called "bait and switch." One product is advertised and then another is substituted in its place. If you've ever had a similar experience, you will understand how Jacob felt when he was taken advantage of by his Uncle Laban. Read Genesis 29:1-30 to learn the story of Jacob in Haran.

Note several things about the story here. As did his father Isaac, Jacob searched for a wife in the land of his ancestors. Just as Rebekah was discovered by Abraham's servant at a

The Hebrew Scriptures: Called by the Father

Genealogy of the Twelve Tribes of Israel

This chart records the Biblical genealogy for the twelve tribes of Israel.

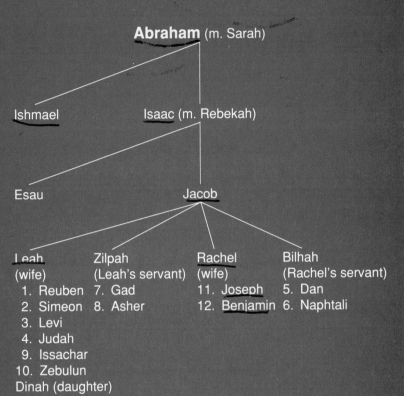

Abraham (m. Sarah)

Ishmael   Isaac (m. Rebekah)

Esau   Jacob

Leah (wife)	Zilpah (Leah's servant)	Rachel (wife)	Bilhah (Rachel's servant)
1. Reuben	7. Gad	11. Joseph	5. Dan
2. Simeon	8. Asher	12. Benjamin	6. Naphtali
3. Levi			
4. Judah			
9. Issachar			
10. Zebulun			
Dinah (daughter)			

Numbers 1-12 next to names indicate birth order of boys.

Manasseh and Ephraim, the leaders of two of the tribes of Israel, are the children of Joseph.

◆

How did Jacob marry Leah + Rachel?

what is Jacob's new name how did he get it and what does it mean.

Thomas was deceived when he bought his stereo. How can you keep from being deceived in a similar situation?

The Jacob stories are concerned with how people and places in Israel received their names. Part of the folk history of any culture consists of answering questions pertaining to how a group derived its name, how certain customs began, why particular holidays are celebrated, and why certain individuals are revered within the group.

The stories about the patriarchs are folk history. They are present in the text, not as literal facts but as a way to communicate background information about the Hebrew people and God's involvement with them.

well in Genesis 24, Jacob met Rachel, alongside a well. Jacob offered to work seven years in order to marry her. After this period of time, Jacob the deceiver was himself deceived. His veiled bride was Leah, not Rachel.

In oral histories, legends, and folk tales repetition was often used for effect. What happened to the father would often also happen to the son. This was done to share with the son the credibility of the father. Through the use of repetition, Jacob is seen as the equal to Isaac, and Rachel was seen as the equal to Rebekah. The promise of God would pass down this lineage. It is significant that Jacob agreed to work seven years. For the Hebrews, the number seven signaled perfection. That Jacob was himself deceived reflects the belief that God's justice prevails.

Jacob's Children

In Genesis 29:31-30:24, the theme of struggle between Rachel and Leah forms the core of these verses. Leah, the "unloved" wife of Jacob, could bear children. Rachel, like

The Hebrew Scriptures: Called by the Father

Sarah and Rebekah before her, was barren. How is this similar to the situation between Hagar and Sarah? What point do you think the story is attempting to make?

Leah gave birth to seven children: Reuben, Simeon, Levi, Judah, Issachar, Zebulun, and a daughter, Dinah. Her servant, Zilpah, gave birth to Jacob's children Gad and Asher. When Rachel proved infertile like Sarah before her, she sent her servant to Jacob. Bilhah had the children Dan and Naphtali. Finally, Rachel had children, the sons Joseph and Benjamin. This brought the total number of Jacob's children to thirteen: twelve boys and one girl. Hebrew tradition holds that the twelve tribes of Israel developed from the twelve sons of Jacob. The envy and jealousy of these women is set out clearly in Genesis 29:31-30:24. Read these verses to fully understand this story.

11. *In what ways did Jacob, Rachel, and Leah suffer because of Laban's villainy?*

Summary

- On his way to Haran to meet Laban, Jacob had a vision of a stairway to heaven at a place called Bethel.

- Later in his life, Jacob had a dream in which he struggled with a stranger until the stranger blessed him with a new name, Israel, which means "one who contends with God."

- Jacob, through the deception of Laban, ended up marrying both of Laban's daughters, Rachel and Leah.

- The twelve tribes of Israel claim descent from Jacob's twelve sons.

SECTION 2
Checkpoint!

■ Review

1. What was Jacob's dream at Bethel?

2. Why was Jacob renamed Israel?

3. How did Laban trick Jacob into marrying Leah?

4. How many years did Jacob have to work for Laban in order to marry Rachel?

5. Words to Know: Bethel, vocation, Peniel, Rachel, Leah, twelve tribes of Israel, Bilhah, Zilpah, Reuben, Simeon, Levi, Judah, Dan, Naphtali, Gad, Asher, Issachar, Zebulun, Dinah, Joseph, Benjamin.

■ In Your World

1. Like Jacob, we "wrestle" with doubts about God, our relationships, and ourselves. Write about a time in your life when you struggled with something or someone. What was the outcome of your struggle? Do you carry a scar, physical or emotional, from this encounter? What did you learn from the experience?

2. What was the cost of Jacob's bargain with the Lord after his first dream at Bethel? Describe a time when you bargained with God. Did you do this kind of bargaining more as a child, or do you find yourself employing this tactic more as a young adult?

■ Scripture Search

1. In the Gospel of John, Jesus refers to Jacob's ladder. Read the entire episode of the call of Nathaniel in John 1:43-51. Whom did Jesus compare to the ladder? What surprising revelation did he make?

2. Read Genesis 30:25-43. How did Jacob outwit Laban? What do you think about having the wile Jacob as an ancestor in faith?

3. Read Genesis 32:4-22 and 33. What was the final outcome of Jacob and Esau's reunion? What does this story reveal about the Hebrew people?

Joseph and His Brothers in Egypt

Wilma Rudolph was the first American woman to win three track-and-field gold medals in the Olympic games. This remarkable feat is even more amazing when you consider the obstacle she was forced to overcome. Rudolph was ill as a child and walked with an orthopedic brace on her right leg until she was eleven years old. Yet, despite this obstacle, her determination to compete made her a star athlete in high school and college and, eventually, an Olympic champion. After Rudolph's retirement from active track-and-field competition, she directed a program in Chicago to promote track and field for women and became a national spokesperson for the sport. Wilma Rudolph proved that weaknesses can often be sources of human strength.

The patriarch Joseph, second youngest of Jacob's sons and the first son born of Rachel, was favored by his father and strongly disliked by his brothers. By the treachery of his brothers, he was sold into slavery in Egypt and given up for dead. God's providence and Joseph's resourcefulness turned his sad circumstances into triumph, just as Wilma Rudolph, through her own efforts and God's grace, turned physical trials into personal and worldwide victory.

Jacob's Favorite

It happens in families all of the time. A child is born who for some reason is given a special place in the family. Maybe it is the first boy after several girls, or the first girl after several boys. Often, it is a child who is born sickly and is not expected to live. The family worries and fights for this child's

Wilma Rudolph overcame tremendous physical obstacles to become an Olympic gold medal winner.

Praying the Hebrew Scriptures

We pray:

Our God, and God of our fathers, God of Abraham and Isaac and Jacob, a heritage has come down to us along all the painful paths our people have travelled.

Our God, and God of our mothers, God of Sarah and Rebekah and Leah and Rachel, a heritage has come down to us.

When others worshiped gods indifferent to goodness, our mothers and fathers found the One God whose law unites all people in justice and love. Amen.

life until he or she is healthy. Or it could be a "miracle" child of older parents. Long after all hope of having a child—or more children—is given up, a baby is born. The newborn is seen as a gift from God and is treated with special honor. When there are older children, they sometime feel slighted or jealous at the attention of the new arrival. Don't they count anymore? Aren't they important and deserving of love? Do you know of families where this has happened?

This familiar story of the younger child becoming the favorite is witnessed in the story of Joseph. From the very beginning of Genesis 37, Joseph is portrayed as Jacob's favorite and rather spoiled son. Although Joseph was younger than ten of his brothers, he was the one who received a beautiful long, flowing tunic from his father as a gift. This gift was a status symbol and marked him as the heir. Just as Jacob stole his brother Esau's birthright, Joseph seemed to be stealing his brothers'. The tragic family tradition continues. Read Genesis 37 to understand all of the details of the story.

The Hebrew Scriptures: Called by the Father

Joseph's Dreams

Jacob's favoritism bred contempt for Joseph among his older brothers. And Joseph didn't seem too concerned about his brothers' feelings, either. He proudly reported his dreams that implied he was to rule over the rest of his family. One dream concerned sheaves of wheat. All the sheaves of wheat in the field surrounded and bowed down to Joseph's sheaf.

The second dream depicted the sun, moon, and eleven stars bowing down to Joseph. Even Jacob was insulted by the implications of this dream: "Can it be that I and your mother and your brothers are to come and bow to the ground before you?" (Genesis 37:10). The more Joseph talked about his dreams, the more his brothers despised him.

Joseph dreamed that all of the other sheaves in the field bowed to his sheave. What do you think this dream means?

Joseph Sold into Slavery

Jacob sent Joseph out to Shechem to check on his brothers' progress with the family flocks. When Joseph's brothers saw him approaching, dressed in his long, beautiful tunic, they became more and more jealous and plotted to kill him: "Come on, let us kill him and throw him into one of the cisterns here; we could say that a wild beast devoured him. We shall then see what becomes of his dreams" (Genesis 37:20).

The biblical account of Joseph's sale into slavery in Egypt, told in Genesis 37:1-36, is really two stories spliced together. The first story consists of vv. 21-24 and 28b-36. In this story, Reuben showed concern for his younger brother by convincing his other siblings to leave Joseph for dead in a cistern, instead of killing him outright. Reuben figured that if Joseph was in a cistern, unharmed but unable to escape, he could return later without his brothers' knowledge to free Joseph and return him to Jacob. In vv. 28b-36, we find that some Midianite traders passing through the area picked Joseph up out of the cistern and took him to Egypt with them.

The second story is intertwined with the first. In vv. 25-28, we see that after plotting revenge on Joseph, the brothers sat down to a meal. While eating, they looked up

Sheaf: a quantity of the stalks and ears of a cereal grass or other material which is bound together.

Midianites: a nomadic people who claimed descent from Abraham. Midian was a son of Keturah, Abraham's third wife (Genesis 25:2). Midian was also the name of a tract of land in northwest Arabia on the eastern shore of the Gulf of Aqabah.

In the stories of Joseph and Jacob we see brother fighting brother out of jealousy. This story addresses a problem which is universal in families.

and saw a caravan of Ishmaelites approaching. Judah suggested that instead of killing Joseph, they should sell him to the Ishmaelites. This way, they would be rid of him and garner a profit without directly taking his life. So they sold Joseph to the Ishmaelites for twenty pieces of silver.

Although the stories differ in their specific details, they agree on the fact that Joseph was sold into slavery in Egypt because of his brothers' jealousy. The preservation of this story in the biblical text reminds us that the Hebrew writers did not hesitate to report the flaws of their heroes. Esteemed ancestors or not, Jacob should not have shown such extreme favoritism toward Joseph, Joseph should not have been so arrogant and boastful, the older brothers should not have been so envious as to want to harm Joseph, and they should not have deceived their father by making it appear that Joseph was dead.

12. *What incidents indicate Joseph's good qualities?*

13. *How did Joseph's brothers convince Jacob that his beloved son was dead?*

14. *How can extreme jealousy or envy lead to physical harm or other types of sinful actions (theft, slander)?*

The Hebrew Scriptures: Called by the Father

There are three main parts to the Joseph saga recorded in Genesis 39-50. The first story is about Joseph and Potiphar's wife. The second is concerned with Joseph's role as a dream interpreter and how that skill enabled him to help the pharaoh and win his freedom from prison. The last and longest story is about the reunion of Joseph with his brothers. Read these chapters of Genesis before proceeding further in the text.

Joseph and Potiphar's Wife

Joseph became a servant of Potiphar, the Egyptian pharaoh's chief steward. Joseph worked so faithfully that he was made an overseer of his master's estate. Potiphar saw that "the Lord was with Joseph," and he entrusted his entire household to him. Potiphar's wife, however, became infatuated with Joseph and tried to seduce him. Joseph resisted this powerful temptation. Read Genesis 39 for all of the details.

One day Joseph was forced to escape the clutches of Potiphar's wife by slipping out of his cloak and leaving it behind him in her hands. Potiphar's wife used the cloak as evidence that Joseph had made improper advances against her. Because of this lie, Potiphar had Joseph thrown into prison.

Besides Joseph, who else in Scripture was forced to go to Egypt to preserve his life?

Ishmaelites: descendants of Abraham's son, Ishmael.

Joseph: The Dream Interpreter

Do you ever have dreams that you try to interpret? You wake up out of breath because you have been running in your dream; or perhaps you are with your friends and order a big pizza, only to discover you've left your money at home. What do these dreams mean? Are they signs from God or simply signs of an overactive psyche? Perhaps you are out of breath because you are avoiding something or someone at school. Maybe the pizza dream expresses your fear of being embarrassed in front of your friends. If you think about dreams, there are usually logical reasons that can be found to explain them.

The story of Genesis proclaimed that all dreams were gifts from God. Joseph, by being able to interpret dreams correctly, is marked as one especially blessed by God. Just as God's favor was granted to Abraham and Jacob, so too was it granted to Joseph. His story continues in Genesis 40 and 41.

While imprisoned, Joseph befriended two of the pharaoh's servants, the cup-bearer and the baker. Both men came to Joseph and asked him to interpret their dreams. Joseph interpreted the dreams of these two men accurately. The cup-bearer was released and the baker was killed, just as Joseph had foretold.

Two years later, Joseph was still in prison. The pharaoh began to have troubling dreams. One dream involved seven fat cows that were eaten by seven thin ones. The second dream was about seven full ears of corn that were consumed by seven lean ears. The pharaoh could obtain no satisfactory explanation for these dreams. Then the cup-bearer remembered how Joseph could interpret dreams. The pharaoh sent for Joseph, who interpreted the pharaoh's dream to mean that there would be seven years of plenty in Egypt, followed by seven years of famine. As a result of Joseph's advice, the harvests of the good years were conserved and stored up against the coming famine, and the Egyptian people were saved from disaster. Joseph, by creating the first recorded food bank, won his freedom.

Joseph married Asenath, the daughter of an Egyptian priest, and had two sons, Ephraim and Manasseh. As God had warned through the pharoah's dream, the years of

Joseph established food banks in Egypt to prepare against famine. What do you know about food banks and soup kitchens today?

Separation and Reconciliation

When two people are angry with each other, a period of separation often follows to allow wounds to heal and anger to calm. The separation need not be physical. It can be mental or emotional separation as well. Which of these procedures would you advise for reconciliation?

- *The person who started the fight should apologize first.*

- *Both parties should admit their guilt.*

- *The injured party should seek out the aggressor to make up.*

- *Neither party needs to refer to the incident if they begin to interact again.*

- *Both parties should express their sorrow by words and actions.*

The journey of Jacob's sons to Egypt is a story of reconciliation. The jealous brothers were brought to esteem and to love their younger brother, who, in becoming a victim, was made their savior. But this account provides good entertainment along with religious instruction. The tricks that Joseph pulled on his brothers before revealing his identity could be fodder for a great movie plot: spy accusations, the taking of hostages, the planting of stolen goods, attempted kidnapping, demands for ransom, and unjust imprisonment are all included. The only difference is that in the Joseph saga, both the "good guys" and the "bad guys" (who eventually turn into good guys) came out on top. Genesis 42-47 describes the story's resolution.

◆

famine devastated not only Egypt but the entire area. As happens today with the famine in Africa, people travel to a source of food, often dying along the road from starvation. In this case, the food was in Egypt and people made the difficult journey. Joseph's correct interpretation of the pharaoh's dream earned him much respect and a position of power in the pharaoh's court.

Joseph and His Brothers

The long story about Joseph's reconciliation with his family in Genesis 42-50 is one of the most beautifully written tales in all the Scripture. As you read these chapters, pay special attention to the following episodes:

- *Chapter 42: first journey—encounter with Joseph and the return to Canaan*

- *Chapter 43: second journey/the goblet*

- *Chapter 44: final test*

- *Chapter 45: the truth revealed*

- *Chapter 46: migration to Egypt—Joseph meets Jacob*

- *Chapter 47: the pharaoh meets Joseph's family—settlement in Goshen*

- *Chapter 48: Jacob blesses his grandsons*

- *Chapter 49: Jacob's testament*

- *Chapter 50: the death of Jacob and Joseph*

These chapters tell how the tribes of Israel moved from Canaan to Egypt and set the stage for the time when the Israelites became enslaved in Egypt. In this touching story, we see how Joseph did not allow misfortune to keep him from becoming an instrument in God's hand for saving his family from extinction.

Summary

- Joseph's brothers sold him into slavery in Egypt.

- Imprisoned falsely, Joseph made the best of a bad situation and won the pharaoh's favor by interpreting his dreams.

- Joseph's dream interpretation saved Egypt from famine and earned him a place of honor in the pharaoh's court.

- The journey of Jacob's sons to Egypt is a story of reconciliation.

The Hebrew Scriptures: Called by the Father

Review

1. Why did Joseph's brothers dislike him?

2. How did Joseph's brothers get rid of him? Discuss both versions of this story.

3. Why was Joseph thrown into prison in Egypt?

4. What did the pharaoh's dream mean?

5. How did Joseph become reunited with his family?

6. Words to Know: sheaf, Midianites, Ishmaelites, Potiphar, pharaoh, Asenath.

In Your World

1. Do you know of anyone like Wilma Rudolph who developed a strength (not just a physical one) as a result of weakness? What weaknesses can you see in yourself, and what are you doing to overcome them?

2. Reread Genesis 37. Picture yourself in the place of any one of Joseph's brothers. What would you have done? Have you ever found yourself in a similar situation where other friends were doing something with which you didn't agree, but you were unsure whether or not you should just ''go along'' with them?

Scripture Search

1. Read Mark 14:1-2, 10-11, 17-21, and 43-46. How can these verses be compared to the sale of Joseph to the Ishmaelites by his brothers?

2. Read Deuteronomy 33:13-16. How does this passage describe the tribal land given to Joseph?

3 Review

■ Study

1. Esau lost both his birthright and his father's blessing. Explain why.

2. Give three examples of Jacob's "opportunism."

3. What happened to Jacob at Bethel and Peniel?

4. Why was Jacob renamed Israel? What did the name imply?

5. Why did Jacob end up marrying both of Laban's daughters?

6. How was Joseph both like and unlike his father?

7. Why might it be considered "poetic justice" that Joseph's brothers tricked Jacob into thinking that Joseph was dead by giving him the bloody tunic?

8. From your reading of Genesis 40, what were the dreams of the pharaoh's cup-bearer and baker? How did Joseph interpret them?

9. Describe Joseph's rise to power in Egypt.

10. Why did Joseph's brothers come to Egypt?

11. What are some of Joseph's good qualities?

12. What is different about Jacob's blessing of Ephraim and Manasseh?

13. How is Joseph blessed by his father?

14. How does Joseph forgive his brothers?

■ Action

1. Your brothers and sisters are called your siblings. Sibling rivalry is conflict between brothers and sisters. List three examples of sibling rivalry in the lives of Jacob and Esau. How, if ever, were these conflicts resolved?

2. List the names of Jacob's twelve sons, and beside each name give its Hebrew meaning as found in the text of Genesis.

3. The theme of struggle is present in most of the biblical material concerning Jacob. He struggled with Esau, then Laban, then his wives Rachel and Leah, and then with a stranger in the night when he was alone at the ford of the Jabbok River. In his confronting of obstacles, Jacob's life was not so different from our own. Think of some struggles and trials that you have endured in your life. How did you get through them? Do any of these conflicts continue to affect you in the present? If so, discuss the situation with a friend and brainstorm creative ways to deal with your struggle.

4. Invite someone who is knowledgeable about dream interpretation to your class or youth group to discuss how best to find meaning in dreams.

■ Prayer

Before he died, Jacob blessed each of his children and Ephraim and Manasseh, Joseph's children. This is how Scripture records the blessing of Ephraim and Manasseh:

"May the God in whose ways my fathers Abraham and Isaac walked. The God who has been my shepherd from my birth to this day, the Angel who has delivered me from all harm, bless these boys that in them my name be recalled, and the names of my fathers Abraham and Isaac, and they may become teeming multitudes upon the earth!" (Genesis 48:5-16).

Write a prayer of blessing for a friend or loved one. Offer your blessing prayer to that person. Use the blessing prayer of Jacob as a model for your prayer.

CHAPTER

4

Moses: Reluctant Hero

OBJECTIVES

In this Chapter you will

- Explore the important biblical themes of election, deliverance, and covenant.

- Learn about Moses' life and his significant role in Jewish history.

- Examine the Exodus and Sinai events and their consequences.

- See how the covenant bound God and the Israelites in a unique friendship.

If you hearken to my voice and keep my covenant, you shall be my special possession, dearer to me than all other people.
—Exodus 19:5

The Hebrew Scriptures: Called by the Father

Choice, Deliverance, and Covenant

David was only eight years old, but he was already a hero. When his house caught fire, David quickly called the fire department and then grabbed his baby sister out of the crib and ran outside. He not only managed to save two lives but also saved the family home. Each time the family would gather to give thanks for their good fortune, David was celebrated for his saving action. The family did not forget how he had rescued them from a great loss.

Have you ever had a close encounter with death and escaped because someone pulled you out of physical danger? Have you ever been on the verge of making a poor choice in your life and someone stepped in with advice or counsel that enabled you to make a better decision? How did you feel toward the person who "saved" you?

God saved the Hebrews, fashioning them into a nation and giving them laws and a land they could call their own—Canaan. God entered into another covenant with them, more detailed than the covenant with Abraham. This chapter will introduce the concepts of election, deliverance, and covenant as seen in the stories of the Exodus from Egypt, the wandering in the desert, and the covenant at Sinai.

> **Election:** the religious conviction that God has chosen a particular person or group of people and established a unique and exclusive relationship with them. Usually election carries with it specific obligations and responsibilities.

Archaeology

When the Israelites began their stay in Egypt, they settled in Goshen, which is also called the land of Rameses (Genesis 47:1 and 47:11). The Israelite slaves were forced to build the supply cities of Rameses and Pithom (Exodus 1:11).

Scholars are unsure of the precise location of the city of Rameses. It probably was located in the northern half of the eastern delta of the Nile River, accessible by ship from the Nile and the Red Sea. This city was the chief residence of the pharaohs for nearly 200 years; Egyptian sources praise the area as a land abundant in fruit, fisheries, and marshlands. More important, Rameses was the starting point of the Exodus, distant from the desert by a two-day march.

Moses: Epic Figure

The Hebrews were God's Chosen People, but their election by God did not mean that they would be free from all physical harm or suffering. After Joseph had his family members migrate to Egypt, they were favored by pharaohs for many years. Then, when "a new king, who knew nothing of Joseph, came to power in Egypt," their "friends" suddenly became enemies and enslaved them (Exodus 1:8). The Israelites were enslaved for over four centuries, until God delivered them from slavery through Moses.

There is more written in the Bible about Moses than about any other person, including Jesus. Like a giant, Moses towers over the whole of the Hebrew Scriptures and ranks as the greatest Jewish hero. Moses holds many titles: prophet, savior, lawgiver, judge, mediator, and leader. The Israelites who repeated his life story and the scribes who wrote it down treated him like an epic hero. Moses became a larger-than-life figure. He represented the pride of the Jewish people and is an example illustrating God's relationship to the Israelites. Moses played the leading role in the most important event in Jewish history—their deliverance from slavery in Egypt to the land of promise.

---

1. *Think of someone in American history who has achieved larger-than-life stature. Why has the person you have chosen been given this status?*

Moses' Early Life

We discover Moses' early history in Exodus 1-2:22. Read these chapters before exploring further.

Originally Joseph's descendants were welcomed into Egypt by the Semitic Hyksos, a foreign invader in control of the country. When the Hyksos were expelled around 1500 B.C.E., the native Egyptians turned against the Hebrews as well. The pharaoh "who knew nothing of Joseph" is identified by scholars as Seti I, who ruled Egypt from

1308-1290 B.C.E. Fearing that the growing strength and unity of the Israelites threatened the safety of his nation, he conscripted the Israelites into labor brigades and gave them the task of building the supply cities of Pithom and Rameses.

Even while under oppression, the Israelites continued to worship their God and to grow into a people. As the Hebrew population increased, the Egyptians worried that

Egyptian civilization is very old. Egypt was once again a powerful nation at the time of the Exodus.

Conscript: to enroll into service by force.

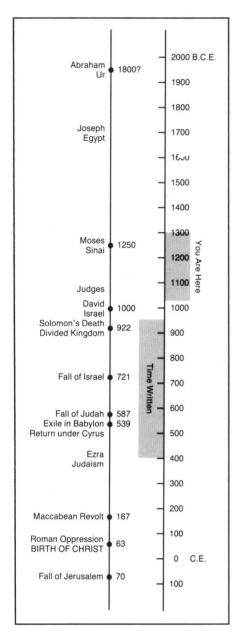

The date for the Exodus is thought to be around 1250 B.C.E.

the Israelites would become too numerous and would want their freedom. Since they provided cheap labor for Seti's building projects, this could not be allowed to happen. Be sure to read Exodus 4:17 which describes the enslavement of the Hebrew people before reading further into this text.

The story of the Hebrew midwives in Exodus 1:15-20 describes people committed to justice. These women risked their lives by disobeying the pharaoh to protect the innocent lives of newborn babies. These women are witnesses for the ages. Their acts of bravery have been followed by people in history who refuse to cooperate with evil: the people who fight against oppressive governments, the men and women who protest abortion, the people who march for peace. Each of these people follows the examples of these midwives. How can you witness for justice?

Moses, from the tribe of Levi, was born during the time when male babies were to be put to death. He, too, was saved by women: first his mother, then his sister Miriam, and finally the pharaoh's daughter. It is women who saved the Israelites from slavery by saving Moses. Often while reading Scripture it is possible to think of the Bible as the story of men. Overcoming the culture of the day, the Hebrew Scriptures do not ignore the efforts of women. Rather, the women are held up as the ones who are found worthy in God's eyes. God works even through the lives of Egyptian women.

Moses was brought up as a prince of Egypt, but he nevertheless knew of his Hebrew origins. One day he saw an Egyptian beating a Hebrew slave, and he stepped in and killed the Egyptian. When the pharaoh heard of this act, he condemned Moses to death. Moses fled from Egypt and traveled across the desert to Midian. There he became a shepherd and married Zipporah, the daughter of Jethro, a priest of Midian.

During Moses' years of safety in Midian, Seti I died and a new pharaoh, Rameses II, came into power. Rameses was even more cruel than Seti, and the conditions of the Israelites in Egypt worsened. But God heard the cries of his people and "was mindful of his covenant with Abraham, Isaac, and Jacob" (Exodus 2:24). It would soon be time for Moses to lead the Israelites to freedom.

The Hebrew Scriptures: Called by the Father

One day as Moses was tending Jethro's flocks near Mount Horeb, he saw flames coming out from the center of a bush, yet the bush was not consumed by the fire. God was present at this place and spoke to Moses from out of the fire. Moses had to keep his distance and remove his shoes, because he was on holy ground, a place of power and danger for human beings.

This was the first in a series of theophanies—appearances of God to humans—that occur throughout the Book of Exodus. God called Moses to a specific task, as Moses' ancestor Abraham had been called hundreds of years before. God had heard the cry of the people and was going to use Moses as the instrument for the deliverance of the Israelites from Egypt. This magnificent call is recounted in Exodus 3:4-17.

Through the spiritual experience symbolized by the burning bush, God called Moses to be the prophet. Using Moses, God would deliver the Israelites from slavery into a land of freedom. Moses, however, was not too keen about his task. He felt uncomfortable being asked to do something for which he did not feel qualified. Moses reasoned with God, pleaded with God. He even used his minor speech defect as an excuse. But God was unyielding. Moses was to go to the pharaoh, along with his brother Aaron, and demand the release of the Israelites from slavery.

The call of Moses on Mount Horeb was the beginning of a personal relationship between God and Moses that led to the deepening of the relationship between God and the Israelites. As a sign of their special relationship, God revealed the divine name to Moses.

There is a close bond between you and your name. Your name identifies you. In some cultures, a name describes the type of person you are. Telling your name to someone is a sign of trust, a first step toward friendship. In a sense, it is putting yourself in the hands of another person. Adam named the animals as a sign that he was master over them. To the Jews, a person's name was a reflection of his or her personality. Thus, to reveal your name to someone was to reveal the secret of your being.

The Name of Israel's God

The people who lived in Moses' day had numerous gods: *Chemosh* (**kehm**-osh) of the Moabites, *Amon-Re* (**ah**-mohn ray) of the Egyptians, and *Baal* (**bay**-ehl) of the Canaanites. Little wonder, then, that when God spoke to Moses, Moses asked for God's name. God responded, "I am who am...the Lord, the God of your fathers, the God of Abraham, the God of Isaac, the God of Jacob" (Exodus 3:14-15). Once the God of the Israelites was named "I Am" or "Yahweh" (the Hebrew consonants for the word in this text are YHWH), the Israelites knew God's personal name. The word *Yahweh* in Hebrew is related to the verb "to be." This verb in Hebrew means more than existence; its use implies active presence. The name "Yahweh," then, reflects the Israelites' belief that God was always present to help them.

Jews have so much reverence for the holy name of God that they do not even pronounce the word "Yahweh." They use the Hebrew substitute "Adonai," which means "Lord" in English. When a Jewish person reads from Scripture and comes to "Yahweh" in a passage, she or he will not say that name aloud, but instead will use "Adonai" out of respect for the name of God.

Why is the revelation of God's name as "Yahweh" significant?

When God revealed a personal name to Moses—I AM, or Yahweh—God showed trust in Moses. God was disclosed as the God who is present to people. Moses' encounter with God at the burning bush motivated him to accomplish a mighty feat—to mold a group of escaped slaves into a community with God as its leader and God's law as its constitution. Moses learned that with God, all things are possible.

2. *Why did the pharaoh order all male Hebrew children to be killed?*

3. *What features of Moses' early life marked him as a hero?*

4. *Why are you offended when people ridicule your name or mispronounce it?*

Summary

- God's Chosen People, the Israelites, were forced into slavery by the Egyptians.

- Moses, a Hebrew slave, was rescued from death by the pharaoh's daughter and raised as an Egyptian prince.

- While defending another Hebrew, Moses killed an Egyptian and had to flee for his life.

- God spoke to Moses from out of a burning bush and gave him the task of liberating the Israelites from oppression in Egypt.

SECTION 1
Checkpoint!

■ Review

1. What does the word *election* mean in terms of the Jewish people?

2. Why is Moses an important figure in the Bible?

3. Why did Seti I order that all male Hebrew children be killed? How did Moses escape this decree?

4. What task did God assign to Moses on Mount Horeb?

5. What does the word *Yahweh* mean?

6. Words to Know: election, Exodus, Moses, conscript, Seti I, Rameses II, Miriam, Jethro, Zipporah, Mount Horeb, Aaron, Yahweh, Adonai.

■ In Your World

1. Moses could have led a life of comfort in the pharaoh's palace, or at least a life of peace tending flocks with his father-in-law Jethro in Midian. Instead, he risked his life for the cause of his people. Under what conditions would you risk your comforts, or perhaps even your life, for a family member? A friend? Your country? A principle? Your faith? Why or why not?

2. Israelites never speak the name of God, "Yahweh," directly. They always use a substitute because they hold God's name in great reverence. Today, however, the name of God is often used very casually. People often say "Oh God" or "God only knows" or "God, that outfit looks awful on you!" Why do people use God's name casually? What can you do to change this practice?

■ Scripture Search

1. Read Matthew 8:4, Mark 7:10, and John 1:17. What role of Moses dominates in these verses?

2. Examine the text of Matthew 2:13-18. Of what part of Moses' life does this passage remind you?

The Hebrew Scriptures: Called by the Father

The Plagues, the Passover, and the Exodus

Moses was a reluctant hero. Even though he was not cooperative at first, he eventually submitted to God's call. However, the road to freedom was a difficult one. Moses endured frustration, humiliation by the pharaoh, and recriminations from his own people before leading the Israelites out of Egypt.

The Exodus story reveals much about the God of the Hebrews as revealed to Moses. This is a God who uses human beings to accomplish the divine will; this is a God who works through nature and natural events; this is a God who saves through unlikely people—midwives and condemned killers, unwilling and disabled spokespersons; this is a God of surprises. Study God's activity in Genesis 6-12:36.

Bricks without Straw

Some heroes are famous because of a skill, a talent, or an outstanding achievement. But the heroes who most inspire admiration are those who risk or give their lives for others.

One night Will McLaughin and his uncle, a minister, were discussing the passage "For this cause came I into this world." Will offered to take his uncle's materials for the next day's sermon to the large new Iroquois Theater of Northwestern University. When he arrived, the building was on fire, and he rushed to the balcony where screaming people were trapped. The fire escapes had not yet been completed, so Will laid a plank from a balcony window to a window of the building next door, enabling many people to escape. By the time Will stepped onto the plank, the fire had weakened it and he crashed to the concrete below. Before he died he said to his uncle, "Maybe your text fits me: 'For this cause came I into the world.' " The university inscribed the passage and Will's name on that plank, and it is cherished as a memento of his saving efforts.

Moses and Aaron reluctantly went to Egypt to face the pharaoh and demand that he release God's people from slavery for three days so that they might worship and offer sacrifice to Yahweh. But Rameses was not too happy about losing his labor force, and since Yahweh was not his god, he saw no reason to fear or obey this Hebrew deity. Rameses dismissed Moses and Aaron and made the work load of the Israelites even heavier by refusing to supply the straw for brick making.

Heroes and Legends

Exodus 15 relates the "Song of Miriam," who was Moses' sister. This song praises God for the mighty works performed in order to save the Israelites. After the successful crossing of the Reed Sea and the destruction of the Egyptian warriors, Miriam, tambourine in hand, led the other Israelite women in song and dance: "Sing to the Lord, for he is gloriously triumphant; horse and chariot he has cast into the sea."

This Song of Miriam is one of the earliest fragments of Hebrew poetry.

Bricks are made today in the Middle East much as they were made over three thousand years ago.

The Hebrew Scriptures: Called by the Father

Egyptian bricks were made from wet clay mixed with straw. Wooden molds with handles were used to shape the clay into bricks, which were then dried in the sun. When the pharaoh refused to supply the straw but still demanded that the daily quota of bricks remain the same, he was giving the Israelites an unbelievably difficult task. They had to gather their own straw and make the bricks in the same amount of time! Needless to say, the Hebrews were not too thrilled with the intervention of Moses and Aaron on their behalf: "You have brought us into bad odor with Pharaoh and his servants and have put a sword in their hands to slay us" (Exodus 5:21). Yet Moses and Aaron heeded God's command and returned to argue their case again before the pharaoh.

---

5. *Have you ever gone through a period when things got worse instead of better before God answered your prayers? How did you feel about God during this time?*

The First Nine Plagues

When Moses returned to face the pharaoh again, a contest ensued. God, Moses, and Aaron were on one side, and the pharaoh and his magicians on the other. The pharaoh demanded a demonstration of power from Moses and Aaron as a sign of the strength of their god, Yahweh. Moses cast down his staff, and it became a snake. The pharaoh's magicians did likewise with their staffs, but Aaron's staff swallowed theirs. Even though the power of Yahweh proved stronger than the magic of the Egyptians, the pharaoh would not relent.

The confrontation between the pharaoh, Moses, and Aaron continued. Theologically, this section of Exodus which recounts God's hardening of the pharaoh's heart poses some problems. That God both saved the Israelites *and* hardened the pharaoh's heart seems to impinge upon the concept of human freedom. Why does this story preserve the idea that God hardened the pharaoh's heart, if

While the plagues of Egypt can be traced to natural phenomenon, such as the locusts in this picture, the Scripture authors saw in them the power of God.

the idea was to have the Hebrews go free? The story indicates that nothing happens without God. If the pharaoh wouldn't let the Hebrews go when faced with the might of God, then God must have had a hand in the process. The story is not concerned with the pharaoh's freedom, only that of the Hebrew's and God's efforts in their behalf.

The first nine plagues (detailed in Exodus 6:28-10:29) are (1) water turned to blood, (2) frogs, (3) gnats, (4) flies, (5) pestilence, (6) boils, (7) hail, (8) locusts, (9) darkness.

The first four plagues affected everyone in Egypt. For the first plague, Aaron stretched out his hand, and the Nile River, along with other water sources, turned into blood. But Egypt still had well water that was protected from this plague, so the pharaoh ignored the pleas of Moses and Aaron. Next, frogs covered the land. This plague did not trouble the pharaoh too much until the frogs began to die and smell badly. For the third plague, Aaron turned the dust of the land into gnats, which coated everything. At this point, the magicians told the pharaoh that they believed these plagues to be from "the finger of God" (Exodus 8:15). Still the pharaoh's heart remained hardened. The fourth plague consisted of a swarm of flies.

The next four plagues injured the Egyptians and their property but did not affect the Israelites. The fifth plague was a pestilence that killed the livestock of the Egyptians. The sixth plague covered the Egyptians with boils; the seventh brought lightning and hail that destroyed crops and animals. The eighth plague covered the surface of the land with locusts, so that "nothing green was left on any tree or plant throughout the land of Egypt" (Exodus 10:15).

The ninth plague, a darkness that spread over the land, caused the pharaoh to summon Moses and Aaron and offer a few concessions, but now Moses and Aaron would not settle for any compromises. The Pharaoh again became obstinate and sent Moses and Aaron away.

Many of these nine plagues correspond to natural phenomena in Egypt. The reddening of the water may have been the result of the infestation of algae, a "red tide," or the clogging of the Nile with reddish silt. When the Nile receded, there were often hordes of frogs left in the riverbed, and the death of these frogs brought gnats and

The Hebrew Scriptures: Called by the Father

flies, which in turn brought various diseases. Hailstorms, locusts, and sandstorms (the "thick darkness") were also common in this area. The coincidence of all these disasters is difficult to prove. The miraculous aspect of the plagues was in their timing and their source. The biblical authors believed that God intervened to save the Chosen People.

---

6. *How can the disasters that befell the Egyptians be considered acts of God if they can each be attributed to natural sources?*

7. *How can the pharaoh be seen as an instrument of God? What does it mean to say that God hardened the pharaoh's heart?*

The Tenth Plague and the Exodus

The final plague, recorded in Exodus 11:1-12:32, was the most severe. The Exodus story tells of the death of the firstborn of Egypt. The Israelites were saved from this plague because they sprinkled their doorways with lamb's blood, as the Lord commanded, so that the angel of death would "pass over": "For on this same night I will go through Egypt, striking down every first-born of the land, both man and beast. But the blood will mark the houses where you are. Seeing the blood, I will pass over you; thus, when I strike the land of Egypt, no destructive blow will come upon you" (Exodus 12:12-13). The pharaoh lost his own son to this plague. Grieving, he begged Moses to leave Egypt with the Israelites.

Without even taking time to put yeast in their bread, the Israelites fled. The Lord preceded the Israelites in their march out of Egypt, represented in the daytime by a column of cloud, and at night as a column of fire.

Meanwhile, back in Egypt, the pharaoh was having second thoughts. He sent his troops after the slaves. The people, seeing the approaching horses and chariots, were terrified. They said to Moses, "Were there no burial places

> **Pestilence:** a contagious or infectious epidemic disease that causes widespread death or illness.

The Seder Meal

The covenant relationship between God and Israel is at the heart of the celebration of Passover. Jews rejoice in their past liberation from Egypt and for God's other redemptions since then. At Passover, the story of the Exodus is retold. The *Haggadah*, the text used during a Passover service, states: In every generation, each person should feel as though he or she were redeemed from Egypt, as it is said: "You shall tell your children on that day saying, 'It is because of what the Lord did for me when I went free out of Egypt.' For the Holy One redeemed not only our ancestors; He redeemed us with them."

This passage shows us that Passover celebrates not only an important event from the past but also an event that must be reinterpreted in the present. Slavery and redemption occur in our own lives, both Jewish and Christian, and the Passover ritual brings hope to those present experiences.

Jews observe three rituals at Passover: (1) the telling of the story of the Exodus, (2) the eating of *matzoh* (unleavened bread), and (3) the refrain from eating *hametz* (leavened bread).

Passover is a family holiday for Jews when they gather together to celebrate a ritual meal, or *seder*. It is through the Seder Meal that Jews all over the world relive the experience of the Exodus. This meal establishes continuity with the past. The Seder Meal includes many rituals, such as eating matzoh and maror (bitter herbs), drinking four cups of wine, and partaking of other foods. The matzoh reminds Jews of the haste in which they fled from Egypt without ample time to allow the dough for their bread to rise. The different foods remind Jews of the bitterness of their slavery and the joy of their liberation by Yahweh from Egypt.

During Passover, Jews rejoice that God saved them from slavery in Egypt.

The Hebrew Scriptures: Called by the Father

in Egypt that you had to bring us out here to die in the desert?'' (Exodus 14:11). But Yahweh, their champion, came to their aid by causing a strong wind to dry up the Reed Sea so that they were able to cross. The exact location of this sea is unknown. The Hebrew *yam suph* actually means ''sea of reeds,'' not ''Red Sea,'' as it is often mistranslated. Some scholars think that the Reed Sea was a marshy area or lake somewhere between the Gulf of Suez and the Mediterranean.

When the Israelites were safely across the sea, they looked back and saw the Egyptian soldiers approaching in their chariots. The wheels of the chariots got stuck in the mud, and the water, perhaps a tidal bore, returned to drown them. The Israelites celebrated with a victory song.

8. *In what ways did God guide the Israelites out of Egypt? Do you feel that God ''guides'' or helps you in your life today? Why or why not?*

Summary

- Moses submitted to God's call and became the savior of his people.

- Egypt experienced ten plagues, the last of which was the death of the firstborn. This final plague broke down the pharaoh's resistance. He then freed the Hebrew people.

- The Passover Meal commemorates God's passing over of the houses of the Israelites and saving them from the tenth plague.

- The Israelites fled into the desert and, with Yahweh's aid, crossed the Reed Sea on the way to the Promised Land.

■ Review

1. Why was the pharaoh's heart hardened against the Israelites?

2. How were plagues five through nine different from the first four?

3. Explain how any three of the plagues correspond to natural phenomena.

4. How were the firstborn of the Israelites saved?

5. What three rituals are Jews commanded to observe during Passover?

6. Words to Know: plague, pestilence, Nile River, Passover, seder, *Haggadah,* Matzoh, Song of Miriam, Reed Sea.

■ In Your World

1. How are the Jewish Passover and the Christian Eucharist related? What parallels are there between the two rituals?

2. Moses is the most important hero of the Jewish people for his role in the Exodus. Think of someone who might be considered a hero today. What qualities does that person have? Are they very different from everyone else? How can you be a hero to other people?

■ Scripture Search

1. Read Hebrews 12:5-11. How does this passage relate to the suffering endured by the Israelites?

2. Skim the Gospel of John to find references to Moses. Write a paragraph detailing your findings.

The Desert and Sinai Experiences

Some experiences either make or break you. Some people experience great difficulties and survive wiser and stronger than they started. Other people experience difficulties and quit, refusing to continue. The Exodus was such an experience for the Hebrews. After fleeing from Egypt, they spent many years wandering in the desert on the way to Canaan. They suffered many hardships and at times even wished that they were still enslaved in Egypt, rather than lost, hungry, and tired in the middle of the desert. Yet God was with them and continued to care for them. God invited them to enter into a further covenant at Sinai, at which time the Ten Commandments were given to them. Instead of being destroyed by this difficult experience, Israel emerged as a people further blessed by God.

Troubles on the Journey

Just as a loving father disciplines his child and allows him or her to face trying situations, the Hebrews felt disciplined by God. Because of what they experienced as divinely directed detours, it took forty years for the Israelites to reach Canaan, the so-called Land of Milk and Honey. The Israelites in their journey underwent an inner transformation. Through their experiences in the desert, they became a unified community. God aided this people, and entered into an alliance with them, offering them divine love and the Law. Moses intervened on behalf of the Israelites, and God used Moses to answer their pleas. Through Moses, God established the Covenant and gave the Law on Mount Sinai.

Read the following imaginary log of the journey to Canaan. It traces the incidents of Marah and Elim, the desert of Sin, the miracle of the quail and manna, and the water struck from a rock. Refer to Exodus 15:22-17:7 as you proceed.

- **Sunday:** *We hadn't seen water for three days, until today. As luck would have it, the water here at Marah was too bitter to drink. The Lord answered Moses' prayer, however, and showed him which reed would sweeten the water (Exodus 15:22-27).*

- **Monday:** *It's been a month since we left Egypt. Now that we're in the middle of the desert, it is difficult to obtain food. We complained to Moses and Aaron, telling them that we wished we had died in Egypt where there was food, instead of coming out here to starve. The Lord told Moses that we would have meat tonight and bread tomorrow. Amazingly, a flock of quail provided us with meat tonight. I'm waiting to see if bread drops out of the sky also: How can it appear in the wilderness of Sin? (Exodus 16:1-15).*

- **Tuesday:** *This morning when we awoke, strange white flakes covered the ground. Moses told us that this was the promised bread and that we should gather enough for our families for the day. He told us not to be greedy; there would be more coming. Only on the day before the Sabbath were we to be allowed to collect a double portion (Exodus 16:16-20).*

- **Saturday:** *Although it was the Sabbath, out of curiosity I went out in the morning to get the flakes that we called manna, but there was none on the ground. I felt as foolish as my neighbor Nathan did when he tried to save two portions' worth on Wednesday and the manna rotted (Exodus 16: 21-31).*

- **Wednesday:** *Today we're encamped at Rephidim, and there is no water here. We grumbled to Moses and were on the verge of stoning him, until he called out to the Lord for help. At the Lord's direction, Moses struck a rock with his staff and water flowed out from it. I truly believe that God is with us (Exodus 17:1-7).*

Praying the Hebrew Scriptures

The following prayer, found in Deuteronomy 6:4, is called the *Shema:* "Hear O Israel, the Lord our God, the Lord is one!" This *Shema* prayer is the most important prayer of Judaism. It expresses the basic principle of the entire Law given to Moses: The Lord is God of the Hebrew people, and is God **alone,** there are no other gods. This is the heart of monotheism, the belief system that set the Hebrews apart from other Near Eastern peoples.

The Hebrew Scriptures: Called by the Father

9. *How might some of the desert experiences of the Israelites be used to illustrate the meaning of Baptism and Eucharist for Christians?*

The Covenant at Sinai

As you read in Exodus 19:20-26, once again God communicated with Moses, this time on Mount Sinai. God set forth the Law and promised to be the God of Israel if the people would worship God and follow the commandments. Yahweh wasn't a god who merely demanded sacrifice of animals on certain days. The God of the Israelites wanted to be worshiped freely. Yahweh asked for a loving response from the Hebrew people, witnessed in trust and faithfulness throughout one's life. The Hebrew people entered into this covenant with Yahweh willingly, accepting God's commandments.

Other peoples became nations because of geographic boundaries, war, or a common form of government. When the Israelites ratified the Mosaic Covenant they became a community formed by their relationship to God. The Israelites were bound together by their faith in Yahweh.

God's Law, which included the Ten Commandments, was seen by the Israelites not merely as a covenant obligation, but as a gift from God. The Law was more than a legal code; it was a way of life. For the Israelites, the Torah was liberating, sacred law, not a confining one. The Ten Commandments, also called the Decalogue (ten words), provided them with the rules of human existence.

Other nations wrote laws to keep order in society. Israel's purpose is clear in the Shema, the greatest commandment and the heart of the Law: "Hear O Israel, the Lord is our God, the Lord alone!" (Deuteronomy 6:4). The Shema demands an exclusive and complete loyalty and love of God. It is the connection of the Mosaic Law with the worship of God that set this Law above all others. The Israelites accepted God as their only ruler and became a

Ratify: to approve, to give solemn authorization.

Torah: this word means "law" or "instruction" in Hebrew. The term also is used to refer to the first five books of the Bible: Genesis, Exodus, Leviticus, Numbers, and Deuteronomy. These five books are the most sacred texts of Judaism.

theocracy. As a theocracy, Israel had no central government or machinery of state. A loosely gathered people of mixed origins, without even a land of their own at this point, the Israelites maintained their identity as a people through their faith in God.

Listed below are the Ten Commandments. The accounts of the bestowal of the commandments and the Shema are found in Exodus 20:1-17 and Deuteronomy 6:4-9. Read these passages and see how the commandments and Shema became part of Israel's life.

1. I, the Lord, am your God. You shall not have other gods before me.
2. You shall not take the name of the Lord, your God, in vain.
3. Remember to keep holy the Sabbath.
4. Honor your father and mother.
5. You shall not kill.
6. You shall not commit adultery.
7. You shall not steal.
8. You shall not bear false witness against your neighbor.
9. You shall not covet your neighbor's wife.
10. You shall not covet your neighbor's goods.

The Ten Commandments has been a theme of artists for many centuries. This is how one movie portrayed Moses bringing the Commandments to the idolatrous Hebrews.

The Hebrew Scriptures: Called by the Father

Think about the values that are being praised and the evils that are condemned in the Ten Commandments.

---

10. *What country today is a theocracy? Why is the United States not a theocracy, even though many people in the United States believe in God?*

11. *How do cultures and ethnic groups in the United States today maintain their identity?*

The Ark of the Covenant

Why do Catholics visit churches and chapels when there are no services? They gather to pray, often in front of the tabernacle. Catholics believe that God is with us, present in a real way through the Eucharist. The Israelites believed that God was with them on their journey as well, especially in the sacred place called the tabernacle. From the beginning, they had experienced God's presence through the events that led to their freedom: the plagues, the passage through the Reed Sea, the food and water in the wilderness. They saw God's guidance visibly as a pillar of cloud by day and a pillar of fire at night. This story continues in Exodus 25-40.

After the Sinai Covenant, the Hebrews received the promise that God would actually dwell in their midst. Instructions were given for the construction of a portable sanctuary, called a dwelling (meeting) tent, or tabernacle, that would house the Ark of the covenant: God's throne. This dwelling was a source of strength for the Israelites because they were able to meet and consult with God because of its presence. In the meeting tent Moses spoke to the Lord face-to-face and presented the people's petitions. This place where God "pitched his tent" with the Hebrew people became the center of their political and religious life. The Ark of the covenant remained with the people about six hundred years, until it was lost in the destruction of Jerusalem in 586 B.C.E.

The Ark of the covenant, housed within the dwelling, contained manna and the tablets of the commandments.

Theocracy: a state or nation governed directly by God and not by any human individual or group.

Hittite Treaties

The Hittites were an ancient people whose empire in Northern Syria collapsed around 1300 B.C.E. Hittite rulers *(suzerains)* and leaders with less power (vassals) made pacts by which the vassals accepted certain obligations in return for the assurance of protection. The Mosaic Covenant conformed to the structure of these Hittite pacts. The Hittite *suzerainty* treaties were almost invariably composed of the following parts:

- **Preamble:** *opening sentences containing the name of the great king who is offering the treaty*

- **Historical prologue:** *recitation of the benefits that this king has already bestowed on the vassal*

- **Stipulations or demands:** *detailed listing of the obligations of the vassal and demands for exclusive loyalty*

- **Deposit of text and public reading:** *depositing of the text in a sanctuary and periodic rereading before the people*

- **Divine witnesses:** *list of witnesses to the treaty (usually a calling together of the gods of nature)*

- **Blessings and curses:** *since the treaty was sacred law, the gods would curse the vassals who broke the treaty, and bless the vassals who upheld it.*

Skim through Deuteronomy 5:10-21; 28:1-19; and 31:14-32:1. Identify the characteristics listed above as they apply to these biblical texts.

The Ark of the Covenant contained manna and the Commandment tablets.
It was a sign for the Hebrews that God was with them.

The ark served as a reminder and pledge of the covenant
which the Israelites had made with Yahweh. The fearsome
presence of the ark is depicted in Numbers 10:35-36:
"Whenever the ark set out, Moses would say, 'Arise, O
Lord, that your enemies may be scattered, and those who
hate you may flee before you.' And when it came to rest, he
would say, 'Return, O Lord, you who ride upon the clouds,
to the troops of Israel.' "

In reading these chapters about the dwelling, be aware of
the common features shared in common with modern
churches. You will encounter some unfamiliar words in your
reading: *Showbread* refers to the twelve sacred cakes that
are renewed every Sabbath and are eaten only by the chief
priest; a *propitiatory* is thought to be the cover of the ark; a
laver is a basin for washing.

The following passages describe the utensils of the
dwelling: Exodus 25-28:5—gold, tabernacle, altar, bread,
lamps, vestments; Exodus 30:1-38—contributions, water,

incense, oil. These passages reveal the uses of the dwelling: Exodus 33:7-11—consultation; Exodus 40:34-38—guidance on the journey; Numbers 7:89—communication; Leviticus 1:1-9—worship.

The Israelites believed that Yahweh was enthroned above the ark. Thus, because of God's presence, the ark was so holy and possessed such power that it had to be treated with the utmost respect and care.

Summary

■ The Israelites encountered many hardships in the desert on their way to Canaan.

■ The Israelites entered into a deeper covenant with Yahweh at Sinai, and it was there that God gave the Law to Moses.

■ The Ten Commandments, part of God's Law for the Israelites, are the rules for human existence.

■ The Israelites believed that God was enthroned above the Ark of the covenant, which was housed in the dwelling, or meeting tent.

Checkpoint!

■ Review

1. Give examples of how God came to the aid of the Israelites on their journey to the Promised Land.

2. What happened to the Israelites in the wilderness of Sin?

3. How did the Ten Commandments resemble Hittite *suzerainty* treaties?

4. What is the *Shema* prayer?

5. What was the purpose of the dwelling? What was the purpose of the Ark of the covenant?

6. Words to Know: Mount Sinai, manna, Torah, Ten Commandments, decalogue, *Shema,* Hittites, theocracy, Ark of the covenant, Meeting (dwelling) tent.

■ In Your World

1. Your baptismal certificate is the document of your personal covenant with God. However, it is not very detailed. Draw up a document that expresses your personal covenant with God. What do you see as God's obligations toward you? What responsibilities do you accept as part of your relationship with God?

2. In the desert, the Israelites were aware of the presence of God in their midst. The Ark of the covenant was protected and revered. Write a story or poem that recalls a time in your life when you felt very aware of God's presence.

■ Scripture Search

1. Read Exodus 17:8-16. How did the Israelites overcome the Amalekites?

2. To appreciate how the Israelites lived by the Law, read and summarize the following passages: Exodus 21:12-23 and 33-35; Leviticus 11:1-8; and Leviticus 16:20-22.

4 Review

■ Study

1. Why is Moses an epic figure?

2. How did Seti I and Rameses II affect the lives of the Israelites?

3. In two paragraphs, describe Moses' life from his birth until his marriage to Zipporah.

4. What happened to Moses on Mount Horeb?

5. What does the word *Yahweh* mean?

6. Why were the Hebrews initially not overjoyed by the intervention of Moses and Aaron on their behalf?

7. List the ten plagues.

8. Why did the pharaoh finally relent and let the Israelites go?

9. How do Jews today commemorate the Passover?

10. Explain how any five of the Ten Commandments can have meaning for us in the twentieth century.

11. List the parts of a Hittite *suzerainty* treaty.

12. Describe the Ark of the covenant.

■ Action

1. Through the ages architects have tried to design suitable places for people to meet God. The meeting tent—constructed according to elaborate directions—was such a place. Describe or draw what you would consider to be an ideal church.

2. Finish the imaginary log of the journey to Canaan that was begun in "Troubles on the Journey" in Section 3 of this chapter. Supply entries for the following passages: Exodus 17:8-15; 18; 19:1-16, 20-26; 32:21-29; Numbers 11 and 12.

3. In the life of every believer, there are "mountain experiences" and "desert experiences." Having read through most of Exodus, what would you say is characteristic of each type of experience? What life events would you put in each category?

■ Prayer

Desert living was a dangerous business for the Israelites after their escape from Egypt. Death stalked their camps in the form of thirst, hunger, dangerous animals, and birds of prey. In open areas, people choked on sandstorms and trembled in the face of thunder and lightning. Their hearts and bones knew heavy fatigue and the threat of marauding nomads, and they were constantly aware of their weakness and vulnerability. Close your eyes for a few moments and picture yourself wandering in the deserts of Arabia. What do you see and hear? How do you feel?

As desert wanderers, the Israelites took comfort from simple pleasures like food, water, secure shelter, and their children's safety. Green trees, fresh fruit, and sleep undisturbed by enemies became luxuries more precious than gold. When the Israelites prayed, they used concrete images rather than abstract words: rocks, trees, water, sky, fire, wind, bread, wine, and wind. For example, Psalm 71:3 states: "Be my rock of refuge, a stronghold to give me safety, for you are my rock and my fortress."

Pray Psalms 3; 4:7-9; 7:2-3; 29:3-9 and 71. As you pray each one, reflect on the real-life situations in these prayers. Use these prayers to address issues in your own life.

Conquerors of the Promised Land

OBJECTIVES

In this Chapter you will

■ See how the descendants of Abraham, led by Joshua after Moses' death, infiltrated into and settled the land of Canaan.

■ Discover the important role of judges like Gideon, Deborah, Samson, and Jephthah in Israel's history.

■ Be aware of God's mercy in coming to the aid of repentant people.

■ Learn about the stories of Judith and Esther, women whose bravery and loyalty saved the people of Israel from destruction.

I will give thanks to the Lord with all my heart in the company and the assembly of the just. Great are the works of the Lord, exquisite in all their delights. Majesty and glory are his work, and his justice endures forever. He has won renown for his wondrous deeds; gracious and merciful is the Lord. He has given food to those who fear him; he will forever be mindful of his covenant.
—Psalm 111:1-5

The Hebrew Scriptures: Called by the Father

Victories in Canaan

Do you know what it's like to be on a winning team? To hold a coveted trophy or medal in your hands? To hear the wild cheering of the crowd? If so, did you acknowledge that thanks were due not only to the other members of your team and your coach but also to God?

As the Israelite tribes overtook the land of Canaan, they knew that it was God who was giving them victory over the other tribes. The scribes who compiled this history arranged and enriched the details of Israelite victories to stress God's faithfulness. The books of Joshua, Judges, Judith, and Esther are prophetic, not historical. They provide religious instructions and encouragement rather than accurate historical details of the past. The overriding truth of these texts is that God was present to the Israelites in their time of need. The God of Moses was faithful to the covenant and asked Israel to do the same.

Desert Wanderers

After the Exodus from Egypt, the Israelites wandered in the desert. Imagine a large tribe of nomads searching for a home. The leaders, Moses and Aaron, led the community in its travels, keeping it together as a people by their faith in Yahweh. The Book of Numbers recounts the story of how this wandering tribe became a people. The Scriptures tell that the Hebrews wandered for forty years before they entered into Canaan, the land promised to them by Yahweh. The Book of Numbers offers many theological reasons for this long journey: Moses' doubt, the people's unfaithfulness, God's unwillingness. There were practical reasons as well.

When they traveled from Sinai to Kadesh, in the wilderness of Paran, the Israelites were close to the Promised Land. In the Book of Numbers (11-14; 20:1-12), you read about many instances of incessant complaining from the Israelites, followed by various punishments from God. Why was the Israelites' dream deferred?

When the people finally neared the Promised Land, God told Moses to send a leader from each tribe to scout the territory ahead. For a period of forty days, these scouts surveyed the land of Canaan. Upon their return, they reported that the land was agriculturally rich but was also occupied and heavily fortified. The scouts also related that they felt tiny compared to the giant stature of the Canaanites. Only two of the twelve, Caleb and Joshua, suggested that they invade. They relied enough on the power of Yahweh to move into Canaan immediately.

The people, on the other hand, were disheartened by the reports from the spies and sought a new leader to take them back to Egypt. Numbers 14:10-45 tells of God's response to the people's lack of faith. They were to wander in the desert for forty years, one year for each day that the scouts were in Canaan. Yahweh decreed that no one over the age of twenty, except for Caleb and Joshua, would enter into the Promised Land: "But as for you, your bodies shall fall here in the desert, here where your children must wander for forty years, suffering for your faithlessness, till the last of you lies dead in the desert" (Numbers 14:33).

Compared to wandering in the desert, the trials ahead in Canaan looked almost inviting! Rather than turning toward the wilderness, the Israelites attempted an invasion of the hill country of the Amalekites and the Canaanites. This attack proved to be foolish and premature. It failed miserably, and the Israelites were left to the fate decreed for them.

Disciplined by the desert and living entirely free from the servitude their parents and elders suffered in Egypt, these strong and young Israelites would become a nation that belonged completely to Yahweh. Even Moses was denied entrance into the Promised Land. In Kadesh, Yahweh had commanded him to draw forth water from a rock (Numbers 20:2-13). Moses' sin, according to the story, was striking the rock twice and then taking credit for the miracle, instead of

The Hebrew Scriptures: Called by the Father

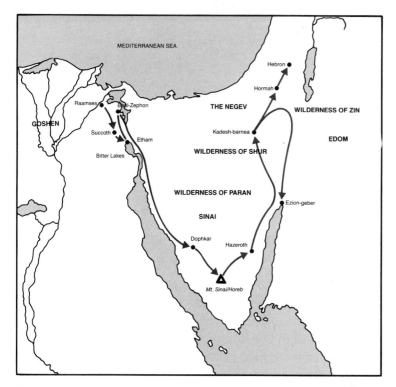

This map shows the journey of the Hebrew people as they traveled east from Egypt.

giving the credit to God. For their sin, Moses and Aaron were to die outside of the Promised Land. Moses, however, was at least allowed to see the promised Land. He climbed to the top of Mount Nebo, surveyed the land his people were to conquer, and died at the age of one hundred twenty (Deuteronomy 34).

The books of Numbers and Deuteronomy tell the story of the Hebrews journey for forty years and thus primarily derive from the oral folk tradition of nomadic people. As you read these books, it is easy to imagine these stories being retold for generations. Stories are repeated and events are explained to reveal theological messages. These two books also show the development of Jewish ritual and law. If you wish to understand the people of Israel, it is necessary to study Numbers and Deuteronomy.

1. *What response did God desire from the people? How did God react when they failed to respond accordingly?*

2. *Why would the Hebrews attribute their wandering in the desert as punishment from God? What are other explanations for this long trip?*

Joshua: On a Mission

Have you ever had the uncomfortable experience of living according to your beliefs when a majority of people disagreed with you? It could be as simple as a classroom experience when you refused to change your answer when everyone else changed theirs. Then, when the teacher announced that the answer you stubbornly refused to abandon was correct, you were rewarded. Or maybe you were at a party and it seemed as if everyone else was drinking, but you refused to drink. When the party was over, you were the one who took your sick friend home and stayed out of trouble. Standing by your beliefs can be difficult, but the rewards are often great in the end.

Joshua and Caleb faced a similar situation. They were the two scouts who had wanted to seize Canaan as soon as the Israelites arrived at its borders. Because of their faith in Yahweh, they were the only two of their generation allowed into the Promised Land after the forty-year period of wandering in the desert.

Joshua assumed the leadership of the Israelites when Moses died, and he was proclaimed a hero. His name, "Yeshua," like "Jesus," means "Yahweh saves." Summoned to the meeting tent with Moses, Joshua had been divinely commissioned to lead the people into Canaan (Deuteronomy 31:14-23). He distinguished himself as an excellent military commander in the desert skirmishes against the people already settled in the land. Joshua led the Israelites into the battles that finally brought Abraham's descendants into the land that was promised to them many years before.

For Example

A statue of Joshua stands today at the United States Military Academy in West Point. He is honored as a military genius in the Academy's Hall of Fame.

The Hebrew Scriptures: Called by the Father

In all likelihood, the tribes of Israel infiltrated Canaan gradually and more or less peacefully, settling in it over a period of three hundred years. During that time, battles were surely fought to claim ownership of the land. In order to affirm that Yahweh had given the land to these people, the sacred author of the Book of Joshua depicted the conquest of Canaan in vivid, dramatic language, as if all Israel had participated immediately in a grand military onslaught under Joshua's leadership. The Book of Joshua, chapters 2-6 and 23-24, recount this story.

That the Israelites' success was due to God's action is evident in the text of the Book of Joshua. In all favorable circumstances, the Israelites interpreted events as God's intervention on their behalf. Likewise, when things went wrong, the Israelites looked at their sinful behavior and saw God's displeasure.

The Israelites believed that God had promised their ancestors—from Abraham through Moses—their own land. They believed this land to be Canaan, the land Abraham settled, where Sarah was buried and where Jacob and his family had left hundreds of years earlier during the time of famine. You may think that it is unjust for God to have fought other peoples so that the Israelites could have this land to call home. Wars, like any evil, are the result of sin. God takes human agents and conditions as they are and accomplishes divine purposes. From a wider perspective, God was leading human beings to a greater destiny than even the Israelites understood.

The Siege of Jericho

According to Joshua 1-3, the first city the Israelites captured was Jericho. Joshua sent two scouts to explore the city. They entered without any trouble and went to a lodging house run by Rahab. Although she was aware that these two men were Israelites and not residents of Jericho, Rahab protected them anyway, hiding them on her roof. When men from Jericho came to question Rahab about her visitors, she pointed them in the wrong direction, out toward

Joshua is considered a great military leader even today.

Archaeologists have discovered that the city of Jericho and its walls were destroyed many times over the centuries, only to be rebuilt each time.

the Jordan River. Rahab was later saved because of her kindness.

According to Joshua 3-6, early the next morning the Israelites prepared to cross the Jordan River and begin their attack on Jericho. The priests marched ahead of the people, carrying the Ark of the covenant. When their feet touched the Jordan, the upstream waters stopped. The waters backed up from the north and disappeared to the south, thereby leaving dry ground on which the people could cross. In memory of this miracle a member from each of the Twelve Tribes brought a stone from the riverbed and set it up as a memorial in Gilgal, the new Israelite camp.

The Israelite siege of Jericho is described very dramatically. The Israelites circled the city and cut off its supplies. Every day for six days, seven priests with rams' horns led the troops out of their camp at Gilgal and marched once with the soldiers around the city. The march was silent except for the sounds of the rams' horns and marching feet. On the seventh day, at sunrise, the Israelites surrounded the city again and circled it seven times. At the sound of a signal horn, the people began to shout and to storm the walls of Jericho. According to Scripture, the walls collapsed and the city was easily taken.

What are we to make of this great success recorded so briefly in Joshua? Archaeological evidence suggests that the cities of Jericho and Ai mentioned in the Bible were already in ruins when the Israelites came to Canaan. The battles described there more likely took place at Bethel. And what about the crossing of the Jordan, so reminiscent of the crossing of the Reed Sea in the escape from Egypt? In 1927 the banks of the Jordan River collapsed, stopping the river's flow. For a time the riverbed beyond the collapse was dry. Could this explain the historical event remembered in the Joshua story? As a story of God's saving action it is certainly a statement of God rescuing the Hebrews from death.

Historically, we do not know if the walls actually fell down as a result of the loud shouting and the blowing of the Israelite horns. This may have been a figure of speech as opposed to a literal truth. The troops under Joshua's leadership may have burrowed under the walls of the city in order to weaken them, their digging masked by the marching feet and resounding horns. No matter what

The Hebrew Scriptures: Called by the Father

Urim and Thummim

The Promised Land was divided among the Twelve Tribes by casting lots, an Israelite method of determining the will of God. The Urim and Thummim were probably the instruments of divination, the means by which lots were cast and the will of God was discerned.

The exact meaning of the words *Urim* and *Thummim* is unknown. They are mentioned together in Scripture five times (Exodus 28:30; Leviticus 8:8; Ezra 2:63; Nehemiah 7:65; and Deuteronomy 33:8). According to these texts, the Urim and Thummim were placed in the breastpiece, a small pocket made of multicolored cloth and twined linen, which the chief priest of the Israelites carried over his heart.

Scholars suggest that the Urim and Thummim were small objects, perhaps in the shape of dice, which were made of precious stones or metal. These objects probably had some symbol impressed upon them that indicated "yes" and "no."

The chief priest would address God with a specific question that required a "yes" or "no" answer. He would then remove the Urim and Thummim from the breastpiece and cast them on the ground or any other flat surface. The chief priest would then interpret the position of the Urim and Thummim as an indicator of God's response to his question.

◆

Gilgal: in Hebrew, this word means "circle." The name of the new camp referred to the circle of stones set up as a memorial to God's intervention on the Israelites' behalf.

Divination: the practice that seeks to foresee future events or discover hidden knowledge, usually by the interpretation of omens or by the aid of supernatural powers.

actually occurred, the authors of this story believed that, because of the Israelites' fidelity, God had helped them overtake Canaan.

The Ban

The Book of Joshua tells that the city of Jericho fell into the hands of Joshua and his troops and that only Rahab and her family were saved from the slaughter. All the people and animals in the city were killed. This practice of completely destroying a city, its inhabitants, and their animals was called the "ban," or in Hebrew, *herem.* The ban was especially connected with warfare. In order to secure success in battle, a vow was made by the Israelite combatants to devote all spoils of victory, living or inanimate, to God. Sometimes women and children were exempted from this barbarous practice. This brutal custom was abandoned later in Israel's history. As is seen in Joshua 7, when the Israelites were defeated at Ai they blamed the defeat on sin; instead of fulfilling the ban, they had taken goods for their own use.

Renewal of the Covenant at Shechem

Once conquered, the land was divided among the Twelve Tribes (Joshua 13-21). Each tribe received a section of land except for the priestly tribe of Levi. Because of the

Archaeology

Before coins were invented, weights were used to measure the value of merchandise. The biblical *shekel,* first mentioned in Genesis 23:15-16, was not a coin but a unit of weight (about 8.4 grams at that time). When Abraham bought the burial plot for Sarah, he did not count out 400 *pieces* of silver but rather he weighed it. The word *shekel* comes from the Hebrew word "to weigh." Another unit of weight, the beka, was valued at half a shekel.

These weights themselves were not always accurate, and a dishonest merchant could cheat customers by chiseling the weights down to an amount lighter than 8.4 grams. Consumers could usually trust what were called "the king's weights," those weights authorized by the government.

At the time of the Exodus, money was not the value of a coin, but rather an amount of weight.

The Hebrew Scriptures: Called by the Father

Lord's commands, the Levites were given cities in every other tribe's portion.

Before Joshua died, he had the tribes renew their covenant at Shechem (Joshua 24:16-28). Because many people had joined the Israelites since the original covenant, the renewal made it possible for them to unite with the first-covenanted people in their solemn promise. Thus a weak people was on its way to becoming a great nation under Yahweh. But future success depended on their faithfulness to Yahweh and the covenant.

---

3. *What qualities are required of someone who strives for a lofty goal? Did the Israelites have these characteristics as a people?*

4. *What are some of the modern memorials developed to witness forever to a people's belief? What are some of Israel's memorials?*

5. *Look at a map of Israel that shows which tribes received what land. Research what you can about each area.*

Summary

- Because of their lack of faith, the Israelites were forced to wander for forty years in the desert before entering the Promised Land.

- Under Joshua's able leadership, the Israelites conquered Canaan.

- After being conquered, the Promised Land was divided among the Twelve Tribes by casting lots.

SECTION 1
Checkpoint!

■ Review

1. Why did the Israelites wander for forty years in the desert?

2. How were Joshua and Caleb rewarded for their fidelity to Yahweh?

3. What sign protected Rahab's house? Why were Rahab and her family saved from the ban?

4. Where did the Israelite tribes, under Joshua's leadership, renew their covenant with Yahweh?

5. What was the purpose of the Urim and Thummim?

6. Words to Know: Joshua, Caleb, *shekel*, divination, Urim and Thummim, Jericho, Rahab, Gilgal, *herem*, Shechem.

■ In Your World

1. Sometimes fear prevents people from achieving their potential. What is at the root of this fear? What advice would you give to people who are fearful?

2. It is amazing how one person can influence thousands, like Moses and Joshua did. Who are some contemporary individuals who have changed the world for the better? How did they accomplish this? What role did faith play in their lives?

■ Scripture Search

1. Read Matthew 1:1-6a and James 2:24-25. What is Rahab's role in salvation history? What point is the author of the Epistle of James making about faith and good works and the function that they serve?

2. Read Psalm 114. What is your reaction to the language used by the writer of this psalm, which was composed about three hundred years after the events described in the Book of Joshua?

Judges: Book of Deliverers

When the Israelites went to war, the tribe involved was led to victory by a leader who then became a local hero. This person, guided by the spirit of God, was called a judge. The biblical Book of Judges names twelve judges. Six of these judges are called "major" because their lives are described in detail in the text. They are Othniel, Ehud, Deborah, Jephthah, Gideon, and Samson. The "minor" judges (will not be studied in this chapter) are Shamgar, Tola, Jair, Ibzan, Elon, and Abdon.

Cycles of Deliverance

The Israelites had been warned by Joshua in his farewell speech: "If you transgress the covenant of the Lord, your God, which he enjoined on you, serve other gods and worship them, the anger of the Lord will flare up against you and you will quickly perish from the good land which he has given you" (Joshua 23:16). However, they had to find out the consequences of unfaithfulness for themselves.

As you read Judges 2:6-3:6, you will see that the Israelites were attracted to idols worshiped by neighboring tribes. Yahweh's people found it just as difficult to be nonconformists as people today who struggle to remain in the "in-groups" or to wear the most "stylish" fashions. Since the Israelites found it much easier to pray to a visible god than to an invisible one, they soon began to worship idols. The Book of Judges tells us that, as a result of their sinful idolatry, God allowed the Israelites to be attacked.

The pattern is repeated throughout the Book of Judges. Almost as soon as the people become contrite to Yahweh

Chapter 5   Conquerors of the Promised Land

The shofar (ram's horn) was blown to call the tribes to battle.

for their idolatry and, in return, received God's forgiveness and help, they would return to idol worship. The following four-phase cycle defined Israel's life during the period of the judges (1200-1120 B.C.E.): (1) sin/idolatry, (2) punishment/oppression, (3) repentance/prayer, and (4) deliverance/victory.

This time is referred to as the "dark ages" of Jewish history because of its conflict, lack of culture, and somewhat low moral standards. Judges 21:25 sums up the mood of the time when it notes: "In those days there was no king in Israel; everyone did what he thought best."

6. *Why do people seek visible signs of God's presence? How do these signs make belief "easier"?*

The Judges of Israel

An Israelite judge was not a judge in the legal sense, although some of the judges served as consultants in tribal matters. Judges were not kings, either. The only judges who led all of Israel were Eli and Samuel, whose stories appear in the Book of Samuel.

It is clear that the judges were military leaders. They are praised in the Bible for their military skills and tactics, but primarily they are remembered because they faithfully did the will of God. Whenever a judge saved the Israelites, it was through God's hands. The judges were honored not because of what they had done, but because of what God had accomplished through them.

Othniel and Ehud

The story of the first judges, Othniel and Ehud, is told in Judges 3:7-30. Begin by reading these verses.

Othniel, a nephew and son-in-law of Caleb, was the first judge or deliverer of the Israelites. He came forward to defend the Israelites from suffering under the oppression of a neighboring tribe, led by Cushan-rishathaim, or "Cushan

The Hebrew Scriptures: Called by the Father

of the double wickedness." This first judge is described in terms typical of all the later judges, whose common characteristics included:

- *being specifically raised up by God;*
- *leading charismatically;*
- *prevailing over Israel's oppressors and giving "rest" to the land.*

No further mention is made of Othniel. The story of the next judge, Ehud, is somewhat more grisly.

Ehud was from the tribe of Benjamin, and led a delegation from his tribe on a journey to Jericho to pay tribute to King Eglon of Moab (the Moabites were demanding bribes from Israel). Ehud, who was skilled with both his right and left hands, had fashioned for himself a double-edged dagger. This weapon was short and could easily be concealed beneath his clothes, an innovation over the usual battle weapons used by the Israelites—the spear, javelin, and curved sword. A man would wear his curved sword visible for all to see on the left side of his body so that the sword could easily be drawn out with the right hand. When the delegation was frisked for weapons, no one thought to search the right side of Ehud. The dagger went by the king's guards undetected.

Ehud asked for a private conference with the king. Because Eglon was a fat man, when Ehud thrust the dagger into his belly, the blade and the hilt went into the king's body, preventing immediate and visible external bleeding. Ehud departed, and when the king's attendants returned to the room they thought the king was merely asleep, and left quietly. By the time the attendants discovered that the king had been killed, Ehud and the delegation of Benjaminites were well on their way. Ehud and many Israelite troops descended on the now leaderless Moabites, and slaughtered them. Moab was brought under the power of Israel for a period of eighty years.

Deborah

One judge, Deborah, was a woman. Her story can be read in Judges 4-5. In this story, Deborah, with the help of the woman Jael, delivered Israel.

For Example

The custom of shaking right hands is thought to arise from this type of situation. By shaking the right hand you reveal that you carry no weapon.

Innovation: a new measure, a change.

Suffering once again at the hands of the Canaanites, the Hebrews recognized this as punishment for their idolatry. During this time in history, Canaan was a minor political state that was constantly at war with its neighbors. It was, however, much stronger than the scattered Hebrew tribes who only banded together when being invaded. The Canaanites had a strong army with nine hundred chariots under the command of Sisera. It's no wonder that the people felt abandoned by God when they were attacked by such a powerful army. Why was God not protecting them?

Barak was a tribal leader. When Deborah told Barak that God wanted him to gather the nearby tribes and overthrow the Canaanites, Barak agreed to attack Sisera's army—on the condition that Deborah also came along. The "Canticle of Deborah" in chapter 5 of Judges (one of the most ancient examples of Hebrew poetry) reveals that heavy rains

The canticle of Deborah is one of the oldest passages of the entire Bible.

The exploits of Samson were probably performed by several different people, but as the legends were passed down through generations, all feats of strength were attributed to Samson. No doubt the tales grew more and more impressive with each retelling of the story. Samson became a folk hero with superhuman powers. In postbiblical Jewish legends, he is often described as gigantic in size, more than 200 feet wide across the shoulders. Although Jewish tradition delighted in describing Samson's physical strength, it also stressed the fact that he was often morally weak. It is a story with theological importance: the strength of the Hebrews comes from faithfulness to God.

flooded the battlefield, rendering the enemy's chariots useless. It was a complete victory for the forces of Israel: every Canaanite was killed.

Jephthah

Often, the judges were not models of virtue. They could be crude and even savage. The warrior Jephthah of Gilead (Judges 11) was an unbeatable hero in battle, yet his life was marked with tragedy because of a foolish vow he had made. Jephthah vowed that if he conquered the Ammonites he would sacrifice to God the first person who came from his house to meet him. When he returned home in triumph and his young daughter came out dancing to welcome him, Jephthah kept his disastrous vow and burned her to death as an offering to God, paying to God what he had promised for victory over the Ammonites.

The story of Jephthah and his daughter illustrates two points: (1) The lack of foresight and failure to think through the implications of one's actions can lead to tragedy; and (2) the power of a vow in ancient cultures was so strong that, once it was sworn, it had to be fulfilled, no matter the cost.

Outline of Gideon's Life

Gideon's life is recounted in Judges 6-8. It is a story that shows God working through the judges. The following brief descriptive outline sets a pattern that is roughly followed in each of the stories about the judges.

Gideon's Call: Gideon is a simple man who is trying to save his father's wheat before the Midianites destroy it. Suddenly an angel commands him to save Israel (God works through the unexpected hero). Gideon asks for a sign that God wants his service, and the sign is granted. This is God's bidding, not the decision of the person. Gideon destroys his father's altar to the god Baal and builds one to Yahweh (through the efforts of the judges Israel turned away from idols). Gideon then summons the tribes against the Midianites (only when the Hebrews return to Yahweh are they united). Gideon asks for a sign that God will save them—the surprisingly wet and dry fleece (proof is offered of God's salvation).

Some Bible Number Facts

Numbers in the Bible serve more important functions than counting. Certain numbers held special significance for the Hebrews.

The importance of the number seven can be traced back to the cosmology of the ancient Sumerians, who recognized seven planets—the sun, moon, Mercury, Venus, Mars, Jupiter, and Saturn. Since the earth was believed to be under planetary influence, the number of planets was viewed as a key to the correspondences between heaven and earth. Seven was the number of the days of the week. For the Israelites, seven was the number of God's perfection. Jews honored the number seven in the branches of the menorah and in the seven-day feast of Passover.

Twelve was also considered a mystical number. The ancients recognized twelve lunar cycles that roughly corresponded to the twelve months of the year. Day and night were divided into twelve-hour periods. The stars were organized into twelve signs of the Zodiac. Jacob had twelve sons. Jesus took twelve Apostles.

Forty stood for one generation or for an extended and uncertain period of time. It usually signified preparation and purification—a holy time—as in the rainstorm of Noah, the wandering of the Israelites in the desert before they were allowed to enter the Promised Land, and Jesus' desert experience after his baptism in the Jordan River.

Interpretation of large numbers is difficult. The immense numbers usually expressed generalities. The Hebrew word for "thousand" can also mean "crowd." The Bible states that Methuselah lived to be nine hundred and sixty-nine years old, and his grandson Noah fathered three sons when he was five hundred years old. These long life spans are symbolic: high numbers signify power, importance, moral living, and faithfulness to God. They are not meant to be interpreted as literal fact.

Gideon Achieves Victory: God reduces Gideon's army from thirty-three thousand to three hundred (the strongest army that Israel can raise on its own cannot win without God, but with God only a small army is needed). There is a surprise attack at night with torches, horns, and the breaking of empty jars (just as God brought down the walls at Jericho, God is with them still). Gideon refuses to become king because Yahweh is the one who rules Israel (it is God who is the savior, not a man).

This same pattern is seen in some detail in the stories of each of the judges. Make a similar outline for yourself of Samson's life and see if you can spot the pattern. You will find his story in Judges 13-16. The judge Samson was a colorful character whose deeds were spectacular but who spent much of his life indulging his own passions and desires. Major headings for the Samson outline might be: Samson Is Consecrated; Samson and the Philistines Battle; Samson's Weaknesses Lead to His Downfall.

7. *What important role did the judges play during this period of Jewish history?*

8. *What is the significance of Deborah being a judge? How is her role different from the other judges?*

This map shows the Hebrew Tribes and their territory at the time of the Judges.

Summary

■ The major judges of Israel were Othniel, Ehud, Deborah, Jephthah, Gideon, and Samson.

■ The Israelites lived through a cycle of sin/punishment/repentance/deliverance during the period of the judges.

■ The judges succeeded through their faith in God's intervention and their own devices.

SECTION 2
Checkpoint!

Review

1. Describe the cyclic pattern of the Israelites throughout the period of the judges.

2. How did Ehud weaken and then defeat the Moabites?

3. What was Jephthah's foolish vow?

4. How did Gideon live up to the title "judge"?

5. What was the importance of the number seven to the Israelites?

6. Words to Know: judge, Othniel, Ehud, Eglon, Deborah, Barak, Sisera, Jael, Jephthah, Gideon, Samson.

In Your World

1. Many of today's films contain excessive violence. Some violence might be necessary to a story, but often it is not. How does the violence in the books of Joshua and Judges compare with the action in films today? Are their purposes different or the same? Explain your answer.

2. What challenging situations or problems can you foresee in your future? Compose a prayer of trust in God to bolster your confidence and help you cope with conflict. In your prayer, refer to God's love for you and the evidence of God's past help. Ask God for help in conquering your particular challenge.

Scripture Search

1. Read Luke 15:11-32. In the time of the judges, how was God like the father of the New Testament prodigal son? How was God different?

2. An old saying goes, "It's not the size of the dog in the fight, it's the size of the fight in the dog that counts." What is the significance of God telling Gideon to make his army smaller? What other Bible stories can you think of where the size of the army or of an individual did not determine the outcome of the conflict? What did determine the outcome?

SECTION 3
Judith and Esther: Women Liberators

Many nations have a treasury of folktales and favorite stories that they tell to illustrate profound truths: Greek, Roman, and Nordic myths about the gods, Aesop's fables, and Hans Christian Andersen's stories are examples. The Jewish people, among the best storytellers in the world, also have their favorite tales. In telling parables, Jesus was following a well-established Jewish method of storytelling.

It is no surprise, then, to find that the Bible contains many exciting and absorbing stories that have little bearing on historical fact. Two of these, the books of Judith and Esther, continue the tradition that God saves those who are faithful to the covenant. In Judith, God uses the hand of a strong woman to keep the Chosen People from being totally destroyed by foreign invaders. In Esther, God uses a loyal and brave woman to spare the Hebrews in Persia from an evil death sentence. It is also significant that God saves the nation through the power of women. Before reading further in this text, read the Book of Judith.

The Story of Judith

The Book of Judith was written much later than one might suspect from the situation described therein, probably in the second century B.C.E. The chief foe, Nebuchadnezzar, who was really the king of the Chaldeans, is called an Assyrian king. It is difficult to identify the conflict and the people described as any specific historical event. Scholars suggest that the glaring errors in the text are the author's way of informing people that the story is not to be taken literally, but instead symbolically. Nebuchadnezzar repre-

Judith is recognized as a heroine. How is her story the story of the Hebrew people?

Praying the Hebrew Scriptures

In prayer, Judith invoked God and pleaded for the safety of her people who were facing apparent annihilation by the Assyrians: "O God, my God, hear me also, a widow...Here are the Assyrians, a vast force, priding themselves on horse and rider, boasting of the power of their infantry...Your strength is not in numbers, nor does your power depend upon stalwart men; but you are the God of the lowly, the helper of the oppressed, the supporter of the weak, the protector of the forsaken, the savior of those without hope...Let your whole nation and all the tribes know clearly that you are the God of all power and might, and that there is no other who protects the people of Israel but you alone" (Judith 9:5, 7, 11, 14).

sents all of the people who try to make themselves into gods. Judith, whose name means "Jewess," stands for the nation of Israel as it should be — devout, careful to observe the Law, and trusting in Yahweh.

The theme of God's intervention in the lives of those who trust in the Lord recurs in a new form in the Book of Judith. God used a woman of faith to destroy the enemy.

The story follows the pattern described below:

Nebuchadnezzar's Goal: King Nebuchadnezzar was determined to destroy the Hebrews because they refused to worship him as a god. As a result, Holofernes, his general, led the Assyrian army on a rampage of destruction.

Achior's Advice: When the Israelites heard of the approach of Holofernes, they prayed, fasted, and did penance. In the meantime, Holofernes asked Achior, the leader of the Ammonites, about the background of the Israelites. Achior warned him that the God of the Israelites shielded them. This angered Holofernes, who saw Nebuchadnezzar as the only god. Holofernes threatened to annihilate the Israelites and sent Achior to be killed with them.

Assyrian Strategy: The Assyrians besieged the Israelite city of Bethulia by capturing the water sources of the city and guarding the mountains so that no one could escape. By the thirty-fourth day of the siege, the Israelites were begging their leader Uzziah to surrender. Uzziah asked them to hold out for five more days.

The Heroine's Plan: Judith flatters Holofernes. She tells him that she fled from her people because they had broken God's law and thus would be destroyed by the

The Hebrew Scriptures: Called by the Father

Assyrians. She says that she will pray every night, and that God will let her know when Israel has sinned. She agrees to tell Holofernes the ideal time to attack and agrees to lead him into the city. Holofernes trusts her.

Good Triumphs: Judith is able to kill the general through God's strength. She directs the Israelite warriors in the next battle and then relates her adventures to the people. Achior converts to Judaism.

---

9. *Why is a woman made the primary character of this story? What do you think is the role of women in society today?*

The Book of Esther: Court Intrigue

The story of Esther is one that features near-catastrophe, hatred, revenge, deadly plots, intrigue, and redemption at the court of the Persian king, Ahasuerus. The text was probably written at the close of the fourth century B.C.E. and explains the origin of the Jewish feast of *Purim*. Neither the people nor the events in the story can be found in other literature or historical records. Whether the events in the tale actually occurred, were greatly exaggerated, or are purely imaginative, the book is part of the Bible and is considered religious literature. It is, however, the only book from the Hebrew Scriptures that is not found in the Dead Sea Scrolls.

Like the Book of Judith, the Book of Esther bolstered Jewish national pride. The purpose of the Israelites' delight in revenge was to demonstrate that evil against God's faithful people returned onto the heads of the plotters of that evil.

At the beginning of the story, Queen Vashti is banished from the Persian court by King Ahasuerus because she will not obey his command to appear before the drunken guests sprawled out at his banquet. The king then holds an empirewide search for a beautiful woman to replace the queen. Esther is chosen to be the new queen, but on the advice of her cousin, Mordechai, she tells no one of her Jewish identity.

> **Purim:** the name means "lots," because Haman used a pur, or lot (dice), to decide when to kill the Jews.

> **Dead Sea Scrolls:** scrolls found between 1947 and 1956, they are the oldest known copy of the Hebrew Scriptures, dating to 100 B.C.E.

Tobit

Like the books of Judith and Esther, the Book of Tobit conveys a message through the medium of a religious novel. In this book, an angel and a fish bring healing. The story of Tobit, probably written in the second century B.C.E., could possibly have its roots in a historical event. As it stands, it is a delightful combination of Jewish tradition and Oriental folklore. It is a classic tale illustrating that goodness is rewarded. Luther wrote about the Book of Tobit: "Is it fiction? Then it is a truly beautiful, wholesome, and profitable fiction, the performance of a gifted poet."

The book centers on Tobit, a devout Jew, whose faithfulness and good deeds result in a release from affliction for himself, his son Tobias, and Tobias' wife Sarah. The author of this text has woven many elements of Jewish folklore into an artistic and appealing tale. The framework of the story provided this author with opportunities to incorporate prayers and psalms along with Jewish wisdom. Although the book is usually listed with historical books, it really is closer in style to the wisdom literature of the Hebrews.

Read the Book of Tobit in its entirety. Watch for themes of respect for law; burial of the dead; God's intervention; intercessory function of angels; purity of marriage; value of prayer, fasting, and almsgiving; and rewarding of the faithful.

◆

Haman, a courtier of Ahasuerus, becomes the king's chief executive officer. Mordechai refuses to bow down to Haman. Enraged at this insult and knowing Mordechai to be a Jew, Haman decides to punish Mordechai and all the other Persian Jews. He convinces Ahasuerus to consent to a decree calling for a massacre of all Jews in the kingdom of Persia. Esther and Mordechai try to counteract this evil, senseless scheme. Esther wines, dines, and charms the king and then reveals that she is a Jew. She pleads for and wins the safety of her people. Ahasuerus promptly hangs Haman and revokes the decree against the Jews. After instituting Purim as an annual celebration, Esther and Mordechai live "happily ever after."

---

10. *How does Esther exhibit courage? What is the source of her courage?*

---

define
Esther
Haman
Moredecan
Ahasurus
Purim

The Celebration of Purim

When Jews celebrate Purim—the feast commemorating the victory of Esther and Mordechai over the evil Haman—the blessings listed below are recited before (1, 2, 3) and after (4) the scroll of the Book of Esther is read aloud to the congregation:

1) "Praised are you, Lord our God, Ruler of the universe, who has sanctified our lives through his commandments, commanding us to read the scroll.

2) "Praised are you, Lord our God, Ruler of the universe, who performed miracles for our ancestors, in those days, in this season.

The Jewish celebration of Purim is a joyous occasion.

Chapter 5   Conquerors of the Promised Land

3) "Praised are you, Lord our God, Ruler of the universe, for giving us life, for sustaining us, and for helping us to reach this moment.

4) "Praised are you, Lord our God, Ruler of the universe, who has championed our cause and passed judgment on our behalf, taking vengeance for us, and punishing all our mortal enemies as they deserve. Praised are you, Lord our God, who saves his people Israel from all their enemies, for you are a redeeming God."

Whenever Haman's name is read, the congregation breaks out into a loud noise to fulfill the curse against Haman: "May his name be erased." The people in the congregation traditionally shake rattles (called *gragers*) or other noisemakers in order to drown out the name of Haman. While the actions of the hero and heroine are applauded, the villain is booed.

For many Jews, the Purim story is seen as a metaphor of Jewish history. Once again, the Jews were at the mercy of an unpredictable local ruler. In the Book of Esther, God's saving hand does not directly appear on the scene to save them from an anti-Semitic plot. In fact, the name of God does not appear at all in this biblical book! Instead, it is a combination of Esther's and Mordechai's own efforts and providence—the hand of God working in their lives—that brings about salvation from Haman's evil schemes.

Summary

- The Hebrew Bible contains books that consist of one self-contained, absorbing story. The books of Judith, Esther, and Tobit are examples of this type of biblical book.

- In the Book of Judith, a woman of strong faith with God's help saves the Jewish people from destruction.

- The Book of Esther demonstrates how evil against God's faithful people returned upon the heads of the plotters.

- The Jewish Feast of Purim celebrates Esther and Mordechai's victory over Haman.

Anti-Semitism: hostility toward or discrimination against Jews as a religious or racial group.

The Hebrew Scriptures: Called by the Father

■ Review

1. How are the stories of Judith and Esther alike? How are they different?

2. Why did Yahweh save the Israelites from the Assyrians? From the Persians?

3. What do the stories of Judith and Esther reveal about the Israelites' attitude toward women?

4. List some of the themes present in the Book of Tobit.

5. Words to Know: Judith, Holofernes, Nebuchadnezzar, Achior, Esther, Haman, Mordechai, Ahasuerus, Tobit, anti-Semitism, Purim.

■ In Your World

1. Judith, Esther, and their fellow Israelites put on sackcloth and ashes and fasted to obtain God's favor. Investigate the Church's teaching on penance and fasting. When, why, and how do Catholics do penance today?

2. Research the history of the Jewish festival of Purim. Be sure to look up the background of "masquerading" on that day and the types of food eaten by Jews during this feast.

■ Scripture Search

1. Read Genesis 34:13-29. How is this story about Shechem's deceit related to chapter 9 of the Book of Judith?

2. Judith and Esther are considered Hebrew prototypes for Mary, the mother of Jesus. From your knowledge of Mary in the Christian Scriptures, what parallels can be found in their lives and hers? (For assistance, read Luke 1:26-38.)

CHAPTER

5 Review

■ Study

1. Why did the Israelites wander in the desert before they were allowed to enter Canaan? Why didn't Moses enter with them?

2. In what ways was Joshua a strong leader?

3. What preceded the people across the Jordan?

4. What did the Israelites do at Jericho when the horn sounded?

5. What was the practice of the ban?

6. What role did the judges play in Israelite history? What were some of their common characteristics?

7. Why were the judges not necessarily models of virtue?

8. How did Jael help the Israelites defeat Sisera?

9. How can someone your age be imitating the Israelite pattern of sin/punishment/repentance/deliverance?

10. What is the source of Judith's and Esther's courage?

11. Describe the qualities that make these people heroes or heroines: Joshua, Gideon, Samson, Esther, Judith, Tobit.

12. What is done during the Purim synagogue service?

■ Action

1. Adapt the stories of Gideon, Samson, Judith, or Esther to a different format such as play, artwork, or dance. If you like, update the stories to modern-day times but retain the themes.

2. Turn the Book of Esther into a play. Assign the part of Haman, Esther, Mordechai, and the narrator.

■ Prayer

Read the prayer in Tobit 13. As you read this prayer, experience the faith and religious background of its author. Do the ordeals and journeys of Tobit and his family apply to your life? When have you felt like Tobit? When has your life seemed as complicated as his? Develop a prayer service using this prayer. Use this prayer service for personal prayer.

CHAPTER

6

Samuel and Saul: Victory and Defeat

OBJECTIVES

In this Chapter you will

- Study the decline of the Israelite priesthood and the subsequent rise of prophecy and kingship within Israel.

- Read about the birth and vocation of Samuel.

- Examine Saul's role in the history of Israel as its first king.

- Learn about Saul's downfall and David's anointing by Samuel to be the next king of Israel.

Sing to the Lord a new song; sing to the Lord all you lands...For great is the Lord and highly to be praised awesome is he, beyond all gods. For all the gods of the nations are things of nought, but the Lord made the heavens. Splendor and majesty go before him; praise and grandeur are in his sanctuary.
—Psalm 96:1,4-6

The Hebrew Scriptures: Called by the Father

Decline of the Israelite Priesthood

What is it that identifies your school as a special place? Does it have a reputation for excellence in sports or academic performance? Is there some special slogan, song, or cheer which shouts out to others that you represent your school? Having a clear identity is an important part of gaining self-respect and reaching maturity.

Israel, too, was becoming aware of its identity. The tribe, now settled on the land of Canaan for some time, was maturing. In the struggle to possess the land, the Israelites gradually adopted the customs of their neighbors and drifted away from the worship of Yahweh. Their worship continued at Shiloh, a central shrine where the ark was housed, but the priests who offered the worship sacrifices were often corrupt, taking the offerings for their own uses and leading the people into false worship.

"There must be a king over us," the people said. "We too must be like other nations, with a king to rule us and to lead us in warfare and fight our battles" (1 Samuel 8:19-20).

Samuel: The Last Judge

Over the centuries, the Israelites' loyalty to Yahweh—the one thing that had united them as a people in the first place—had weakened. The leaders of the Israelite tribes bickered amongst themselves and placed their individual needs above the good of Israel as a whole. With a decline in moral standards and a divided army, fending off invasions from the east and the south proved difficult. When the Philistine tribes grew in number and strength and began to push inland from the coast, Israel found itself threatened.

> **Philistines:** a seafaring people who lived along the coast of the Mediterranean Sea.

As in the past, Israel saw its hope in God fulfilled in an unlikely leader. The last judge, Samuel, was a holy and deeply respected person, whose influence on the Chosen People was great enough to have one entire scroll named after him (later split into two separate books, 1 and 2 Samuel). Samuel led the Israelites from near-disaster into the most glorious period of their history. He summoned military forces powerful enough to contain the invading Ammonites, Amalekites, Moabites, and Edomites. Not strictly a military leader, through prayer and sacrifices Samuel led his people to victory over the Philistines who had captured the Ark of the covenant and threatened Israel's existence.

Samuel is one of the few biblical characters whose story we know from infancy to death. He is depicted in the biblical text as a man of God and a person of prayer. He responded to God's call with generosity and courage. The last judge of Israel, Samuel was also its first prophet since Moses.

Samuel reawakened Israel's conscience by turning the people away from idol worship and back to Yahweh.

---

1. *Name some modern-day individuals who seem to be prophets. What is their message?*

2. *Discuss how a decline in moral standards can put a nation in danger.*

Archaeology

Among all ancient peoples, war was linked with religion. It was seen to have been commanded or approved by the gods. In a broad sense, then, every war could be considered a "holy war."

Israel, however, did not fight in order to spread its faith in Yahweh by force. Israel was not fighting directly for its religious survival, but for its existence as a people. When the Israelites took up arms they were called the "armies of Yahweh" (Exodus 12:41) or the "troops of God" (1 Samuel 17:26). The Israelites believed that Yahweh fought on their side; this by itself made their wars essentially "religious."

The Birth and Call of Samuel

As with most of the great leaders of the Hebrews, Samuel was recognized as a special gift from God even prior to his birth. Compare his birth in Samuel 1-2:21 with those of Isaac and Joseph.

Elkanah, an Israelite from the tribe of Ephraim, had two wives. One of them, Peninnah, had many children. The other wife, Hannah, was childless. Disgraced by her barrenness, Hannah cried out to the Lord for a son. During

The Hebrew Scriptures: Called by the Father

Samuel was the last judge to lead Israel.

a visit to the Israelite sanctuary at Shiloh, Hannah vowed that if Yahweh would give her a son, she would dedicate him to God's service. Her prayer to God was answered and she bore a son, whom she called Samuel, which means "name of God" in Hebrew.

Hannah brought Samuel to Eli, the priest at Shiloh, and told him: "I prayed for this child and the Lord granted my request. Now I, in turn, give him to the Lord; as long as he lives, he shall be dedicated to the Lord" (1 Samuel 1:27-28). Under the care of Eli, the chief Israelite priest, Samuel learned how to serve God. While still a child, Samuel began his career as a prophet. God called him by name repeatedly during the night (1 Samuel 3).

Prophet: an official spokesperson for God. A prophet does not necessarily foretell the future, but that may be one of his or her functions.

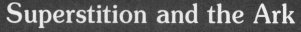

Superstition and the Ark

Superstitious people believe that a rabbit's foot is lucky and that the number thirteen is unlucky. Similarly, many Israelites developed superstitions about the Ark of the covenant.

Frightened after losing a key battle with the Philistines, the Israelite warriors had carried the ark with them into war. The now-elderly Eli was frightened. The Philistines, with their iron weapons and speedy chariots, had a distinct military advantage. Eli knew that the men of Israel were idolators who believed that the ark would work like magic to defeat this sea people. Not even the holy ark, however, could replace genuine worship.

Just as walking under a ladder makes some people expect bad luck, the Philistines saw the ark as an omen of evil, and they were extremely suspicious of its power. Triumphant at having captured the shrine city of Shiloh, they placed the ark before their god Dagon in their own city of Ashdod. However, strange things happened each time the ark was moved. Even the Philistine gods fell off their pedestals. Finally, recalling the stories of the Egyptian plagues, the Philistines returned the ark to the borders of Israel and sent atonement offerings of gold images.

Even with the ark, the Israelites superstitiously believed that the Canaanite gods, Baal and Ashtaroth, would reward them with a good harvest. The Israelites offered sacrifices to these Canaanite gods, forgetting Yahweh's faithful care. Samuel led a revival in Israel in which the people renounced their allegiance to the Canaanite gods and offered sacrifices of repentance to Yahweh, the true God.

It is easy to be superstitious, to allow fate or lucky numbers to control your life. Taking responsibility for your own actions is much more difficult. Israel's strength, like yours, lay in its faithfulness to God. When they counted on the ark over faithfulness to the covenant, they failed.

At first, Samuel did not understand what was happening. He ran to Eli, who kept sending him back to sleep. Eventually Eli realized that it was the Lord who was calling Samuel, so he gave the young boy instructions on how to answer Yahweh. The next time that God called him, Samuel responded with "Speak, Lord, for your servant is listening" (1 Samuel 3:10).

The message given by the Lord to Samuel was a painful and difficult one to relate. God told Samuel that Eli and his household were destined for oblivion because of the immorality and corruption of Eli's sons and because of Eli's failure to restrain his sons from doing evil in the sight of the Lord.

Samuel's first prophecy came true during the wars between Israel and the Philistines. Eli's sons, Hophni and Phinehas, foolishly used the Ark of the covenant in an attempt to force God to protect their armies in battle. Instead, they were annihilated by the Philistines, who captured the ark. At the doubly depressing news of the capture of the ark and the death of many Israelites, including his two sons, Eli fell over backward and broke his neck.

Infants are universally considered special. Samuel was recognized as being someone who was special even before his birth. What other heroes of Israel are recognized in the same way?

3. *Why is the story of Hannah so important? How is Hannah's faithfulness a witness to God's presence with Israel?*

4. *Samuel's call from God was clear. What are some ways in which God may be calling you?*

Summary

- The Israelite priesthood deteriorated because of corruption and idolatry.

- Samuel's first prophecy was against the household of his teacher, Eli, chief priest of the Israelites.

- Samuel rose up to replace Eli and became judge and prophet of Israel, leading it to victory over neighboring tribes.

■ Review

1. Why did the Israelite priesthood decline?

2. In your own words, tell the story of Samuel's conception, birth, and dedication to God.

3. In what way was Samuel truly a man of God?

4. How did the Philistines obtain the ark? What did they do with it?

5. Although he was not a military leader, Samuel still led the Israelites to victory. How did he lead them?

6. Words to Know: Samuel, Elkanah, Peninnah, Hannah, Eli, Hophni, Phinehas, prophet, Philistines, Shiloh, Ashdod, Dagon.

■ In Your World

1. Samuel obeyed Eli, even though Eli was not always a good priest. Who communicates God's will to you? How does this person's behavior and attitudes affect this communication? What does the statement "Praying is listening" mean? How can you understand the will of God in your life?

2. Why do you think the elder Eli so willingly received Samuel's criticism? In what circumstances might a teenager today be required to show courage in standing up for the Lord?

■ Scripture Search

1. Read 1 Samuel 4-6; 2 Samuel 6; and 1 Kings 8. After reviewing these passages, answer the following questions:
   a) How was the ark depicted as the visible sign of God's presence?
   b) How did the people, both the Israelites and Philistines, react to the ark?
   c) How was the ark to be approached? What happened to Uzzah?

2. Read 1 Samuel 2:1-10 and then read Luke 1:46-55. How is Hannah's prayer of exultation in 1 Samuel similar to the Magnificat in Luke?

Call for a King

Samuel inherited Eli's position and worked to bring about a religious renewal in Israel that would reject idolatry and result in the sole worship of Yahweh. There was a need in Israel for a stronger, more unified form of government. Continually harassed by the nations surrounding it, Israel had no governing body capable of maintaining an army to defend it. However, Samuel's own sons, like those of Eli, were also corrupt and unfit to succeed their father in office.

Monarchy in Israel

The American Revolution was fought for independence from Britain. One of the reasons for going to war was political representation. American settlers wanted control over their own lives. They didn't want to be ruled by a king across the ocean or, for that matter, a king at home. When the war was won, the thirteen states began to establish a form of government they could live with, which resulted in the Articles of Confederation. These articles gave total independence to each separate state. But this arrangement quickly proved unworkable. Within twenty years of their adoption, the Articles of Confederation were dropped in favor of the Constitution and the Bill of Rights. The states had learned that unless they surrendered some of their independence to a central authority, they would never be able to solve simple problems between states or even to defend themselves as a whole.

Israel found itself in a similar situation to that experienced by the United States. With no one person in authority over the Twelve Tribes, they were only loosely joined by their common faith. If Israel was to overcome the hostile attacks

Chapter 6   Samuel and Saul: Victory and Defeat

With the U.S. Constitution, the states surrendered some of their authority to the federal government. How is this situation similar to that of the Hebrews at the time of the monarchy?

of surrounding nations, each tribe would have to surrender some of its independence to a strong central government and king.

There were not only political ramifications to this decision. The covenant with Yahweh proclaimed God as the only king of Israel. In Israel's tribal confederation, God had been the sole source of law and the request for a monarchy seemed to contradict the faith of the Israelites. The story of how Israel resolved these difficult issues is explored in 1 Samuel 8-10.

Envying the strength of other nations, the elders asked Samuel to appoint "a king over us, as other nations have, to judge us" (1 Samuel 8:5). Samuel saw the potential for trouble if Israel tried to imitate the government of their Canaanite neighbors. Samuel knew of the flaws of human kings, who were often treated like gods and held absolute power.

The author of the biblical text gives many historical reasons for Israel's desire for a change in rule: the continual Philistine attacks, the weakening of the priesthood, the aging of Samuel, and the corruption of his sons. The author also provides practical reasons for having a king but makes it clear that monarchy was Yahweh's wish as well. God reveals Saul to Samuel in prayer. Saul was appointed by God, through the authority of Samuel, to be the first king of Israel.

Samuel listened to God and left the people free to bind themselves to a human king. He anointed Saul, but only after warning the nation of the abuses that could creep in when human beings rose to power. The theme that runs through all the biblical books dealing with the history of the Israelite monarchy (1 and 2 Samuel, 1 and 2 Kings, and 1 and 2 Chronicles) confirms Israel's original belief that everyone, even the king, is subject to God's law.

5. *To what kind of abuses can absolute power lead?*

6. *How is it possible for good parents to raise children who do not follow their beliefs?*

The Hebrew Scriptures: Called by the Father

History of the Term "Israel"

The following list will provide a clearer idea of the many meanings of the term "Israel" as they appear in the Hebrew Scriptures and in world history.

1. After Jacob wrestled with a stranger at the Jabbok River (Genesis 32), he was renamed Israel.
2. Tribes who claimed descent from Jacob and the other patriarchs called themselves the people of Israel. The term "Hebrews" is also used to designate these tribes, but usually the word *Israel* is used to designate these people as a whole.
3. As related in 2 Samuel, the ten tribes of the Northern Kingdom were called Israel, whereas the two southern tribes were called Judah. When unified by David (1000-962 B.C.E.), the kingdom was called Israel.
4. After Solomon died (842 B.C.E.), the kingdom was once again divided and Israel was the name given to the Northern Kingdom. The Assyrians conquered the Northern Kingdom in 722 B.C.E. At the time, the nation of Israel ceased to exist for nearly 200 years.
5. The Southern Kingdom was captured in 587 B.C.E. and its inhabitants were exiled to Babylon. The exiles returned from Babylon to the southern province of Judah in 539 B.C.E. Individually they were called "Jews," but as a whole the nation was once again called Israel.
6. Israel today means the land and the people as a nation. All Jews consider themselves part of Israel no matter where they live. Some Jews today see the modern state of Israel as a continuation of the ancient nation, while others believe that Israel today is only a political entity. The true Israel, according to the latter view, will not exist until the coming of the Messiah.

◆

Saul was anointed with oil and with the spirit of the Lord. He became both a king and a prophet over Israel, and his reign was marked with both successes and failures. Saul had many good qualities, although it seems that history mainly recalls his faults both as a ruler and as a fragile human being.

The passages listed below vividly recount Saul's first military success, his boldness in taking Samuel's place at the altar of sacrifice before going into battle against the Philistines at Michmash Pass, the war against the Amalekites, the ultimate rejection of Saul, and God's election of David to replace Saul as king of Israel.

Victory Over the Ammonites

Saul's military campaign is described in 1 Samuel 11:1-11. When a force of Ammonites laid siege to Jabesh-gilead, the elders of that town sent messengers to Saul to report this threat. The spirit of God came upon Saul, and he forced all the tribes of Israel to unite against the Ammonites. After Saul and his troops defeated the Ammonites, Saul was accepted by the people as a military leader and as king of Israel. In the midst of all the celebration, Samuel warned the people not to rebel against the commandments of God. Fidelity to God's Law was still the key to Israel's success, not the power of an earthly king.

Saul Offers Sacrifice in Samuel's Place

Saul's problems really begin when he assumes Samuel's duties as priest. Read 1 Samuel 13 for the story.

The Philistines assembled for battle against the Israelites at Michmash Pass. Saul and his men waited at Michmash for Samuel to arrive and offer sacrifices and peace offerings on God's altar. The priest was the only person allowed to offer sacrifice on the altar.

When some of Saul's troops began to desert him, Saul usurped Samuel's role as priest and disobeyed the Lord by offering the prebattle sacrifice himself. In his impatience, he brought down upon himself the anger of Samuel who

Heroes and Legends

Saul reigned for twenty years, more a warrior-hero than a king. An unusually tall and strong man, he was far from a giant in social status, disposition, or character. He began his career with many advantages: he had been anointed by God, counseled by Samuel, and accepted by the elders of Israel. He was also something of a military genius. Yet he lacked self-confidence, and his sense of inferiority and insane fits of jealousy led him to desperate acts. Saul nevertheless understood the evil that he had done and was continually torn by a guilt that eventually led him to take his own life.

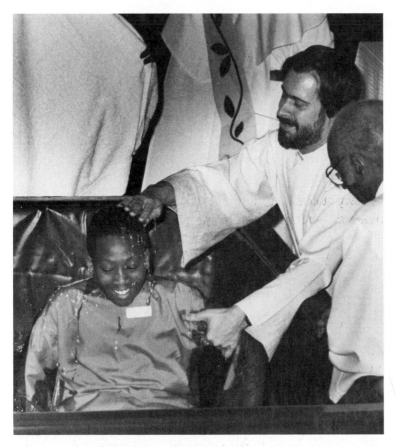

When a person is baptized, he or she is anointed with oil as a priest, prophet, and a king. In a similar way, Saul was anointed by Samuel as the first king of Israel.

reacted to this foolish act by prophetically pronouncing that Saul's kingdom would not endure. Because of Saul's pride and lack of faith, his descendants would never rule in Israel.

Saul Disobeys God's Command

Military leaders are often elected to positions of authority or they physically take the power of dictator or king. While capable of leading an army to victory, military leaders are often inefficient political leaders. Saul fits this description as it is recorded in 1 Samuel 15.

The Amalekites had long been the sworn enemy of Israel, especially since they forced Moses and the Israelites to detour through the desert by forbidding passage through their land. When Samuel told Saul to attack the Amalekites

Saul was a man of his time. He undoubtedly believed in magic and superstition. Saul usurped the authority of Samuel and offered the pre-battle sacrifice because of superstition. By these and similar actions, Saul lost his ability to lead Israel.

and put them under the ban, Saul disobeyed this second command of God. Saul made a show of conformity by ordering all the people killed, but he saved Agag, the Amalekite king, whom he greatly admired. To win favor with his men, Saul also allowed them to keep the best animals for themselves, offering the excuse that he intended the men to sacrifice the sheep and oxen when they returned home. Samuel again prophesied that God would reject Saul and then parted company with him. Samuel knew that he would never see the king again, and he grieved for Saul, "because the Lord regretted having made him king of Israel" (1 Samuel 15:35).

The Hebrew Scriptures: Called by the Father

David's Anointing

God then sent Samuel to Bethlehem. In 1 Samuel 16:1-13, Samuel goes to the house of Jesse to offer sacrifice. Samuel meets seven of Jesse's sons, one after the other, but realizes that none of those seven was chosen by the Lord to be the next king. Jesse sends for his youngest son, David, who was still out with the flocks. Samuel then chooses David to be the next king of Israel, and anoints him with oil. The spirit of the Lord comes upon David.

7. *How did the incident at Jabesh-gilead establish Saul as a military leader in Israel?*

8. *What prophetic pronouncement did Samuel make about Saul?*

9. *Samuel said, "Obedience is better than sacrifice." How might a person offer sacrifice but not follow the Law?*

Summary

- The tribal elders requested a change in government in order to unify Israel against its enemies.

- Samuel anointed Saul to be the first king of Israel.

- Saul's reign was marked by both military successes and personal failures.

- Samuel anointed David as God's choice for the next king of Israel, even though it would be a number of years before Saul's death.

SECTION 2
Checkpoint!

▪ Review

1. List some of the reasons why Israel desired a change in government.

2. Why was Samuel hesitant to appoint a king over Israel?

3. When was Saul accepted as king?

4. Name the two specific instances in which Saul disobeyed God's commands and incurred Samuel's anger.

5. Trace the different meanings of the term "Israel."

6. Words to Know: Saul, Jabesh-gilead, Ammonites, Michmash, Amalekites, Agag, Jesse, David.

▪ In Your World

1. The elders would not have accepted a king without Samuel's approval. How important is it to have the Church's blessing on the important events of your life? Discuss how you feel about the need for Church approval.

2. Samuel looked over all the sons of Jesse and chose the youngest and most unlikely son to be the second king of Israel. What unlikely people do you know who have been chosen for important missions in life?

▪ Scripture Search

1. Read 1 Samuel 14. In two or three paragraphs, summarize this chapter about Jonathan's heroic exploits against the Philistines.

2. Reread 1 Samuel 13:15-18. Using a map, draw soldiers to represent the positions of the Israelite and Philistine contingents before the Philistine invasion.

The Hebrew Scriptures: Called by the Father

SECTION 3
The End of Saul's Reign

Of the emotions that enrich our lives, most come in pairs. You can name the opposites of joy, despair, and fear. Our capacity for a pleasant emotion also includes our capacity for an unpleasant one. People who love deeply can also hate fiercely. Saul became sad, melancholy, withdrawn, and subject to fits of anger and depression. One of the most destructive emotions is jealousy. The Hebrew Scriptures present Saul as a very jealous person. As you read about Saul's exploits in the following passages, determine for yourself how Saul, in trying to destroy others, destroyed himself. Read the introductory material to each passage before reading the biblical text itself.

Saul's Downfall

The characters in the Hebrew Scriptures are not stereotypes, lacking uniqueness or individuality. They are real flesh-and-blood people, with strengths and weaknesses just like all other human beings. As a history of God's presence with the Chosen People, the Scriptures are not concerned with presenting people without flaws. As has been discussed earlier, the Scripture stories reveal that God brought victory out of defeat using very flawed people. In this way, God's power is made known.

The old saying, "The victors write the history books!" is very appropriate here. David was the greatest king in the history of Israel. He succeeded Saul as the king, replacing Saul's descendants. The unflattering portrayal of Saul's leadership and David's success in Chapter 18 reflects as much on who was king when the story was written as it does on what actually happened. However, it is clear that Saul saw David as a political rival and attempted to kill him.

The Victory March

It was a great day in Israel when Saul's armies marched home, victorious over the Philistines. Everyone ran out to greet the soldiers. One young warrior in particular, David, attracted attention. People danced in the streets and sang: "Saul has slain his thousands, and David his ten thousands." Saul became jealous of David's talents and popularity (1 Samuel 18:6-9).

All night Saul must have tossed and turned, unable to sleep because he was consumed with the thought of David's growing popularity. By morning he was overcome by a deep depression. Raving like a madman, he paced back and forth in front of his royal seat, carrying his spear as if ready to pounce on some invisible enemy. Across the room from Saul, David gently strummed his harp and made music to soothe his king. Twice Saul tried to spear David, and twice he missed his target (1 Samuel 18:10-16).

David and Jonathan

The story of David and Jonathan is one of the most beautiful tales of friendship ever written. On the one hand, Jonathan's friendship with David is not easy to explain, considering the fact that Jonathan was the rightful heir to the throne of Israel as Saul's oldest son. On the other hand, David's complete trust—even to the extent of placing his life in Jonathan's hands—is just as difficult to explain. After all, Jonathan had good reasons to do away with his political rival. David also had good reasons to mistrust Jonathan, since it was Jonathan's father who was trying to kill him (1 Samuel 18:1-5, 19:1-7, 20:1-9, 35-42).

The Fugitive and the Slaughter

After the second attempt on his life David fled the country, taking refuge with the hated Philistines. Saul deliberately hunted him down in order to kill him. Ask yourself how the people must have felt when their anointed king, Saul, suddenly and senselessly massacred priests whom he had once sheltered on the pretense that they had aided David in his flight from Saul's court.

The Hebrew Scriptures: Called by the Father

Israel's Music

David is portrayed as Israel's most inspired musician. He soothed Saul in his dark, tormented moods. At the death of Saul and Jonathan, he chanted an elegy, a poem of grief for the dead. As king, he had such a heart for the music of worship that he commanded musicians to march along with the ark as it was carried in solemn ceremony to Jerusalem. David established a special group to sing the psalms of Israel at their religious festivals. He himself composed psalms— songs of praise to be accompanied by the harp.

His son Solomon followed his lead, setting aside rare cabinet wood imported from Ophir for harps and lyres. Cantors led the people in song. Since Israel's system of musical notation was limited, cantors or lead singers had to memorize hundreds of melodies. The cantors were such important figures in Israel that they were paid as professionals with money and produce. They were expected to understand their music and their religious tradition, be skilled in singing, have a flair for leading the people in song, and be sensitive to whatever would help the people to pray.

The tradition of good leadership in congregational worship continued in Israel for hundreds of years after David's reign. New psalms were added to the nation's repertoire until 300 B.C.E., when the psalter—Israel's songbook— was completed.

The Catholic Church encourages people who play an instrument—as well as those gifted with good voices or ability in musical direction—to lend their talents to worship. If congregational singing is to accomplish its purpose of praising God and making a joyful noise unto the Lord, then every voice is needed. Saint Augustine said that when you sing, you pray twice. You, too, can be like David. All that is required is a willingness to share your gifts with others.

The importance of liturgical music can be traced to the music of King David.

Repertoire: list of the pieces that a group is prepared to present.

This massacre was Saul's final rejection of all that Israel believed. He might as well have been a worshiper of foreign gods, for to the Israelites he was no longer a worshiper or servant of Yahweh. However, David was not totally innocent in this story. He deceived the priest, Ahimelech, within earshot of Doeg, one of Saul's henchmen. Doeg then reported David's deception to Saul. David was responsible, in a sense, for the deaths of Ahimelech and the other priests (1 Samuel 21:2-22:23).

Jealousy affects everyone from students to rulers. Saul was jealous because David had the trust of the crowd.

10. *How do you feel when you've worked hard on a project only to have someone else who only helped a little be given the credit? Discuss whether Saul's feelings of jealousy were justified or not.*

11. *If you were one of Saul's sons, the same age as David, how might you feel about the popularity of someone who could take your rightful place as the next king?*

12. *What does it mean to say that "the victors write the history books"?*

13. *Discuss the significance of David seeking shelter with the Philistines? How was David responsible for the deaths of the priests at Nob?*

David and Saul

Saul continued to search for David. He brought troops with him to the desert area near Engedi, where there were many caves. Saul entered one of the caves, unaware that David and some of his men were hidden in the inner recesses. Nevertheless, David spared Saul's life, even when he had the perfect opportunity to kill him.

1 Samuel 24:1-23 and 26:1-25 shows David in a fine light, still possessing reverence for the office of the king, even when the king of Israel was persecuting him and sought his death. David is not the usurper of the throne. Instead of killing Saul when he had the chance, David

simply sliced off a piece of Saul's cloak with his sword, then let Saul leave the cave. He then followed him, waving the piece of cloak as if to say, "I could have killed you, but I mean you no harm." David is later shown in another situation in which he could have killed Saul. Again, David spared Saul's life and only removed Saul's spear and water jug from the sleeping king's side as a sign that he had been there.

The end was near for Saul. The Philistines pressed their attack upon the Israelites near Mount Gilboa. When Saul saw that his sons had been killed and his own death at the hand of the enemy was imminent, he asked his armor-bearer to kill him. When the armor-bearer would not fulfill Saul's command, he fell on his own sword and died. As you read of the final hours of Saul's life, try to capture the internal agony that caused him to turn his violent emotions upon himself. Think of how he felt when he learned that not only had the Philistines won the battle, but by slaughtering Jonathan and Saul's other sons they had destroyed his dynasty as well (1 Samuel 31:1-13).

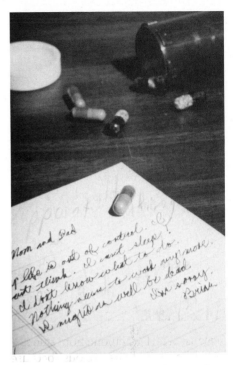

Many teens today give up hope when things go against them, much like Saul. A fundamental Christian belief is that we can depend on God, no matter what happens.

Samuel and Saul: Two Very Different Men

Samuel is seen as a true man of God. A child of his mother's prayer, a boy who knew how to listen and do courageous things for the Lord, Samuel became a great leader. He consistently brought victory and peace to his people by leading them to God. As an elderly prophet, he consulted the Lord when the nation wanted a king. As Samuel had rebuked Eli, so he was to judge Saul. Saul's mistake was to reject Samuel, who stood for the true religion of Israel.

Once Samuel's work was finished, he gracefully stepped aside and let others take over. This is a sign of his humility and prayer—it was not he who was important but Yahweh. He died quietly in his hometown and was grieved. Samuel's public role in Israel was an extension of his own deep convictions—that true religion, happiness, and stability are not to be found in external things such as hereditary priesthood or a particular form of government, but in keeping God at the center of life. In the darkness of faith, the beacon that kept Samuel's (and Israel's) ship on its steady course was constant communication with God.

Saul, in contrast, was a tragic figure. Although he possessed a giant's body, he did not have the heart he needed to lead wisely. Unlike Samuel, Saul was a military leader whose personal life was not rooted in God. He could not believe that God had chosen him just as he was, or that God wanted to use him. Lacking faith, Saul counted on his making the correct sacrifice in order to succeed. In many ways he was little different from those who offered sacrifices to idols. He could not believe that others might like him for himself. Even when accepted by his fellow Israelites for leading them successfully in battle, he was continually fearful of losing his soldiers' loyalty. Saul was not able to use David's talents as a gift to enhance his own reign; rather, he regarded David as a threat.

A religious man in the beginning, Saul gradually forgot the Lord who walked beside him. As a result, Saul felt his weaknesses keenly, and eventually steered himself and his people off course. Instead of leading Israel to peace, he introduced violence into his court and his nation and finally turned that violence toward himself. In the end, Saul's life reflected the destruction that can result from faithlessness.

Praying the Hebrew Scriptures

One of the psalms of thanksgiving attributed to David is Psalm 18 (which also appears in 2 Samuel 22). David is thought to have written this beautiful poem as a hymn to the saving power of the Lord. Some scholars believe that David wrote this psalm as a young man after he learned of Saul's death. The psalm says: "I love you, O Lord, my strength. O Lord, my rock, my fortress, my deliverer. My God, my rock of refuge, my shield, the horn of my salvation, my stronghold" (Psalm 18: 1-3). Take a moment to read through the entire text of Psalm 18. Think about the ways in which this psalm is a prayer of thanksgiving.

Summary

- Saul became jealous of David's skills and popularity and plotted to kill him.

- Saul failed in his attempts to kill David, only harming himself and other innocent people.

- The story of the friendship between David and Jonathan is one of the most moving accounts in the Hebrew Scriptures.

- David spared Saul's life twice.

SECTION 3
Checkpoint!

■ Review

1. Why was Saul jealous of David?

2. The friendship between Jonathan and David seems difficult to explain. Why?

3. What happened to the priests at Nob?

4. Where might David have gotten the inspiration for the songs that he sang at court?

5. What political reasons might David have had for not killing Saul and for praising him at his grave? Explain.

6. Words to Know: Jonathan, Nob, Ahimelech, Doeg, Mount Gilboa, elegy, Solomon, cantors, repertoire.

■ In Your World

1. Imagine that David and Saul were to be represented by animals. Decide which of the following would best symbolize each man: serpent, panther, fish, dog, lion, horse, bear, chameleon. Draw a coat-of-arms for both David and Saul, incorporating the animals and titles you would find appropriate for each man. Explain your choices.

2. Write or act out a skit showing a situation in which a young person would need courage to stand up for something required of him or her by God.

■ Scripture Search

1. Read 1 Samuel 25. Summarize the story of Nabal, Abigail, and David.

2. Saul's visit to the witch at Endor is recounted in 1 Samuel 28:3-25. This type of divination had been banned from Israel by Saul himself. What happened at the "seance," and what was foretold? How is this related to the present-day use of palm readers, Tarot cards, or Ouija boards?

■ Study

1. How was Samuel's birth similar to the births of Isaac and Joseph?

2. Why was Samuel considered to be both a judge and a prophet?

3. What is the difference between superstition and true faith?

4. The Israelites had been led by their religious leaders for centuries. How did Saul break that tradition? What was the result of this action?

5. What faults led to Saul's behavior? What contributed to his insane jealousy?

6. Why is David considered a patron of liturgical music?

7. In one paragraph, summarize the content of Psalm 18.

8. Why was David partly responsible for the slaughter of the priests at Nob?

9. List several reasons why David showed reverence for authority in his encounters with Saul.

10. In your own words, describe the power of David and Jonathan's friendship.

11. How did Saul and his sons die? What is the significance of their deaths in this manner?

12. What was the difference between Samuel and Saul in terms of their trust in God's guidance?

■ Action

1. Read 1 Samuel 4-7 and trace on a map the movements of the ark from its capture to its return.

2. Who is responsible for the music in your parish? Interview this person. Is he or she paid as a professional? Ask about the problems and satisfactions of the job. Make a report on your findings.

3. Investigate how one of the following people discovered his or her vocation from God: Saint Francis of Assisi, Saint Joan of Arc, Mother Teresa of Calcutta.

■ Prayer

Two women were walking along a crowded city sidewalk. Suddenly one of them said, "Listen to the lovely sound of that cricket." The other woman replied, "How can you expect me to detect the sound of a cricket amidst the roar of traffic and the noise of all the people around me?" The first woman did not respond; she simply dropped a quarter onto the pavement. Immediately, a dozen people began to look around them. "We hear what we listen for," the first woman said.

   What does this brief story say about your relationship with God? With your own heart? With other people in your life? Prayer is listening to God amid the noise in your life. Take a few moments to jot down when and how you listen to God. Read Psalm 18 quietly. Think about each verse. How does God speak to you through the psalm?

A Man After God's Own Heart

OBJECTIVES

In this Chapter you will

- Examine Israel's rise to power under David's leadership.

- Discover how David's character, administrative ability, and strong personality made him Israel's greatest king.

- Learn how David had total trust in God and total confidence in himself.

- Recognize that even as strong and blessed a person as David still had personal flaws and weaknesses and needed to repent for his sins.

One thing I ask of the Lord, this I seek: to dwell in the house of the Lord all the days of my life that I may gaze on the loveliness of the Lord and contemplate his temple.
—Psalm 27:4

The Hebrew Scriptures: Called by the Father

When David marshalled his forces in the mountains, it is the first record example of guerrilla warfare. This tactic is used even today when a smaller force is fighting a larger, better equipped force.

Summary

- David was considered the ideal Israelite king.

- David inspired loyalty in his troops and in his friends.

- The story of David and Goliath represents the victory of the young nation of Israel against the powerful Philistines.

- In his dealings with foreign enemies, David relied on God but also used his own ingenuity to preserve his life.

■ Review

1. Despite his flaws, why was David a model king?

2. What condition did David have to meet in order to marry Michal?

3. How does the story of David and Goliath symbolize something greater than the characters involved?

4. Why were embalming and cremation not practiced in Israel?

5. How did David succeed as a double agent? For which two sides did he work?

6. Words to Know: Michal, Achish, Goliath, Philistines.

■ In Your World

1. In a format of your choice, retell a modern version of the story of David and Goliath.

2. David's friendships had all the qualities that bring out the best in people. Point out examples of the following qualities in your own friendships: (a) a friend thinks of the other's good; (b) a friend helps the other to grow; (c) a friend provides support in hard times; and (d) a friend is loyal.

■ Scripture Search

1. The urgent need to provide the dead with a proper grave is the focus of the story of Rizpah, in 2 Samuel 21. Summarize this story in a few paragraphs and explain its importance to the history of Israel.

2. Read 2 Samuel 1:19-27. Why did David mourn the deaths of Jonathan and Saul?

Israel's Finest Hour

The hour of glory was at hand: Israel was about to become independent. The charismatic King David would bring to fulfillment God's promise made to Abraham centuries earlier: "I will give this land to you as a possession" (Genesis 15:7). Under David's leadership, Israel's borders would extend from Mesopotamia to Egypt. They were never to reach farther.

Under David's reign, Israel abandoned its nomadic way of life entirely. The nation's control of the great east-west trade routes enabled agriculture and commerce to flourish. Links with important seagoing nations of the Mediterranean were established, and the literature and architecture of Israel developed. Under David's direction, Israel experienced its finest hour.

David Assumes the Throne

At Saul's death, David returned to Hebron, the center of the southern tribes. There, after mourning Saul and Jonathan, he was crowned king of Judah (2 Samuel 2:1-7). With amazing swiftness, he reorganized the scattered army and dealt a fatal blow to the Philistines (2 Samuel 5). During his seven-year reign in the South, he was no longer bothered by the Philistines, but his armies skirmished frequently with the remaining members of Saul's family. His next task was to win over the ten northern tribes ruled by one of Saul's surviving sons, Ishbaal. The fact that Saul's son was named after the Canaanite god (Baal) may have been a sign of Saul's idolatry.

Ishbaal was backed by Saul's general, Abner. Instead of forcing himself militarily on the North, David waited patiently. His instinct proved correct. As a result of internal

David was made king of Israel when he was thirty-eight years old.

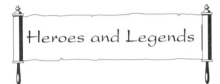
Joab, the eldest son of David's sister Zeruiah, was the commander of David's army. Because of his military vision, Joab achieved an importance in Israel that was second only to that of King David. Joab's military victories began with the defeat of Abner at the pool of Gibeon (2 Samuel 2:12-24). Joab and his troops also captured the Jebusite stronghold of Zion by a daring assault through a water shaft (2 Samuel 5:6-12). The Jebusites had cut a tunnel into the rock on which the fortress was built in order to reach fresh water outside the city walls. When the water level was low, Joab and his men came into the city through the shaft and took Zion. Because of his bravery and ingenuity, Joab was made supreme commander of the armies of Israel.

conflicts, both Ishbaal and Abner were killed (2 Samuel 2:12-4:12). Weakened by corruption, the House of Saul begged for David's protection. At the age of thirty-eight, David became the unchallenged ruler of all Israel, both North and South. David ruled for thirty-three more years, inaugurating a welcome time of peace in the land. David moved the capital of Israel from tiny Hebron to the more central and strategic city of Jerusalem (2 Samuel 6).

To cement national unity, David revived devotion to Yahweh by establishing the ark in the midst of the people. He dreamed of building a temple to house the ark, but this task was to remain for his son, Solomon. Through the prophet Nathan, however, God promised David a house: a kingdom that would last forever.

David as Brilliant Leader

In a few years, you will be eligible to vote. Which of the following qualities would you consider helpful in a political leader: intelligence, courage, military genius, a sense of humor, administrative ability, friendliness, loyalty, diplomatic ability, character, understanding of people, artistic interest, personal charm, speaking ability? Which one of these qualities would be the most important?

David is portrayed as being graced with all of these gifts. He believed that God called him to serve Israel, and he

The Hebrew Scriptures: Called by the Father

made the most of these God-given talents. He also knew how to be patient and wait for the right moment to act.

Anointed as a young man, David did not claim the throne until after Saul's death. He learned the ways of kingship, not in the court, as might be expected, but as a fugitive, getting to know the people and learning the battle strategies of the enemy he intended to defeat. Even after Saul's death, David waited until the elders elected him king of Judah before assuming power. For seven years he learned to govern Judah before accepting the responsibility of leading Israel.

After receiving the Lord's signal, David ascended to the throne of Israel fully prepared. His royal achievements included the creation of a central government, expansion of national boundaries, cultural progress, religious unification, and the establishment of a shrine for the Lord.

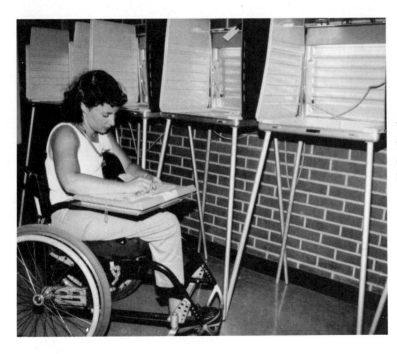

When you are eligible to vote, what criteria will you use to make an informed decision: looks, personality, courage, integrity?

Jerusalem

To weaken tribal leadership, David concentrated political power in himself. This kind of concentration of power can be dangerous if it is in the hands of an inadequate leader. David, however, seemed fully competent to handle the

God's Promise to David

If you have ever worked to achieve some goal, how did you feel when the job was done? Blessed with success in every undertaking, David remained restless. He felt guilty for living in a beautiful palace while the crude ark was the sign of Yahweh's presence. He dreamed of building a magnificent temple. God solved David's problem with an unexpected and mysterious pronouncement made through the prophet Nathan: "I will build a house for you...Your house and your kingdom shall endure forever before me; your throne shall stand firm forever" (2 Samuel 7:27; 16). From this time forward, Israel looked to David's descendants for its final deliverance.

Put yourself in David's place when he was frustrated and God made him a momentous promise. Read through 2 Samuel 7, and answer the following questions:

- *What was David's concern in this chapter?*

- *What answer did the Lord give?*

- *The promise given to David is one of the most important in the Hebrew Scriptures. How is it connected with the covenant made with Abraham and Moses?*

- *David was astonished by God's promise. What greater and even more astounding gifts has God given us since then?*

responsibility that came with such power. In a brilliant move, he captured the old Canaanite fortress of Zion, held for centuries by the fierce Jebusites, and made it his capital city—Jerusalem.

The new "City of David" was less vulnerable to attack, and its central location made it acceptable to both the northern and southern parts of the kingdom. From there, David would govern wisely and launch a dynasty that was

The Hebrew Scriptures: Called by the Father

to last for more than four hundred years. Eventually, Israel would come to consider the name "Zion" as meaning "the fulfillment of God's promise."

Over the years, the House of David became a symbol of God's enduring love for Israel. It was believed that the messiah would be descended from the royal lineage of David. Jesus is often called "Son of David" in the Christian Scriptures. In different ways in the Gospel according to Matthew (Chapter 1) and Luke (Chapter 2), David is named as a direct ancestor of Jesus.

---

4. *Patience allowed David to conquer the northern tribes. What virtue do you possess that wins people to your side? How can you develop further virtues?*

5. *What are the skills necessary for a person to be a leader? How can you be a leader today?*

6. *Catholics honor Mary as the daughter of Zion. How does the name apply to her?*

Administrator and Military Leader

David was a keen judge and administrator. He knew how to delegate authority and had a sharp eye for talent and character. By personally choosing his chancellor, cabinet, armed forces commander, and other officers, he surrounded himself with people he could trust. He was careful to place honest people in charge of public welfare and distant outposts.

David was also an inspired military leader. He replaced untrained military volunteers with a standing army of professional soldiers headed by his own generals. He accomplished two things by this action: (1) he eliminated the power of the tribal chieftains; and (2) he ensured the military strength he needed for expansion. David and his forces conquered some neighboring lands completely, and set up occupation forces in other lands. Before his death, David gradually subdued all his foes and saw Israel increase to 60,000 square miles—ten times the territory he had inherited.

David was an exceptional administrator and military leader, much like Napoleon, 2,800 years later. Investigate Napoleon's life and compare it to King David's.

Dynasty: a succession of rulers of the same line of descent who maintain power for several generations.

Messiah: the anointed one of God who would rule Israel forever. Applied to Jesus.

For Example

David gained the favor of other nations by taking foreign concubines. These women would be the younger daughters of powerful rulers. By taking these women into his house, David would enter into political alliances with the rulers of these countries. Early in the history of the Hebrews, tribal leaders and kings were expected to have many wives and concubines. This practice ceased following the return from the Babylonian captivity.

Unlike Saul, who had been content with a rustic fort for his headquarters, David dreamed of a better life for himself and his people. With the treasures of conquest pouring in, David could afford to hire the expert carpenters and stonemasons from the coastal city of Tyre to build a magnificent house of cedar. Taking his cue from other kings, he increased the number of his concubines, both foreign and Hebrew. He also ordered scribes to keep the historical records that developed into the two books of Samuel, the nation of Israel's first literary work.

The Ark Comes to Jerusalem

Some people believe that all a leader needs is a forceful personality. But when several top U. S. presidential aides were once asked what quality was most needed by a president, their unanimous response was "character." By this, they implied that high office requires high moral principles. David was successful, the biblical author says, because "the Lord went with him" (2 Samuel 7:3). David possessed a strong moral character and never outgrew his humble obedience to God. He sought God's guidance in every decision, and then, with faith in God's help, he insisted on honesty in his administration.

David saw Israel as twelve tribes held together only by a common faith in Yahweh. To reinforce Israel's sacred heritage, David rescued the ark from its forgotten residence in a private home and brought it to Jerusalem with pomp and ceremony (2 Samuel 6). Thus the City of David—Zion, now called Jerusalem—became Zion, the City of God, for the Lord was present once again in the midst of the people.

David insisted that those who worked with him also have integrity. He was willing to risk being ridiculed when he forgave his enemies and showed his love for God publicly. As you shall see later in this chapter, David was not perfect. He did make moral mistakes, but he ultimately accepted responsibility for his failures. Unified in military strength, government, and religion, Israel quickly became the most powerful small nation in the Near East.

When the ark entered Jerusalem, David was at the pinnacle of his political and religious powers.

---

7. *Why did David want to bring the ark to Jerusalem? What are ways in which modern leaders attempt to use religious objects for political gain?*

Summary

- Israel achieved greatness as a nation under David, an excellent military, administrative, and religious leader.

- After Saul's death, David became king of Judah. Later, he won over the ten northern tribes and was crowned king of all Israel.

- David retrieved the ark and brought it to his new capital, Jerusalem.

- David was graced with all the gifts of leadership, yet he still remained humble and obedient to God.

■ Review

1. Why was Israel able to abandon its nomadic existence under David's rule?

2. What made David a good administrator?

3. How did Joab become commander of David's troops?

4. What prophecy did God speak through Nathan about David's house?

5. Name some of David's leadership qualities. Why is "character" an important aspect of leadership?

6. Words to Know: Hebron, Zion, Jerusalem, Ishbaal, Abner, Joab, Nathan, Gibeon, Jebusites, dynasty, messiah.

■ In Your World

1. How was the government of David's Israel like the government of the United States? How was it different?

2. At the present time, what "arks" or signs of God's presence do Christians have in their midst? What leaders does the Church pray for at the Eucharist? Why is Mass an appropriate time to pray for good leadership?

■ Scripture Search

1. David understood the psychology of victory: the side with the most confidence is the likeliest to win. Read 2 Samuel 5:17-25 and 2 Samuel 8. From where did David's—and the Israelite army's—confidence come?

2. Humor is seen in the David stories. Tell how you see humor in these accounts: (a) 1 Samuel 17; (b) 1 Samuel 29; (c) 2 Samuel 7:1-17; (d) 2 Samuel 5:6-12.

David's Private Sins

A letter arrived at the church without a return address. It read:

> Dear Father,
>
> Twenty-five years ago I was an altar boy at your parish. One day when no one was watching, I stole $20 from the collection basket. I am ashamed of myself for that act and I have never been able to forget it. I ask your forgiveness, and I especially ask God for mercy. As a sign of my remorse, here is $50 for the church. Now that I have returned what I stole so many years ago, maybe I can find peace.
>
> "A Sinner."

Everyone makes mistakes. Even the great King David had weaknesses. David's public successes were marred by his private sins and their dire consequences. The biblical authors did not hide the faults of their national heroes. The sinful side of so great a person as David was not ignored, either. It is in these stories of David where we sense his dependence on God most fully.

David and Bathsheba

David, middle-aged and perhaps somewhat bored with life, had reached the peak of his career. His court, with its fine cedar walls and ornate stone pillars, its large harem and quarters for many officers of state, began to resemble the luxurious courts of the great Oriental rulers. David succumbed to the lure of power and began to use his kingly office for his own purposes rather than in the service of God and God's people (2 Samuel 11).

It all began with idleness. For the first time, David did not accompany his men into battle, and then curiosity led him

Everyone sins. Catholics celebrate God's forgiveness in the sacrament of Penance.

תְּפִלָּה
Praying the Hebrew Scriptures

Psalm 51 is believed to have been written by David after Nathan confronted him about his sin with Bathsheba. Read these verses and put yourself in David's place as he repents of his sin and asks God's forgiveness.

"Turn away your face from my sins, and blot out all my guilt. A clean heart create for me, O God, and a steadfast spirit renew within me. Cast me not out from your presence, and your holy spirit take not from me. Give me back the joy of your salvation, and a willing spirit sustain in me ... My sacrifice, O God, is a contrite spirit; a heart contrite and humbled, O God, you will not spurn" (Psalm 51:11-14,19).

into temptation and sin. While his troops battled the Ammonites, David stayed at his court. Walking on the roof of his palace, he spotted a beautiful young woman bathing nearby. He made inquiries about her and discovered that she was Bathsheba, the wife of a Hittite named Uriah. Uriah was not from an Israelite tribe, but he was fighting in David's army. In fact, he was one of David's best soldiers.

Abusing his authority, David sent messengers to bring the woman to him. David committed adultery with Bathsheba, and she became pregnant. At first, David sought to hide his crime. He concocted a plan that would bring Uriah back from battle. David thought that if he let Uriah spend some time with his wife, that might make it plausible that Bathsheba became pregnant through her husband, instead of through David. However, David was frustrated by an Israelite tradition: many soldiers remained continent (abstained from sexual relations) while on a military campaign.

The Hebrew Scriptures: Called by the Father

Uriah, though not an Israelite, kept this tradition and refused to go to his wife while his fellow soldiers were in combat.

Thus David had to resort to another plan. He sent Uriah back to his commanding officer with a sealed note that contained an order from David that Uriah be placed at the front line. Uriah was killed in battle, and David quickly married the newly widowed Bathsheba. A son was born to them, and David presumed that he was beyond reproach.

The prophet Nathan came to ask David's help in solving a dilemma. Nathan asked David to judge the case of a rich man who had many flocks of sheep. The rich man, even with all those sheep of his own, stole the one small lamb that belonged to his poor neighbor. David declared that the wealthy man deserved death for his crime. Little did David know that Nathan's story was a parable of his own crime, for Nathan then said to David: "You are the man!" (2 Samuel 12:1-25). David confessed his sin and repented, but he was not released from the consequences of his action.

---

8. *How did David misuse his power? What were the consequences of his actions?*

9. *How do lies trap a person, even when there may not be witnesses to the event?*

Although it is impossible to judge another person's sinfulness, David's lust for Bathsheba seems sinful: He wanted what was wrong, he knew it was wrong, and yet he did it anyway.

> **Parable:** a brief story that illustrates a moral or religious principle and is intended to move the listener to action.

The Psalms are poems set to music. Although the original melodies are unknown, there are many new arrangements for singing the psalms today.

The World's Most Popular Songs

What songs are popular today? What do you like about these songs? The beat? The lyrics? The music itself? Most songs are short-lived. The "top ten" often changes from one week to the next. You may only know a few of the "golden oldies" that your grandparents cherished, and you probably only recognize a few of the songs to which your parents listened when they were your age. Some songs, like "Greensleeves" and "Amazing Grace," are special in having survived for several hundred years.

The psalms, Israel's religious songs, are extremely special. They've lasted three thousand years and are still revered wherever Jews and Christians gather to pray. You will find them in the Book of Psalms (or psalter) in the Hebrew Scriptures. Although all one hundred and fifty psalms are attributed to David, who was a talented harpist, no one knows who all of the composers were. The psalms were written over a period of six hundred years and refer to all stages of the history of Israel. They molded the traditions and the faith of the people as much as the Torah itself did.

Psalms are songs accompanied by stringed music. They mirror David's great worshipful heart, which delighted in the glory of God. The lyrics of the psalms touch the heart. They comfort us with God's greatness and nearness and show us that God protects those in danger and is concerned with all who call on the Lord. They inspire hope as they proclaim God's mercy and forgiveness.

The Hebrew Scriptures: Called by the Father

The remainder of David's reign was filled with jealousy, murder, and rebellion within his own family (2 Samuel 13:15:17).

One of David's sons, Absalom, rose up in rebellion against him. David's men refused to let their king engage in battle with Absalom. David then sent his troops ahead to quell this rebellion, but even as he sent them he told his generals, "Be gentle with young Absalom for my sake" (2 Samuel 18:5).

As Absalom tried to escape the battlefield following his failed rebellion, his long hair became entangled in the branches of a terebinth tree. His mule ran out from underneath him, leaving him hanging in midair and defenseless. When an informant saw that Absalom was trapped, he reported the youth's predicament to Joab who, along with his men, ignored David's earlier plea for mercy toward Absalom and killed David's son.

When told of Absalom's death, David mourned him from a room in his palace above the Jerusalem city gate, weeping and saying, "My son, Absalom! My son, my son, Absalom! If only I had died instead of you, Absalom, my son, my son!" (2 Samuel 19:1). To David, the success of his men in subduing the rebels paled in comparison to the news of his son's death. Following this tragic event, David acted once again as a strong leader, reconciled the fragmented Israelite tribes in the north and south, and unified Israel once again.

After 3,000 years Absolom's tomb still stands as a monument marking David's sorrow at the death of his son.

---

10. *What are the implications of Absalom's rebellion and death for David's rule and for Israel's future?*

The biblical authors included David's grievous sins in their account of David's reign: his selfishness in taking Bathsheba from Uriah, one of his own loyal soldiers, and the cold-blooded plans for Uriah's murder. But if these sins show David at his worst, his sincere repentance revealed him at his best. He did not try to continue the cover-up by silencing Nathan permanently. Nathan wakened the king's conscience by means of a story, and only spoke the truth that David recognized within his own heart—that the God of Israel held authority even over the king.

With courage, David faced his sin and accepted the consequences. He regretted the injustice done to Uriah, the child, and Bathsheba. But his overriding concern was the the offense against his Lord who had so blessed him. "I have sinned against the Lord," he said simply (2 Samuel 12:13).

After these incidents, David's private and public life fell apart. Nathan's prophecy did indeed come to pass: "The sword shall never depart from your house" (2 Samuel 12:10). In every generation, David's family would know violent death. The death of his child, wickedness among his children, and the rebellion of his own son led to a trail of suffering that was to extend beyond his own lifetime and well into the future, ultimately leading to the collapse of the nation. Yet for all his misfortunes, David grew stronger in character and in his allegiance to God.

Summary

- David's public successes were marred by his private failures.

- David committed adultery with Bathsheba, and then, to conceal his crime, he had her husband Uriah killed.

- The prophet Nathan revealed David's guilt by means of a parable.

- David's rebellious son, Absalom, was killed by Joab and his men.

Checkpoint!

■ Review

1. How were David's public successes marred by his private sins?

2. Why did David's first plan to cover up his adultery fail?

3. Why is Psalm 51 so powerful?

4. What did Nathan's parable mean?

5. How did Absalom die?

6. Words to Know: Bathsheba, Uriah, parable, psalm, Psalter, Absalom.

■ In Your World

1. Why is it hard to forgive yourself? Why is it almost impossible to accept God's forgiveness if you cannot forgive yourself?

2. What good has come out of apparently bad things in your life? How did you handle one of those bad situations? What knowledge did you gain about yourself, other people, and God through these experiences?

■ Scripture Search

1. A second version of the story of David appears in 1 Chronicles 10-29. This text was written six centuries after David died. This later version erases David's faults and paints his character in glowing colors. Name some of the differences between the story of David's life in 2 Samuel and the account in 1 Chronicles. Explain why these stories would be different.

2. Look up the following verses in the Book of Psalms: 69:2-3; 47:2-3; 35:1-5; and 13:2-3. Match these psalm verses with the following emotions: anger, fear, sadness, happiness. Write four psalm verses of your own that mirror one or more of these emotions.

7 Review

■ Study

1. Why did commerce and agriculture flourish in Israel during David's reign?

2. Why were the Israelites afraid to leave bodies unburied for long periods of time?

3. How did David inspire loyalty in his friends?

4. What was the meaning of kingship for the Israelites?

5. Who were Abner and Ishbaal? How did they die?

6. What is the older name of the city of Jerusalem?

7. List three of David's qualities of leadership. Cite an example from the story of his life that illustrates each of the qualities you have chosen.

8. What are the psalms? Why do the lyrics of the psalms touch people deeply?

9. How did David first plan to cover up his sin of adultery? What was David's second plan and how well did it succeed?

10. How did Nathan waken David's conscience?

11. How did David repent of his sin? What were the consequences of his sin?

12. What was David's reaction to Absalom's death?

■ Action

1. Find a modern counterpart to the story of David and Bathsheba in literature or current events. What are the consequences for sin today?

2. Draw an upside-down pyramid entitled "David's Growing Role in God's Plan." Place David as a young shepherd at the lowest point to represent his starting role, then rearrange his other achievements (listed below) so that they move up the pyramid to "Repentance and Glory" at the top: King of Israel; Reorganization of Government; King of Hebron; Final Victory over the Philistines; Sin and Shame; First Victory over the Philistines; Unembittered Exile; Repentance and Glory; Service at Saul's Court; Dream of a Temple and God's Promise; Victory over Goliath; Victory over All Enemies; Transfer of the Ark; Successful Escape.

3. Read David's final instructions to Solomon in 1 Kings 1-4. Write an essay on what it means to be a man or woman of God according to the sacred ideal presented in these chapters.

■ Prayer

How can we pray together with a psalm? You may find the following method helpful in your prayer.

The group should sit in a circle. One person reads the psalm out loud while the others listen. Then, people in the group should read the psalm silently to themselves, perhaps two or three times, thinking about the meaning of the words. After this period of private reflection, one person and then another speaks a verse that has made a particularly strong impression. The psalm verse can be repeated word for word from the biblical text, or the volunteer can rephrase the verse in his or her own words.

By using this technique, the words and images of the psalms take on a new significance. They are filled with the life of the individual who is reading the verse. They become personal prayers which then have the power to resonate within the listening group. Periods of silence are frequent during this type of group prayer. Don't be afraid of these moments. Time is needed to absorb the words of the text and the words of our brothers and sisters in Christ who are praying with us.

Solomon: The Magnificent Failure

OBJECTIVES

In this Chapter you will

- Learn about David's last days and Solomon's anointing as the third king of Israel.

- Become aware of the Wisdom Movement of the Hebrew Scriptures.

- Understand the importance of the Jerusalem Temple for the Israelites.

- Study how Solomon's injustice and compromises led to civil war.

You have shown great favor to your servant, my father David, because he behaved faithfully toward you, with justice and an upright heart; and you have continued this great favor toward him, even today, seating a son of his on the throne...Give your servant, therefore, an understanding heart to judge your people and to distinguish right from wrong.
—1 Kings 2:6, 8-9

The Wisdom of Solomon

In the rule of Solomon, the son and successor of David, the golden age of Israel reached its most prestigious point. Before his death, David saw that Solomon was made king, although Solomon's older half brother Adonijah, a legitimate heir, had already claimed the throne for himself. Unlike his father, Solomon was "born to the purple," a king who was conscious of his royal role from the time of his ascent to the throne in 961 B.C.E. to his death forty years later.

He is remembered as a model of wisdom who united practical know-how with the ultimate knowledge that all success comes from God. Solomon began his reign by asking the Lord for wisdom and an "understanding heart." His vast knowledge earned him the title of "patron" for the Wisdom Movement in Israel and gained him credit for much of the Bible's wisdom literature. His later practice of idolatry became a reminder to Israel of its call to remain faithful to Yahweh.

As you study this chapter, there are a few issues to keep in mind about these Bible verses. First, although the books of Samuel and Kings are much closer to being historical texts than any other books of the Bible that you have studied thus far, their purpose is still to tell the story of God's role in the life of the Hebrew people. What happened is not the important question but rather "why did God cause this to happen?" As you read these texts, understand that they have been interpreted into theological language. Second, remember that stories of David and Solomon were probably written at the king's command. If they are favorable to the king, don't be surprised. A saying goes, "There are at least two sides to every story." We see Solomon's side in

> **Wisdom literature:** the collection of wise sayings that teach how to succeed in life.

these stories. Finally, these texts were edited nearly four hundred years after they were written by people whose interest was fidelity to Yahweh. These editors gave us the books we have today.

The King Is Dead

The story of the end of King David's rule is found in 1 Kings 1:1-40, 49-53. Although he had led Israel with confidence and passion, David died weak, feeble, unsure, and unable to make or influence decisions. His practice of polygamy complicated the issue of royal succession. With more than one wife (in David's case, many wives and concubines) it was difficult to determine which of the king's sons would follow him to the throne. As David's health declined, controversy over his successor added more stress to the end of his life. Adonijah, the son of his wife Haggith, sought the throne. David had not yet publicly declared a successor, so Adonijah began to act as if he were to be the next king. He gathered a large following to himself and gave a banquet to celebrate his supposed ascent to power. With the help of Joab, the commander of the army, and Abiathar, the priest, Adonijah declared himself king.

When the prophet Nathan became aware of Adonijah's plot, he stirred up a movement to make Solomon king. Nathan had Solomon's mother, Bathsheba, tell David of Adonijah's treachery. Bathsheba reminded David that he had promised the throne of Israel to their son, Solomon.

Scholars do not know whether David truly had promised to make Solomon king, or whether this so-called earlier "promise" was invented by Nathan in collusion with Bathsheba or even added later to explain Solomon's rise to the throne. Whatever motivated him to action, David commanded his ministers to anoint Solomon as king, blocking Adonijah's coup.

Adonijah's banquet guests abandoned him when they heard that Solomon had been anointed. Afraid that he would be punished or killed for trying to usurp the throne, Adonijah fled to sanctuary at a sacred shrine and refused to leave the altar until Solomon personally assured him that he would be safe from harm.

Archaeology

After eliminating his enemies, Solomon turned to other tasks of kingship. He launched an extensive building program in Israel that included two palaces and a magnificent temple. He fortified the walls of strategic cities throughout the land, establishing them as "chariot centers" for defense. He charged tolls on all the trade routes through Palestine, and to build up the economy he hauled imports from distant ports in Ophir and Arabia in fleets he had built in partnership with the king of Tyre.

Excavations at Hazor, Meggido, and Gezer have uncovered city walls dating back to the tenth century B.C.E., all of the same pattern. This supports the authenticity of the biblical text's descriptions of Solomon's building program.

The Hebrew Scriptures: Called by the Father

Like any modern world leader who is loved and respected, David was mourned at his death. Solomon wasted little time in getting rid of any competitors for the throne.

David's deathbed instructions to Solomon are recorded in 1 Kings 2:1-8. He "rested with his ancestors" and was buried in Jerusalem (1 Kings 2:10). After his father's death, Solomon consolidated his power by removing his enemies. He had Adonijah and Joab killed, and installed Zadok as priest, deposing Abiathar but letting him survive, because he "carried the ark of the Lord God before my father David and shared in all the hardships my father endured" (1 Kings 2:26).

1. *How would polygamy complicate the issue of royal succession?*

2. *How can someone be wise, as Solomon is reported to have been, and yet be so cruel and cunning?*

Polygamy: the practice of having many wives.

Usurp: to seize and hold in possession by force and without right.

If you were given one wish—anything you wanted—what would it be—clothes? a new car? money? a career as a sports, recording, or television star? Solomon was faced with such a momentous decision, and he is remembered for having chosen with care (1 Kings 3:4-14).

In the beginning of his reign, Solomon was as humble and devoted to the Lord as his father had been. One night God told Solomon in a dream to ask for whatever he wanted. Solomon asked for an understanding heart to judge right from wrong. His request so pleased the Lord that he promised even more than Solomon had asked. God promised Solomon wisdom, long life, riches, and honor, as long as Solomon followed God's statutes and commandments.

When he awoke, Solomon realized that God had come very close to him that night. To celebrate God's goodness, Solomon gave a banquet for all his followers in Jerusalem. As the royal judge of Israel, he sought to be as good to his people as God was to him.

Solomon's wisdom in dealing with human nature is illustrated in the story about two mothers who claimed the same child as their own (1 Kings 3:16-28).

Two women came before Solomon with a seemingly insolvable dilemma. Both of the women lived in the same house and had recently given birth. One of their infants was

For Example

In ancient Israel, the king was also the chief justice in the land.

The case of the women and the child has been used to show how Solomon was a wise king. What do you think of his judgment?

found dead—but which one? Each woman claimed the surviving baby as her own, and unfortunately there were no family members or witnesses who could identify either infant.

Solomon guessed that the real mother would act to save the life of the child, so he ruled that the live infant should be cut in two and split between the women. The woman whose child had died accepted the verdict, whereas the infant's real mother begged the king to give the infant to her rival rather than to see it be killed. Solomon then awarded the infant to its real mother, and all Israel was "in awe of him, because they saw that the king had in him the wisdom of God for giving judgment" (1 Kings 3:28).

---

3. *How would the choice of wisdom be a valuable gift for a leader? For yourself?*

4. *What do you think of Solomon's decision about the baby? Would his decision have proven wise if both mothers had insisted on killing this infant? How would you have solved the dilemma?*

Israel's Wisdom

Short sayings that capture the wisdom of the people are present in every culture. Which of the following can you complete?

- *Necessity is the mother of...*
- *An ounce of prevention is worth a pound of...*
- *The early bird catches the...*
- *Do unto others as...*
- *An apple a day...*

How many more of these do you know? These sayings are so popular because they are bits of down-to-earth folk wisdom. Israel, too, had its folk wisdom, which it recorded years ago in texts such as the Book of Proverbs.

What has been called the Wisdom Movement of the Hebrew Scriptures had its beginnings under Solomon, the

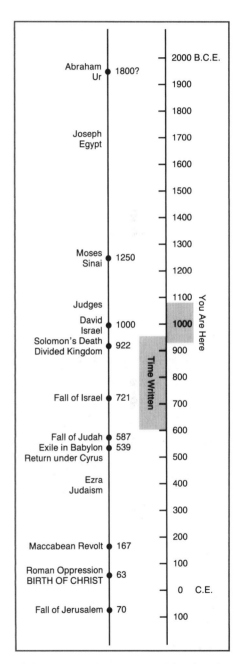

Unlike most other scriptural books, the Book of Kings was probably written close to the historical time it describes.

God: The Source of Israel's Wisdom

Although it borrowed from the wisdom of other nations, Israel's wisdom was different, because it was based on the belief that full wisdom belonged to God alone. For Israel, divine wisdom was seen in creation and was personified as an eternal heavenly being who always accompanied God. "The Lord begot me, the firstborn of his ways," Wisdom says (Proverbs 8:22).

In the Book of Proverbs, wisdom is sometimes personified as a beautiful woman who leads people to a full life. This heavenly power of wisdom is God's gift, bestowed on the talented and skillful. A wise person knew that "the fear of the Lord is the beginning of knowledge" (Proverbs 1:7).

The Book of Wisdom divides the human race into two classes: the foolish and the wise. It regards youth as generally foolish, but capable of becoming wise. An adult without wisdom, however, is a hopeless fool, doomed to failure and earthly unhappiness. Mature wisdom is the acceptance of God's deeds in faith, especially calamities, accidents, and other misfortunes. The higher wisdom is the fulfillment of God's Law.

Thus, Hebrew wisdom goes far beyond merely practical sayings. It teaches the lesson of the prophets: Unless you love and obey God even in small things, your daily life will be without meaning or joy.

sage of Israel and its promoter of the arts. In his court, three thousand proverbs were preserved by the scribes. Because authorship was attributed to the patron of a work, other books of sayings and longer wisdom tales, added years later, were also attributed to Solomon.

The Book of Proverbs is the first of the biblical books known as the wisdom writings. It probably was not completed until five hundred years after Solomon's reign, in the early fifth century B.C.E. Other wisdom books include Job, Psalms, Ecclesiastes, Wisdom, Sirach, and the Song of Songs—a long, beautiful poem in which human love symbolizes God's love for humanity.

Israel borrowed sayings and stories from neighboring cultures. Many examples of this popular form of writing survive in texts from Mesopotamia and Egypt. As a result, many proverbs are purely secular—no more than practical suggestions on how to get along in life, win friends, or accept frustration gracefully. The later texts, like Wisdom and Ecclesiastes, show greater depth. The Book of Job asks some hard questions, like, Why do the wicked so often succeed and the good fail? Why must we suffer? Generally, though, the wisdom texts tried to give practical advice. Through concise sayings and clever stories, the authors of these wisdom books attempted to treat the problems of life in a very practical way.

---

5. *Why would texts be attributed to Solomon even though they were written hundreds of years after his death?*

Summary

- Adonijah's plot to become king was foiled by Nathan and Bathsheba, who worked to have Solomon anointed king after David.

- In a dream, God promised riches, wisdom, long life, and honor to Solomon if the king kept God's commandments.

- Solomon was famous throughout Israel for his wise judgments both in practical, simple matters and in more complex matters.

- Solomon was the patron of the Wisdom Movement in Israel.

■ Review

1. How was Adonijah's plan foiled?

2. By what judgment did Solomon resolve the dispute between the two women who claimed the same baby?

3. Name some of the books of the Wisdom Movement.

4. What kinds of advice does wisdom literature offer?

5. Why is God the source of Israel's wisdom?

6. Words to Know: Adonijah, Haggith, Wisdom Movement, proverbs, Abiathar, Zadok.

■ In Your World

1. What characterizes a wise person? In two paragraphs, describe someone that you know who possesses those characteristics.

2. Write a modern version of the ideal wife, husband, child, teenage student, employee, employer, or diplomat based on Proverbs 31:10-31.

■ Scripture Search

1. Solomon was rewarded for his faithfulness. Are the good always rewarded and sinners punished? Read what Jesus said about this in Luke 13:1-5 and John 9:1-3. Is there a connection between having wisdom and being successful?

2. Read 1 Kings 5:1-14. List some examples of Solomon's practical wisdom.

If you inherited or won an immense sum of money, how would you spend it? Would any of it go to others? Would any of it go to your church? Why or why not?

"The glory of Israel for the glory of the Lord!" This might have been the motto of the young king Solomon as he took up his royal duties. He wanted to make Israel a respected nation. His plans included raising splendid buildings, like the Temple and palaces for himself and his Egyptian bride.

Solomon's Building Program

Solomon's dream took shape as a massive twenty-year building program financed by public taxes and accomplished largely by the workmen of Israel. Local resources were not enough for Solomon's ambition, however, since he needed fine woods, precious metals, and quarried stone from other countries. Native architects and skilled artisans were also lacking. For these he turned to the more advanced and prosperous civilization of Phoenicia, where his friend Hiram, king of Tyre, met his needs in exchange for grain and olive oil.

The largest project was the king's own palace—a magnificent building called the House of Cedar that took thirteen years to complete. Larger than the Temple, it featured a luxurious grand ballroom with cedar pillars and ceiling beams (1 Kings 7:1-11).

Solomon built a second palace for his most important wife, the pharaoh's daughter. In order to gain favorable diplomatic relations with foreign nations, Solomon brought many wives and concubines from other countries into his harem. Traditionally, Egyptian princesses did not leave their country to marry. But in the tenth century B.C.E, when the

Egyptian dynasty was weak, this rule was broken. Solomon received his bride and brought her to Israel. By building her a separate palace, Solomon demonstrated both his desire to stay on friendly terms with Egypt and the extent of Israel's international influence.

---

6. *What is the significance of the fact that Solomon's palace was larger than the Temple?*

Modern building techniques make even difficult jobs seem easy. Given the primitive tools of his day, Solomon's building projects were very impressive.

Construction and Dedication of the Temple

The Bible cites what might have been fragments of documents exchanged between Solomon and Hiram in 964 B.C.E. when they made arrangements to erect the Temple (1 Kings 5:17-23). The elaborate details of the Temple and its furnishings are carefully chronicled in the documents. From this time on, the Temple became the center of activity for Israel. It symbolized their unity and national identity, and it attested to their faith. God's glory filled the Temple when the ark came to rest there.

In the middle of the many descriptive details found in 1 Kings, there was a warning from the Lord to Solomon: "As to this Temple you are building—if you observe my statutes, carry out my ordinances, keep and obey all my commands, I will fulfill toward you the promise I made to your father David. I will dwell in the midst of the Israelites and will not forsake my people Israel" (1 Kings 6:12-13). In other words, God's presence with the people did not depend on the physical building of the Temple, no matter how magnificent, but on whether the Israelites maintained a faithful relationship with God.

When the Temple was completed, Solomon ordered all the leaders of Israel to gather in Jerusalem for the dedication of the New Year Festival. Joyfully, the priests carried the ark of the Lord and the vessels of the Meeting Tent to the new Temple. Today, in modern Judaism, this feast is called Rosh Hashana.

The Hebrew Scriptures: Called by the Father

Details of Solomon's Temple

The building of the Temple occupied Solomon for seven years (1 Kings 6; 7:13-51). He made a contract with Hiram, the king of Tyre, for the timber which was to be brought from Lebanon. The woodwork was prefabricated so that "no hammer, axe, or iron tool was to be heard in the Temple during its construction." All the stones used in building Solomon's Temple were cut to shape in quarries near Jerusalem. Constructing the Temple was a monumental feat.

The measurements of the Temple building were modest by our standards: ninety feet long, thirty-five feet wide, and forty-five feet high. The main purpose of the structure was to house the ark, not to function as a gathering place for people. Only the high priest entered its innermost sanctuary once a year.

The Temple was divided into three parts: (1) the **vestibule,** or entry room; (2) the **nave,** or principal chambers; and (3) the **Holy of Holies,** or the inner sanctuary. The building was fronted by a porch supported by huge bronze columns, probably meant to represent the pillars of fire and cloud that guided the Israelites in the desert.

Double doors of olive wood led to the Holy Place, a high room that measured sixty-five by thirty-five feet. In this windowed room were kept all the rich apparatus for worship. These treasures were often stolen and carted off to foreign lands during invasions.

Two double doors led into the Holy of Holies, or Most Holy Place, where the Ark of the covenant was kept in absolute darkness.

The bronze altar of sacrifice at which Solomon and the priests offered whole burnt offerings (or *holocausts*) was in the court in front of the Temple on a platform.

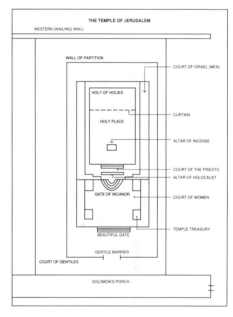

Solomon's Temple was to become the center of Jewish life.

Solomon then led the people in a solemn prayer of dedication: "Can it indeed be that God dwells among men on earth? If the heavens and the highest heavens cannot contain you, how much less this Temple which I have built!" (1 Kings 8:27). After the dedication, God appeared again to Solomon, renewing the covenant to David in which God promised to establish David's line forever (1 Kings 9:45).

---

7. *Rosh Hashana marks the date when the Temple was dedicated. It is also celebrated as the Jewish New Year. What is the significance of these facts?*

Heroes and Legends

The major source of cedar wood in biblical times was the mountainous regions of Lebanon. Both David and Solomon imported large quantities of cedar for their palaces and for the interior of the Temple. Cedar was used for roofing, ceilings, paneling, carved work, and supporting beams. Masts for sailing vessels were often made of cedar because of its resistance to decay. The phrase "cedars of Lebanon" is frequently used in Scripture to represent strength, splendor, and longevity.

There is a tragic note to this story. Because they were so suitable for construction, the cedars of Lebanon were cut down with no thought for the future. Today, the remaining trees are of no value for construction. What was once a lush forest is now a desert. The phrase "cedars of Lebanon" now suggests ecological disaster.

Temple Worship

Once the Temple was built by Solomon, it was put to use. The central purpose of the Temple was to offer animal sacrifice. This was practiced to show thanksgiving for God's gift of life. There were other reasons, however, to sacrifice an animal. The following five reasons are listed in the first five chapters of the book of Leviticus.

Holocausts (Leviticus 1). An animal was totally burned on the altar after the priest had laid hands on it and sprinkled its blood on the altar. If offered by the community, it represented the people's praise of God. If offered by an individual, it usually represented atonement for sin.

Grain offering (Leviticus 2). This offering also included cakes baked with unleavened bread, presented with oil and incense. Although all was offered at the altar, only a small portion of it was burned by the priest. The rest was used to feed the priest and his family.

Peace offering (Leviticus 3). An animal was used in this sacrifice, but it was not totally burned. The remaining food was shared as a meal by the offerer and his family and guests. This sacrifice was often used to seal a promise or vow.

Sin offering (Leviticus 4). The Hebrew Scriptures contain many laws relating to cleanliness. A person was

The Hebrew Scriptures: Called by the Father

considered unclean, for example, if he or she touched a dead body, committed a sin, contracted certain diseases, or made an oath he or she did not intend to keep. In the sin offering, the fat of the animal was burned, and its blood was sprinkled on the altar. Two doves were substituted if the individual was poor. If the sin offering was made on behalf of the whole community, a bull was used.

Guilt offering (Leviticus 5). This offering was required in addition to a holocaust in cases of serious sin. It involved a male ram brought to the priest who would burn its fat and sprinkle the blood on the altar. The sinner was also expected to right the wrong he or she had done.

Every day, special morning and evening sacrifices were offered in the Temple. On important feast days, the numbers of sacrifices increased. Sometimes there were processions with the Ark of the covenant; music, led by cantors who were accompanied by lyres, harps, and cymbals, always played an important role. This practice of sacrificing animals lasted until the Temple was destroyed at the time of the Exile. The practice of sacrifice was resumed after the Temple was rebuilt in 516 B.C.E., and did not stop until the Temple was completely destroyed by the Romans in C.E. 70.

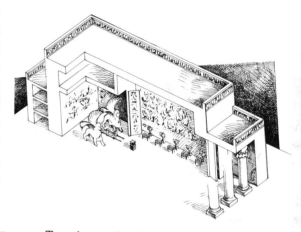

Temple sacrifice became a key element of religious practice during Solomon's reign.

Summary

- Solomon embarked on a major building program in Israel that included the construction of two palaces and the Temple.

- Both physical and human resources were imported into Israel from other nations in order to fulfill Solomon's ambitious plans.

- The Temple became the center of life for the Israelites.

- The Temple consisted of three main parts: the vestibule, the nave, and the Holy of Holies.

- The main purpose of the Temple was to offer animal sacrifice. This continued until the final destruction of the Temple in C.E. 70.

■ Review

1. How did Solomon finance his building program?

2. What were the three main parts of the Temple? How long did it take to build?

3. What was kept inside the Holy of Holies?

4. What effect did the physical Temple building have to do with God's presence to Israel?

5. What qualities does the phrase "cedars of Lebanon" bring to mind?

6. Words to Know: holocaust, vestibule, nave, Holy of Holies, Hiram, Tyre, cedars of Lebanon, *Rosh Hashana.*

■ In Your World

1. How important is money to your happiness? What do you think makes people genuinely happy?

2. Research the architecture of medieval cathedrals, like Chartres or Notre Dame. Write a report on the similarities and differences between their layout and the floor plan of Solomon's Temple.

■ Scripture Search

1. What does Jesus say about the value of material wealth in Matthew 6:19-33?

2. What does the Book of Revelation say about the new Jerusalem and the Temple? Read 21:2-4, 9-14, and 22-27. Why is this important to Christians?

Solomon's Strengths and Flaws

If Saul was the brawn and David the heart, then Solomon was the brain of Israel's kings. Yet even when he was at the peak of his power, his success was never total. In his new sophistication, Solomon belittled the faith that he had inherited from his father and instead equated his personal worth with the magnificent buildings and large court. His reputation in foreign nations became more important to him than his reputation before God.

Military and Trade

Once the Temple and palaces were completed, Solomon extended the city walls in order to enlarge and defend Jerusalem. Making use of the most advanced military weapons of the time, he built a force of hundreds of chariots and thousands of drivers as the main arm of his military strength. He stationed some of the chariots in Jerusalem and strategically placed the rest in six fortified cities throughout Israel to discourage foreign invaders. The six fortified cities were Hazor (north); Meggido (at the mountain pass); Gezer, Beth-horon, and Baalath (western lookouts); and Tamar (south).

Solomon capitalized on Israel's vulnerable position between two empires and turned what had been a disadvantage into an asset. He developed a monopoly on the trade routes. Excavations of vast stables at Meggido, one of the "chariot cities," show that Solomon engaged in a profitable horse and chariot trade as well.

Hiring craftsmen from the Tyrean shipbuilding yards, Solomon built a fleet on the Gulf of Aqaba. These vessels,

Recent archaeological discoveries support the biblical account of Solomon's building program.

Praying the Hebrew Scriptures

Psalm 132 was probably used in services which years later commemorated Solomon's dedication of the Temple. Here are some verses from that psalm: "The Lord swore to David a firm promise from which he will not withdraw: 'Your own offspring I will set upon your throne; if your sons keep my covenant and the decrees which I shall teach them, their sons, too, forever shall sit upon your throne. For the Lord has chosen Zion; he prefers her for his dwelling...Her priests I will clothe with salvation, and her faithful ones shall shout merrily for joy.'"

maintained by the Israelites under the direction of expert seamen from Tyre, brought gold, precious stones, and sandalwood from Ophir. The king had another fleet that transported cargoes of gold, silver, ivory, and animals from Arabia. In southern Palestine, Solomon undertook the most extensive copper mining and refining known in the ancient Near East. A refinery fleet carried the smelted metal to distant shores (1 Kings 9-11).

During Solomon's kingship, Israel developed a large commercial fleet.

The Hebrew Scriptures: Called by the Father

8. *How did Solomon's relationship with Hiram benefit both Israel and Tyre?*

The Queen of Sheba

The famous exchange of gifts between Solomon and the queen of Sheba—a country in Arabia—is recorded in 1 Kings 10:1-13, and reveals the extent of Solomon's ambition and fame. Not content to control the sea routes on the Red Sea, Solomon was also interested in land caravan trade routes with southern Arabia. Developing such strong trade must have had a devastating effect on Near Eastern commerce. It is no wonder that Solomon was the talk of the region. At home, however, the wealth that poured into Israel appeared to be a symbol of God's approval.

The queen of Sheba, having heard of the wealth of Solomon's court and of his wisdom, surveyed his palace and asked Solomon to solve some riddles. She was curious

The queen of Sheba's visit to Solomon shows the prestige and power of Israel during his reign.

Ophir: a country in modern-day Africa.

Star of David/Seal of Solomon

The origin of the Star of David, now recognized as an emblem of Judaism, is obscure. One legend is that King David bore a hexagram-shaped shield when he fought Goliath. Originally a pagan ornament, the hexagram was later named both the Star of David (in Hebrew, *Magen David*) and the Seal of Solomon. By the Middle Ages, the symbols were used as protection against evil; the terms "Seal of Solomon" and "Magen David" were interchangeable in magical texts. By the nineteenth century, the Star of David was used widely, appearing in Jewish ritual and on synagogues. The Seal of Solomon, often depicted as two interlacing triangles, continued to be linked to magic ceremonies. One interpretation is that its cojoining light and dark triangles represent the unity of body and soul.

In 1897, the Star of David was adopted by the Zionist Congress as its emblem. But it was not until World War II, when the Nazis forced European Jews to wear a yellow star as a badge of shame—and, ultimately, death—that it took on its power as a symbol. In 1948 it was chosen as the central design in the flag of the state of Israel.
(Adapted from *Mysteries of the Bible*, copyright © 1988. The Reader's Digest Association, Inc. Reprinted by permission.)

The Star of David has been used as a sign of derision (during World War II) and as a sign of power (on the flag of the modern nation of Israel).

as to whether Solomon was as wise or as rich as had been reported to her. The queen of Sheba recognized Solomon as favored by God when she said: "Your wisdom and prosperity surpass the report I heard...Blessed be the Lord, your God, whom it has pleased to place you on the throne of Israel" (1 Kings 10:7, 9).

The Hebrew Scriptures: Called by the Father

Solomon Yields to Temptation

Filled with pride by prosperity and power, Solomon yielded to the temptations of his newly acquired riches (1 Kings 11:1-13). While claiming only to be open-minded to other ways of life, in actuality Solomon was all too eager to please Israel's neighbors. By building shrines to the gods of his foreign wives and participating in idol worship himself, Solomon compromised his faith. His own "inner temple" was becoming hollow, filled with false gods. He acted unwisely, forgetting that true success comes not from wealth, achievements, or great armies, but from faith in the living God.

Beneath Israel's blossoming landscape, the restlessness of the people smoldered. Solomon's extravagant buildings and luxurious court life were made possible only by excessive taxation and forced labor. These demands on the Israelites created volcanic pressures that would fuel another civil war (1 Kings 11:14-43). The threat to Solomon came not from outside of Israel, but from within—from his own people who had been forced to suffer for Solomon's goals. As Solomon strayed from God, he grew deaf to the cry of the Israelites, who carried the tax and labor burdens of his excessive life-style.

Solomon learned that Jeroboam, the foreman of forced-labor teams in the North, was planning to lead the ten northern tribes in rebellion. Solomon ordered his death, but Jeroboam escaped to Egypt before the orders could be carried out. Later, after Solomon's death, Jeroboam would emerge as a leader in Israel. When Solomon died, his son Rehoboam succeeded him. With Solomon's death, the nation of Israel came apart in civil war. The biblical authors realized that it was the corruption of Israel's religious tradition that had brought about the collapse of the monarchy.

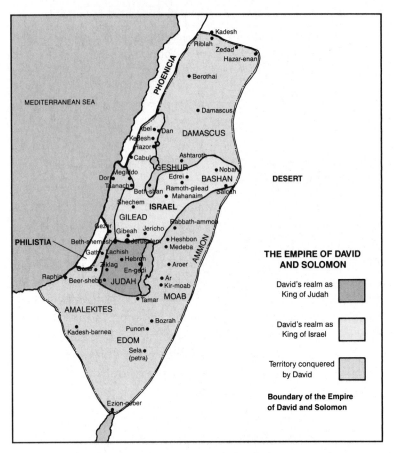

This map shows the kingdom of Israel during the reign of David and Solomon. Compare this map to a modern map of the nation of Israel.

Summary

- Solomon built up Israel's defenses and expanded trade routes.

- Solomon compromised his faith by building shrines to the gods of his foreign wives.

- Forced labor and excessive taxation during Solomon's reign led to unrest among the people of Israel.

- Israel was near rebellion when Solomon's son Rehoboam succeeded him as monarch.

The Hebrew Scriptures: Called by the Father

■ Review

1. For what two reasons did Solomon extend the walls of Jerusalem?

2. Name three of the six Israelite cities that were fortified with chariots.

3. Why did the queen of Sheba visit Solomon?

4. How did Solomon's greed and excessive building program cause problems?

5. What did the Seal of Solomon represent?

6. Words to Know: queen of Sheba, *Magen David,* Seal of Solomon, Jeroboam, Rehoboam.

■ In Your World

1. Jesus referred to the temple of his body (John 2:19-21) and Saint Paul, in 2 Corinthians 6:16, called Christians "temples of God." What do these statements mean to you? How are you a temple of God to other people? Do you treat your body with the same respect as you would a church building, since you "house" God in yourself? How do people disrespect the gift of their bodies?

2. Decide which of the following popular "idols" seem most attractive to you: sexual satisfaction, travel, freedom to do whatever you want, drugs and/or alcohol, stereo, freedom from pain, clothes, money, good looks, popularity. Why did you make your particular choices? These things—if used in moderation—are not necessarily always harmful. How can you develop the wisdom to use them in moderation?

■ Scripture Search

1. Make an inventory of Israel's assets during the golden age of Solomon. Use 1 Kings 10:11-29 to make your list. Categorize the items under the following headings: Practical Things, Luxury Items, and Basic Necessities.

2. What did Jesus say about the queen of the South (Sheba) in Matthew 12:42? Why is this statement important?

8 Review

■ Study

1. Adonijah and Joab were killed by Solomon for plotting against King David. Why was Abiathar's life spared?

2. Why was Solomon considered to be a wise person?

3. Read Ecclesiastes 3:1-8. What wisdom do you find there?

4. From the story in 1 Kings 3, how would you describe wisdom? What is a listening heart?

5. Who was the only person allowed into the Holy of Holies?

6. Why did Solomon build two palaces?

7. What types of materials did Solomon's fleet transport?

8. Why was the queen of Sheba impressed with Solomon and Israel?

9. Outline Solomon's achievements.

10. What sins led to Solomon's downfall?

11. Compare and contrast the reign of Solomon with either Saul's or David's reign.

■ Action

1. Search through the books of Proverbs, Ecclesiastes, Wisdom, and Sirach. Select three of your favorite sayings from each book. Copy out these verses. Rewrite in your own words four of the sayings that you have chosen, or create four "wisdom" sayings of your own.

2. Draw, sculpt, or construct a scale-model of Solomon's Temple. Be sure to include the vestibule, nave, and Holy of Holies.

■ Prayer

The following antiphon can be used in a prayer service as a litany praising the omnipresence of God.

Leader: Lord, where shall I find you? Your place is hidden and high.
All: Yet where shall I not find you, whose glory fills all space?

Leader: Far space is your dominion, yet you dwell in the human heart.
All: You are the refuge of those close by, the haven of those far off.

Leader: You are enthroned in your house, though unconfined by the heights.
All: Your hosts adore you, but you transcend their praise.

Leader: All space cannot contain you, still less an earthly house. Yet though exalted above us in high and lonely majesty...
All: You are closer to us than our own spirit and flesh.

Leader: In the wonders of your creative power, I perceive you.
All: In the holiness of your sanctuary, I find you.

Leader: Does God truly dwell in us? Our origin is dust, how can we presume?
All: O holy God, we can, for you dwell whenever we sing of your glory.

(Antiphonal reading adapted from *The Gates of Prayer,* 1975. The Central Conference of American Rabbis.)

The Nation Divided

OBJECTIVES

In this Chapter you will

- Become aware of the problems that caused Israel to split into two kingdoms and eventually collapse as a nation.

- Understand the role of the prophets in Israel as they attempted to call the people back to their covenant promises.

- Discover the mission and message of Elijah, Elisha, Isaiah, and Micah as they fought idolatry and wickedness in the Southern Kingdom of Israel.

- Examine the lives of Amos and Hosea, who fought for moral and social reform in the Northern Kingdom of Israel.

This people draws near with words only and honors me with their lips alone, though their hearts are far from me...Therefore I will again deal with this people in surprising and wondrous fashion.
—Isaiah 29:13,14

Prophets and Kings

When the nation of Israel began walking the path of idolatry toward self-destruction, God sent prophets to try to persuade them to forsake their evil ways and return to the faith of Abraham and Moses. God had already informed the Israelites that infidelity to the covenant would result in disaster. When the people began to worship idols, live immorally, and act without concern for justice, Yahweh sent messengers called prophets to challenge their infidelity.

The history of the three centuries between Solomon's reign and Israel's restoration (922-539 B.C.E.) revolves around Israel's kings and prophets. The prophets' role was to call Israel to remember the one God, the covenant, and the Mosaic law. The prophets spoke their message directly to the kings, who needed to be reminded of the obligations of their office. The Israelite kings were not above the law, but often they acted as if they were, oppressing the powerless, acting arrogantly, and seeming to be drunk with their own power.

Although the prophets were heeded by only a few and were unable to prevent Israel's collapse, they did save her from extinction. Their words still have an effect on those who hear them.

Two Nations

Solomon's death in 922 B.C.E. led to the division of the kingdom into two parts. The ten northern tribes rebelled against Solomon's son, Rehoboam, who had made the following threat: "My father beat you with whips, but I will beat you with scorpions" (1 Kings 12:11). This type of talk did not win Rehoboam any friends in the north. These tribes chose Solomon's foreman, Jeroboam, as king, and they

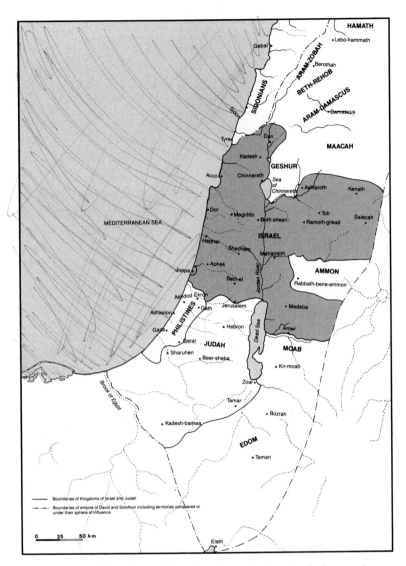

The Northern Kingdom of Israel is shown in the shaded area above.

Archaeology

Baal, the most significant Canaanite god, was revered for his mighty exploits. Myths about him were recorded on clay tablets uncovered by archaeologists in 1928 at the Canaanite city of *Ugarit* (or *Ras Shamra,* the "hill of fennel").

In the Ras Shamra texts, Baal is symbolized by a bull. He is the god of rain, storm, and fertility; a fierce fighter; and an active god. It is easy to see how an agricultural people, whose lives depended on the fertility of the land, might be attracted to Baal. Since the Israelites lived alongside a large Canaanite population, worship of this Canaanite god often attracted the people of Israel.

became the separate kingdom of Israel. The southern tribes of Judah and tiny Benjamin formed the kingdom of Judah under Rehoboam.

Fighting between these two kingdoms was almost continuous. After the division, Israel was unable to defend itself from invasion and became easy prey for neighboring countries that vied with one another for the territory. Israel and Judah would now pay for Solomon's display of power.

The political division that separated Israel into two kingdoms also inspired religious rebellion. In order to

The Hebrew Scriptures: Called by the Father

prevent his people from worshiping in Jerusalem, the holy city of the kingdom of Judah in the South, Jeroboam established the city of Shechem as the capital of the kingdom of Israel and built new sanctuaries to God in Dan and Bethel: " 'If now this people go up to offer sacrifices in the Temple of the Lord in Jerusalem, the hearts of this people will return to their master, Rehoboam, king of Judah, and they will kill me.' After taking counsel, the king made two calves of gold and said to the people: 'You have been going up to Jerusalem long enough. Here is your God, O Israel, who brought you up from the land of Egypt' " (1 Kings 12:27-28).

Initially, the golden calves were meant to represent the invisible divine majesty of Yahweh, but they soon became objects of idolatry: "This led to sin, because the people frequented these calves in Bethel and in Dan" (1 Kings 12:30).

Even if Jeroboam's original intent was good, in the end the people turned to idolatry, violating God's Law. They confused Yahweh with the idol of Baal, the Canaanite god. Encouraging idolatry was the greatest sin of Jeroboam and all the subsequent northern kings. God chose this time of turmoil to speak to the Chosen People through the voices of the prophets.

Jeroboam established shrines to Yahweh in Dan and Bethel. Why would these statues of bulls be confused with the god Baal?

---

1. *Why was the choice of a calf (or bull) to represent God's invisible presence an unwise idea?*

2. *What images represent false gods in today's world?*

Elijah and Elisha

Before the age of the classical prophets—those whose writings are in the Scriptures—there were other prophets in Israel, people like Elijah and Elisha. Elijah was truly a man of God. Although his words were not recorded, his deeds and actions are saved in the Hebrew Scriptures. As God's champion and Baal's foe, Elijah is a hero in Jewish history. He and his successor Elisha were dynamic in combating the religious and immoral policies of Ahab and Jezebel.

Northern Kings

The author of the book of Sirach says this about the kings of Judah, the Southern Kingdom: "Except for David, Hezekiah, and Josiah, they were all wicked; they abandoned the law of the Most High" (Sirach 49:4). The kings of the Northern Kingdom were even worse. Their story is briefly recounted in 1 Kings 15:25-34 and 16:1-4, 8-13, 23-33.

The northern kings who followed Jeroboam did not curb idolatry. Most of them "did evil in the Lord's sight" (1 Kings 15:26). Many were assassinated. The story of the northern kings after Jeroboam (922-915 B.C.E.) is full of wickedness and murder.

Jeroboam's son Nadab (901-900) succeeded him as king of Israel. Like his father, Nadab was an idolater. He was killed by Baasha, who then destroyed the entire family of Jeroboam. When Baasha died (877), his son Elah became king (877-876), reigning for two years over Israel. Elah's chariot commander, Zimri, murdered him and assumed the throne, killing all of Baasha's relatives. However, Zimri's reign was short-lived. He lasted seven days (876), and was then besieged by Omri, the general of Israel's army. Sensing defeat, Zimri committed suicide.

After further political conflict, Omri became king (876-869). Many historians consider him one of the most important kings of Israel because of his political accomplishments. He founded Samaria as his new capital and improved the economic condition of the people through building and trade. War with the Southern Kingdom of Judah ended for a time during his reign. With stability on the home front, Omri was able to develop strong international alliances. When he died, Omri was succeeded by Ahab (869-850), who was the most harmful northern king of all.

The Hebrew Scriptures: Called by the Father

The amazing stories of Elijah and Elisha reflect their exalted reputation. They belong to a class of inspired prophets and reformers who upheld strict belief in and worship of Yahweh. They made the tradition of Moses come alive at a time when Israel had forgotten the meaning of its covenant with God, abandoning Yahweh for Baal.

Elijah Confronts Ahab and Jezebel

The texts concerning the prophet Elijah and his confrontations with Ahab and Jezebel are found in 1 Kings 18:16-19:18 and 21:1-28.

Jezebel was a Phoenician princess who brought her faith in Baal to her new home in Ahab's court. Her chief offense was imposing the cult of Baal on Israel. Jezebel exerted great influence on Ahab. A temple to Baal was erected in Samaria, and worship of Baal was furthered through the work of the "prophets of Baal," who served as religious and political advisors to Ahab. At first, the people of Israel did not consider this to be a threat. However, Jezebel changed their attitude when she killed or chased into hiding many of Yahweh's prophets.

In a famous showdown with the prophets of Baal, Elijah exposed Baal as a false god (1 Kings 18:18-46). The prophets of Baal called on their god to bring fire down upon a sacrificial bull, but no one answered. Elijah called on Yahweh to do the same, and God responded with a fire that consumed Israel's sacrifice. The people proclaimed Yahweh as the true God, seized the prophets of Baal and killed them. This enraged Jezebel. She sought to kill Elijah, who took refuge on Mount Horeb. It was here, near a cave, that Elijah encountered Yahweh personally. God came not in the form of fire or earthquake or strong wind, but in a tiny, whispering sound: a still, small voice (1 Kings 19).

Jezebel also increased the powers of the king. She supported the notion that the king was above the law of God and, therefore, had unlimited power. The text of 1 Kings 21 illustrates the wickedness of Jezebel and Ahab. A man named Naboth rejected Ahab's offer to buy or exchange his vineyard for another. When Ahab returned to the palace and told Jezebel that his bargaining had failed, Jezebel acted surprised that the king did not simply take

Elijah called upon God to consume his sacrifice. Elijah went to great lengths to prove the power of God.

over the property. After all, he was the king, wasn't he? Jezebel fabricated a charge of treason against Naboth and had him arrested and later executed. Ahab then appropriated Naboth's property, and this caused Elijah to prophesy: "The dogs shall devour Jezebel" (1 Kings 21:23).

Elisha Succeeds Elijah

At God's direction, Elijah chose Elisha as his successor in the prophetic mission. Later, as Elijah and Elisha were walking together, a flaming chariot descended from the sky and whisked Elijah away. Elisha picked up Elijah's cloak and proceeded to carry out Elijah's prophetic mission. The stories about Elisha's career as a prophet are mainly contained in the first thirteen chapters of the second book of Kings.

Elijah is said to have been taken to God in a fiery chariot.

The Hebrew Scriptures: Called by the Father

In these texts, Elisha performs many miracles to help individual Israelites. The power of God through Elisha is depicted as life-giving. Elisha also helps the nation as a whole by anointing Jehu, a man called by God to be king of Israel. Jehu proceeded to wipe out Baal worship in Israel by: (1) assassinating Joram, Ahab's son and the current king; (2) participating in Jezebel's death; (3) destroying Baal's temple in Samaria; and (4) slaughtering all of Ahab's descendants and all Baal worshipers in Samaria. Thus, a terrible period in Israel's history came to a shameful, savage end.

3. *In what ways does God come to you in prayer? Is it as a still, small voice in your heart; a strong, external power; an image of some kind; or something else? Be specific.*

4. *Can bloody wartime deeds (like those of Jehu) be justified because they were done in God's name? How is God's name used to excuse horrendous behavior?*

Summary

- Due to political strife, the once-unified nation of Israel became two kingdoms: Israel (north) and Judah (south).

- Jeroboam established sanctuaries in Dan and Bethel, yet he encouraged idolatry among the people by installing golden calves in these shrines.

- Elijah the Prophet campaigned against Ahab, Jezebel, and Baal worship in Israel.

- Elisha succeeded Elijah as Israel's prophetic voice.

■ Review

1. What happened to the kingdom of Israel after Solomon's death?

2. What was Jeroboam's big mistake?

3. Why was Ahab just as evil as Jezebel, even though she initiated many of the crimes committed during his reign?

4. How was Elijah a man of God?

5. Name some of Omri's accomplishments.

6. Words to Know: Rehoboam, Jeroboam, Baal, Dan, Bethel, Shechem, Ugarit (Ras Shamra), Omri, Elijah, Elisha, Ahab, Jezebel, Naboth, Jehu.

■ In Your World

1. Think of occasions when someone's words made you angry, disappointed, or happy. Using these examples from your own life as illustrations, write an essay on the power of words.

2. Why do people often react negatively to reformers?

■ Scripture Search

1. The story of Elisha and the Shunammite woman is told in 2 Kings 4:8-37. What might be a logical explanation for this miracle?

2. Read the account of the death of Jezebel in 2 Kings 9:30-37. How did her death fulfill Elijah's prophecy?

Amos and Hosea: Messengers of God

What kind of motivation works better—threatening punishment or appealing to love? Would the results of these two types of motivation be the same for children as for adults? Which type works best for you?

God attempted to keep the Northern Kingdom faithful to the covenant by using two different messengers: Amos, a herdsman and keeper of sycamore trees, was sent to proclaim prophecies with fierce words; and Hosea, who was married to an unfaithful wife, was sent with words of love, forgiveness, and promise.

Jeroboam II ruled Israel from 786-746 B.C.E. During this time, Israel experienced a rebirth in wealth and power to rival that of Solomon's time, although internal corruption was progressing like a cancer within the political body. The privileged took advantage of the poor, and since judges were also corrupt, the poor had little hope of receiving justice. This situation existed because the people had lost their understanding of covenant law. Faith no longer guided their lives; worship was merely a matter of religious rites, performed mechanically, with no real personal commitment. To this society, Amos and Hosea announced both condemnation and hope.

Today, when most people think of prophets, they often imagine an old man preaching damnation and the end of the world. Amos's predictions could certainly fit in this category.

Amos was not a professional prophet—that is, he was not hired by the king to explain God's mysteries. Rather, he was a simple herdsman and keeper of sycamore trees who lived in Tekoa on the fringe of the Judean wilderness. Although Amos lived in the Southern Kingdom, he proclaimed his message to the people of the Northern Kingdom. When he heard God's call, Amos felt chosen by God to rebuke Israel and its rulers for breaking the law of Yahweh.

In the middle of the eighth century B.C.E., this stern man of the desert pounced on the sophisticated city people of Bethel like a lion and roared the Lord's words. Amos dared to call the aristocratic women of the city fat, lazy cows, comparing them to the cattle from the region of Bashan. He denounced immorality and luxury, condemning the way the wealthy lived at the expense of the poor.

When Amos pronounced his predictions of retribution for Israel—the overthrow of the sanctuary, the collapse of the royal house, and the captivity of the people—the priest of Bethel enlisted Jeroboam II's help in banishing Amos. Amos, however, continued to warn of future political upheaval. His strength as a prophet came from the way in which he challenged Israel's imbalanced, fragile society built on injustice with the message of the covenant.

Although the Book of Amos ends with the promise of restoration, it is primarily a book that predicts suffering for the Northern Kingdom. It was Amos who gave new meaning to the idea of the "day of the Lord." This phrase originally meant the day when Yahweh would intervene to save the Chosen People from their oppression. According to Amos, however, this day would be "darkness and not light" (Amos 5:18). He further warned, "Prepare to meet your God, O Israel" (Amos 4:12) in a tone which suggested that Yahweh would not be happy with his people because of their selfishness and neglect of the poor and powerless within Israelite society.

Read quickly the nine chapters of the Book of Amos in order to get a better understanding of the prophet's message of divine judgment. Pay special attention to the form of the oracle to Moab in Amos 2:6-16. Notice how the formal opening of this prophecy repeats the opening of the prophecies to the seven neighboring countries. Be able to summarize the general form of the prophecy to Israel.

———————————————————

5. *Why was Amos an unlikely prophet? How would you judge the validity of a modern-day prophet's words?*

———————————————————

The Role of the Prophets

The prophets taught that Israel must live up to its covenant obligations or face consequences. The people of Judah thought that if they carried out the rituals of formal religion, worshiping according to the law, it wouldn't matter if their lives were filled with perversions and injustice. The prophets proclaimed that God wanted people's actions, not their deeds. Yahweh desired mercy, not sacrifice. The nation of Israel was dependent on God's faithfulness, the prophets explained. The prophecy concerning David's house pointed to a higher kingdom and to a future Messiah, not to a guarantee of Israel's national success.

The prophets were spokespersons for God. The word *prophet* comes from the Greek for "to speak in place of." The Hebrew word for prophet is *nabi,* which means "mouthpiece." *Nabi* is derived from another Hebrew word which means "to spring forth" or "to bubble up." In the recorded words of the prophets, it is clear that they spoke God's words, not their own. As ambassadors for God, their messages were often phrased in diplomatic language: "Thus says the Lord." Their words could also be direct and embarrassing as well.

The prophets came from a society that was in danger of collapse from within. Prophets were called by God and compelled to declare the divine will in the current affairs of the people. In so doing, they made the past understandable, the present endurable, and the future hopeful.

In many cases, the prophets' predictions were natural outcomes of the actions of the people. They were like a

Prophets were not fortune tellers. Rather, they were interpreters of reality. They explained the consequences of people's actions.

parent's advice to a young child: "If you touch that hot pan, you'll get burned." The prophets spoke to Israel in much the same way: If you break the Law and forget Yahweh, you will be crushed. The Israelites heard the words of the prophets verified and experienced their fulfillment as history unfolded.

---

6. *How can you speak for God today?*

7. *What are some of the prophetic statements made by people today? What is the importance of these statements?*

The Hebrew Scriptures: Called by the Father

True and False Prophets

The Hebrew Scriptures use the word prophet to refer to many types of people who, in one way or another, were believed to reveal the message of God to the Chosen People. The various groups of prophets are categorized in the following ways.

Classical prophets: These people's words were recorded and remembered in the Hebrew Scriptures. They demanded that the Israelites live according to the covenant and faithfully worship Yahweh. They often spoke to their audience in depressingly harsh and defeatist terms, criticizing the immoral behavior of the people. These prophets did not hesitate to challenge the king, either. These men of power did not enjoy being told that their administrations were corrupt and their policies evil. For this reason, being a classical prophet was risky.

Professional or ***ecstatic prophets:*** While their works and words were generally not preserved in Scripture, these prophets and prophetesses are mentioned in the stories. Unlike the classical prophets, they often lived and worked in groups and used special techniques—hypnotic music, drink, or dance—to work themselves into ecstasy, an emotional state or trance in which they would prophesy. Although classical prophets like Ezekiel sometimes had psychic experiences, in general they were not ecstatic. Elisha was probably a professional prophet. Once, when he wanted to prophesy, Elisha called for a musician. When the musician played, the power of the Lord came upon Elisha (2 Kings 3:15).

False prophets: There were also false prophets in Israel who were paid for their prophecies and who spoke only the soothing, flattering words the people wanted to hear. Their dangerous falsehoods and the fact that they prophesied for money angered the classical prophets. (See 1 Kings 22.)

Hosea, a contemporary of Amos, had the same message to deliver as did Amos, yet his message was not nearly as harsh. He did not speak with the abrupt anger of Amos. Hosea recalled God's love for Israel, and all of God's efforts to coax her back to faithfulness. In his marriage to the unfaithful Gomer, Hosea symbolically lived out the estranged relationship between Yahweh and Israel. Do not be misled by Hosea's different approach to proclaiming the message. Hosea was indeed a firebrand; his message was just as forceful as Amos's message.

Hosea's family life reflected the love, despair, and hope of Yahweh's relationship with Israel. Gomer, the woman Hosea loved, deserted him for other men. In much the same way, Israel deserted Yahweh for Baal. Gomer's adultery was a parable for Israel's chasing after strange gods after it had promised to be faithful to Yahweh. Hosea condemned Israel's priests and leaders. He called the country "an unturned hearth cake" (Hosea 7:8), burned on one side, unbaked on the other. With this image, Hosea symbolized both the uselessness of the people and the vast difference between the rich and poor in Israel.

Although he was hurt and angered by Gomer, Hosea was willing to forgive her and take her back. Yahweh, too, was hoping to take back a repentant Israel. This was the point Hosea tried to impress on the people. When the people showed no sorrow for their behavior and were unwilling to change it, Hosea foretold Israel's destruction. Deaf to Hosea's words of forgiveness and content without Yahweh and Yahweh's demands, Israel rushed headlong into destruction.

As you read through the Book of Hosea, pay special attention to these passages: 2:15-22 and 11:1-4. These beautifully express God's love for the people of Israel.

---

8. *How is the relationship between God and Israel like a marriage? How are both relationships affected by faithfulness?*

Heroes and Legends

The prophet Hosea and his wife Gomer had three children. Hosea gave them symbolic names reflecting God's displeasure with Israel. The first son was named Jezreel, as a reminder of the bloodshed by Jehu at Jezreel when he slaughtered all of Ahab's family and the supporters of Baal. The second child, a daughter, was named Lo-ruhama, which means "She is not pitied." The child represented the people of Israel for whom God no longer felt pity. The third child, a son, was named Lo-ammi, meaning "Not my people." This was the most frightening image for Israel, since it implied that God would break the covenant because of Israel's unfaithfulness.

Hosea spoke of God as being a faithful spouse.

Summary

- Yahweh sent Amos and Hosea to prophesy against corruption and immorality in Israel.

- Amos predicted dire consequences for Israel's behavior. He was banned from the sanctuary in Bethel because of his words.

- The word prophet comes from the Greek for "to speak in place of." The prophets announced God's will to the people.

- In his marriage to Gomer, Hosea lived out the broken relationship between God and Israel. Just as Hosea's wife was unfaithful, so was Israel unfaithful to Yahweh.

SECTION 2
Checkpoint!

■ Review

1. What two different strategies did Amos and Hosea employ to bring Yahweh's message to Israel?

2. What were the sins of Israel that Amos and Hosea condemned?

3. In what ways do classical, ecstatic, and false prophets differ?

4. How do the names of Hosea's children symbolize Yahweh's view of Israel?

5. What did Hosea's image of the unturned hearth cake represent?

6. Words to Know: classical, ecstatic, and false prophets; Amos; Hosea; Gomer; Jeroboam II; Jezreel; Lo-ruhama; Lo-ammi; Nabi.

■ In Your World

1. Just as your parents and teachers don't enjoy correcting you, you probably don't like to tell your friends that what they're doing is wrong. However, in conscience, you are obliged to do so in a kind, loving manner. How would you speak to a friend who was: a) stealing from other students; b) abusing his or her body with alcohol or other drugs; or c) spreading false rumors about another person?

2. If Amos and Hosea were to read today's newspapers, they would find that the human race hasn't changed much since their time. What aspects of contemporary society would anger them?

■ Scripture Search

1. Amos 7, 8, and 9 consist of symbolic visions. Read these chapters and describe or draw a picture of two of these visions.

2. Read Hosea 4-5 and 8-9. What evils was Hosea condemning?

Isaiah and Micah: God's Ambassadors to Judah

Robert Kennedy once said, "Moral courage is a rarer commodity than bravery in battle or great intelligence. Yet it is the one essential vital quality for those who seek to change a world that yields most painfully to change." Isaiah and Micah, prophets from the Southern Kingdom of Judah, were men of moral courage. They attacked the very same evils as did Amos and Hosea, the prophets of the Northern Kingdom. Both Isaiah and Micah sought to rescue the faith of the people of Israel from idolatry and unjust living. They were ambassadors of Yahweh to the people of Judah. They challenged the people to live as God had called them to live, faithful to the covenant and the commandments.

Hezekiah's Reforms

Judah, the Southern Kingdom, followed a course similar to that of Israel in the north. The Judeans in the south survived as a kingdom for more than a century longer than the Northern Kingdom. Israel was conquered in 722 B.C.E. by Assyria, while Judea was conquered in 587 B.C.E. by Babylon. Depending on the king, idolatry was either upheld or purged. Jehoshaphat and Uzziah were two kings who initiated reform and brought Judah to a time of prosperity. Under Ahaz, however, Judah became a state subject to the rule of Assyria, which instituted pagan practices in all of their lands.

Supported by the southern prophets Isaiah and Micah, Ahaz's son, Hezekiah, reversed this pattern. He attempted

Praying the Hebrew Scriptures

A story is told about a sparrow lying on its back in the road. A person passing by asked the sparrow why he was lying there. "I heard the heavens are going to fall," replied the sparrow. "Oh," said the passerby, "do you really think your spindly legs can hold up the heavens?" "One does what one can," said the sparrow.

The prophets' actions resembled those of the sparrow. They did what they could to stop the fall of the kingdom of Israel. Micah 6:8 gives us an idea of what we can do: "You have been told, O man, what is good, and what the Lord requires of you: only to do the right and to love goodness, and to walk humbly with your God." Think about the ways in which you can walk humbly with your God.

Judah (shaded area) remained a kingdom until 587 B.C.E.

to gain independence from the Assyrians by closing the shrines of Yahweh that were corrupted by Assyrian practices. Hezekiah also attempted to rally the Israelites around the monarchy and the holy city of Jerusalem.

Hezekiah's reform was short-lived, however. The prophets failed to stir the consciences of the majority of the people. Judah grew less able to defend itself against military attack. By the time Babylon became a powerful nation under Nebuchadnezzar in 604 B.C.E., replacing Assyria as the leading world power, Judah was vulnerable.

The Hebrew Scriptures: Called by the Father

The writings of Isaiah and of his disciples, including work done by individuals known only as Second and Third Isaiah, are found in the lengthy biblical Book of Isaiah. Chapters 1-39 are called Isaiah. Chapters 40-55 are believed to be the work of Second Isaiah. Chapters 56-65 come from a much later historical period than the eighth century B.C.E., and are often called Third Isaiah.

Isaiah: Adviser to Kings

Isaiah indicates that he was a respected member of the royal court with access to the king. When Assyria was the dominant world power, Judah's King Ahaz ignored Isaiah's warning to have nothing to do with Assyria. Isaiah used extreme means to get his point across to Hezekiah, Ahaz's successor (Isaiah 7:1-6; 20:1-6). Hezekiah heeded Isaiah's protest against attacking Assyria after Isaiah walked through Jerusalem barefoot and stripped like a prisoner of war. Isaiah did, however, encourage Hezekiah to stand firm against Assyrian aggression and to resist surrender. Isaiah predicted that if Hezekiah waited, God would save Judah. Somewhat miraculously, a plague weakened the massed army of Sennacherib. However, the kingdom of Judah was eventually destroyed in 587 B.C.E. (2 Kings 19:20-35).

Isaiah was involved in the politics of Israel. He encouraged the kings and the people to depend only on the One who is dependable. He said, "Woe to those...who put their

Isaiah communicated his warnings to the king through dramatic actions.

The Book of Isaiah

The Book of Isaiah with 66 chapters makes it one of the longest books in the Bible. Scholars have divided the book into various sections in an attempt to understand the many different types of sayings within the text. The following outline shows the principal divisions of the Book of Isaiah.

A. **The Book of Judgment**
   1. *Denouncing the sin of Israel and Judah (1:1-6:13)*
   2. *God will be the savior of Judah against the Assyrians (7:1-11:16)*
   3. *Hymn of thanksgiving (12:1-6)*
   4. *Prophecies against the nations threatening Judah (13:1-23:18)*
   5. *Universal prophecies (24:1-27:13)*
   6. *The Lord alone provides salvation (28:1-33:24)*
   7. *The Lord, Zion's avenger (34:1-35:10)*
   8. *Historical section on Sennacherib's siege of Jerusalem (36:1-39:8)*

B. **The Book of Consolation**
   1. *Prophecies of mercy and salvation (40:1-41:29)*
   2. *The Servant of the Lord passages (42:1-44:28)*
   3. *God's power demonstrated (45:1-48:22)*
   4. *Hymns of praise (49:1-55:13)*
   5. *Return of the captives (56:1-59:21)*
   6. *The glory of new Jerusalem (60:1-22)*
   7. *Consolation of Zion (61:1-62:12)*
   8. *God destroys idol worshipers but saves the faithful (63:1-64:12)*

Find each of these divisions in the Book of Isaiah and explore why they are titled in this way.

◆

trust in chariots...but look not to the Holy One of Israel nor seek the Lord!" (Isaiah 31:1).

Isaiah is best known to Christians for his prophecies about Emmanuel, a Hebrew name meaning "God with us." When Judah was finally destroyed, Isaiah spoke of a future king from the line of David who would bring peace. Because of this prophecy the people were still able to hope and believe in God's faithfulness. Isaiah also taught that the tragedies of the Israelites were not a sign that God had

The Hebrew Scriptures: Called by the Father

abandoned them, but rather were the result of the people's failure to trust in God's promises.

The Transcendence of God

The sixth chapter of the Book of Isaiah vividly described Isaiah's call from God. At first, Isaiah seems unwilling to accept his vision. Like Moses, he felt unable, unworthy, and unprepared to be God's spokesperson. But after Isaiah's lips were purified by an angel, the voice of the Lord came from heaven and charged Isaiah with the task of confronting the inhabitants of Judah.

To Isaiah, God was holy and transcendent. Second Isaiah further developed this theme when he wrote, "As high as the heavens are above the earth, so high are my ways above your ways and my thoughts above your thoughts" (Isaiah 55:9). The Hebrew word for holy means "cut off," separated from anything worldly or evil.

Unfaithfulness and sin were hateful to Isaiah as affronts to the holiness of God. He verbally attacked the upper classes of Judah, predicting that the nation would be reduced to a remnant of its once mighty state because of its selfish habits and immorality.

Isaiah is purified with fire to proclaim God's word. How can you be purified from sin?

9. *What is your concept of God? Explain why you think of God in human terms, or in other-worldly terms.*

Micah

Micah, another southern prophet, denounced his people more strongly than Isaiah had. The Book of Micah is only seven chapters in length. Begin your study of this prophet by reading these chapters and noting the key points of his message: the coming judgment of the Lord because of Israel's sins; the glory that awaits Jerusalem when it is restored to glory by God; God's case against Israel for being unfaithful. Be aware especially of Micah's prayers.

As you read this brief prophetic text, examine how Micah made the point that Israel was to care for the powerless in

Transcendence: existence far above and beyond the normal state of being.

society—the poor, the oppressed, the widows, the orphans. Micah predicted ruin for Judah because of its social and economic abuses. Although it is believed that Micah's words moved King Hezekiah to penitence and reform, Micah predicted doom for the kingdom as a whole. However, like Isaiah, he also anticipated a faithful remnant and a new ruler from Bethlehem (Micah 4:6-5:4).

The Power of Words

Words are powerful. They can wound or heal; they can even kill or give life. According to the mentality of the ancient Near East, God's Word was God—an active, dynamic presence. Speaking for God, Jeremiah described God's Word: "Is not my word like fire...like a hammer shattering rocks?" (Jeremiah 23:29).

The might of God's Word was evident at creation, when through the words of God the universe came into being. The Christian Scriptures affirm this understanding of the power of God's Word as being "living and effective, sharper than any two-edged sword. It penetrates and divides soul and spirit, joints and marrow; it judges the reflections and thoughts of the heart" (Hebrews 4:12).

Israel did not take the prophets' criticism lightly. As a result of their harsh words and outspokenness in pointing out Israel's faults, the prophets were persecuted. Although they knew the danger they faced in speaking God's words of truth, they spoke them without hesitation or fear.

Prophets often spoke God's harsh words to the people of Israel. God's words were considered "like a hammer shattering rocks."

Summary

- Hezekiah tried to reform the Southern Kingdom of Judah, but his attempts ultimately failed.

- Both Isaiah and Micah were ambassadors of God to the people of Judah.

- Isaiah's concept of God was one of "otherness." God was transcendent.

- Micah promised ruin for Judah because of its social and economic abuses.

The Hebrew Scriptures: Called by the Father

■ Review

1. What reforms did Hezekiah institute in Judah at the urging of Isaiah and Micah?

2. What does it mean to say that God is transcendent?

3. How was Judah saved from destruction at the hands of Sennacherib?

4. Explain the message Isaiah and Micah delivered to Judah for God.

5. Discuss how words carry great power to hurt and to heal.

6. Words to Know: Hezekiah, Isaiah, Micah, Assyria, Sennacherib, Emmanuel.

■ In Your World

1. Prophets saw that work done for the poor was work done for God. How can you help the poor? What opportunities to put your faith into action are available to you now?

2. Probably more than once you have regretted ignoring a warning. Often human beings live recklessly, and then have to suffer the consequences of their actions. Think of some instances in your own life when you ignored a warning: "Stop fooling around like that or someone will get hurt!" or "Be careful of that crowd; they're into drugs!" or "The gas gauge is on 'E'; shouldn't we fill up?" What happened to you because you ignored those warnings?

■ Scripture Search

1. Read the following passages in Isaiah: 3:8-26; 5:1-7; 6:1-9; 10:20-22; 11:1-4; and 35:4-6. Match each of these six passages with one of the following themes that is characteristic of that text: a) God is holy; b) Only a remnant of Israel will survive; c) God will eventually restore the people to happiness; d) Judah will be destroyed for its wickedness; e) A future ruler from the house of David will bring justice and peace; f) God, who has cared for Israel, has received nothing in return.

2. Find verses in Micah 5 and 6 that reflect the six themes listed above.

9 Review

■ Study

1. Explain how the national fortunes and the religious fidelity of the Israelites were linked during the period of the prophets.

2. Why was Elisha considered a miracle worker?

3. List the kings of Israel between Jeroboam and Ahab.

4. What storm god is depicted in the clay tablets found at Ras Shamra?

5. What was the role of the prophets?

6. How did the professional prophets work themselves into a state of ecstasy?

7. Why is evil so enticing to people? Which is easier—to do good or to do evil? Give reasons for your answer.

8. Why is Hosea such a tragic figure?

9. What names did Hosea give his children? What does each one mean? What do you think Hosea would name his children if he lived today?

10. How did Isaiah advise Hezekiah?

11. What advice does Micah give in 6:8?

■ Action

1. Write prophetic messages for today. These messages could be related to topics such as poverty, pornography, sexual abuse, racism, crime, abortion, drugs, and the environment. Entitle your list "Prophecies for Today."

2. What does the term "Sunday Catholics" mean? How are Sunday Catholics like the Israelites rebuked by Amos and Hosea? What attitudes can you maintain to keep you from becoming one of them?

3. Imagine that you are a prophet. What would be the hardships of your life? What would be the rewards?

■ Prayer

Saint Basil the Great, a fourth-century bishop, said this to wealthy Christians: "The bread which you do not use is the bread of the hungry. The garment hanging in your wardrobe is the garment of him who is naked. The shoes that you do not wear are the shoes of one who is barefoot. The money you keep locked away is the money of the poor. The acts of charity you do not perform are so many injustices you commit."

As you read these words, consider how they apply to your own life. As a Christian, you are called on to bring about the kingdom of God by influencing the world around you. As you pray, ask these questions: How can you help those in need? Take a few moments to think about all that you have. What material "things" are absolute necessities? What could you give up? How can you live out Basil's ideas?

Prophetic Voices in Exile

OBJECTIVES

In this Chapter you will

- Learn how the Israelites became exiles in Babylon.

- Identify Jeremiah as the suffering prophet and Ezekiel as a prophet of visions who promised a new covenant.

- Understand why Jeremiah is viewed as the "martyr" prophet, and a person whose whole life was dedicated to doing God's will.

- See how Ezekiel called for a change of heart and emphasized a return to law and ritual.

My God, my God, why have you forsaken me, far from my prayer, from the words of my cry? O my God, I cry out by day, and you answer not; by night, and there is no relief for me...Be not far from me, for I am in distress; be near, for I have no one to help me.
—Psalm 22:2-3,12

The Exile

Pompeii, Sodom, Hiroshima, Jerusalem—what do these cities have in common? Pompeii was destroyed when the volcano Mount Vesuvius erupted; Sodom was leveled by an earthquake and a fire; Hiroshima was devastated by an atomic bomb during World War II; and Jerusalem was destroyed by the Babylonians.

Even more disastrous for the Hebrews than the destruction of Jerusalem was the fact that they were taken from the Promised Land and forced to live in exile in Babylon. When the Northern Kingdom was destroyed by the Assyrians, its people were scattered to many different lands. Scripture ceases to treat the Northern Kingdom as a people of God. The people of the Southern Kingdom, Judah, would eventually return to Jerusalem as a people with restored dedication to the Lord. The difference in the outcomes between the two kingdoms can be credited to the work of the prophets during the Exile.

Judah Becomes a Vassal State

After Assyria had destroyed the Northern Kingdom, it made Judah a vassal state. King Hezekiah was forced to pay tribute to the Assyrians. Judah remained a vassal of Assyria through the lengthy reign of Manasseh, Hezekiah's son.

Manasseh encouraged the worship of the Canaanite god Baal, and the pagan practice of human sacrifice. The Scriptures relate that "[H]e immolated his son by fire. He practiced soothsaying and divination, and reintroduced the consulting of ghosts and spirits. He did much evil in the Lord's sight and provoked him to anger" (2 Kings 21:6). This constituted a rejection of the reforms that his father Hezekiah had worked so hard to institute. Manasseh's son Amon succeeded him on the throne, but he only lasted for two years before he was assassinated by his own servants. In 640 B.C.E., Amon's son Josiah became the King of Judah.

Assyria had destroyed the Northern Kingdom, as Amos and Hosea had prophesied, in 722 B.C.E. Now Judah was also under the dominion of the Assyrians, though they had little time to enjoy the spoils of their conquest while fighting off the Egyptians, Babylonians, and Medes. The preoccupation of the Assyrians with their enemies in the north allowed Judah to be free of the burden of paying tribute for a few years. For a brief time, around 630 B.C.E., it again

Archaeology

Babylonian rulers kept written records of important events. These documents are significant since they complement much of the historical material in the Hebrew Scriptures. These records were written on clay tablets, cylinders, stone obelisks, and even the faces of smooth rocks. The following is an excerpt from the Babylonian Chronicle, which tells of the capture of Jerusalem in 597 B.C.E.:

"In the seventh year...the Babylonian king mustered his troops, and, having marched to the land of Hatti (Palestine), besieged the city of Judah, and on the second day of the month of Adar took the city and captured the king."

Jerusalem was completely destroyed ten years later.

Much of what we know from this period in history has been learned from clay tablets recovered from Babylon and Egypt.

The Hebrew Scriptures: Called by the Father

became an independent kingdom. For an account of this time period, read 2 Kings 18-19 and 21.

The career of the prophet Jeremiah spanned the reigns of five Judean kings. The first of these kings was Josiah, who ruled from 640 to 609 B.C.E. Josiah was a very important king for Judah because he instituted many religious reforms. In 621 B.C.E., about eighteen years into his reign, Josiah began repairing the Temple in Jerusalem. During these repairs, a "Book of the Law," most likely some form of the Book of Deuteronomy, was found in the Temple. When Josiah heard the words in this long-lost book, he tore his clothes and said, "For the anger of the Lord has been set furiously ablaze against us, since our fathers have not kept the word of the Lord and have not done all that is written in this book" (2 Chronicles 34:21). Josiah had the people renew the covenant with Yahweh. He cleansed the country of foreign cults, removed from the Temple the altars to gods other than Yahweh, and rededicated the Temple to the sole worship of Yahweh.

---

1. *Why was Manasseh a disappointment as king?*

2. *Josiah cleansed Judah of foreign cults before rededicating the Temple. What is the significance of these actions? Provide examples to back up your answer.*

The Book of Deuteronomy

The book that played the most important role in Josiah's reform was Deuteronomy, the fifth book of the Hebrew Scriptures. The literary style of Deuteronomy differs from the other four books that make up the Pentateuch, or Torah. It is a lengthy farewell speech that resembles a sermon. Although the speech is attributed to Moses, who supposedly delivered it on the banks of the Jordan River just before the Israelites entered the Promised Land, it was, in fact, written several hundred years after the Exodus and the death of Moses, probably during the Babylonian exile (ca. 560). It was a common practice in the ancient world to

The Day of the Lord

The "day of the Lord" referred to the future intervention of God in the human affairs of Israel. This day was believed to be one in which God's power and justice triumphed. In Amos 5:18, the oldest passage in which this term appears, the "day of the Lord" specifically referred to a day of punishment for sinners. Amos did not believe that the "day of the Lord" would mean salvation for Israel. He foretold a day of misfortune and darkness, "gloom without any brightness." Amos wanted the Israelites to know that they would not always enjoy salvation and deliverance. Because of their evil ways, some of them would face disaster and judgment.

Later, in the era of Jeremiah and Ezekiel, the phrase "day of the Lord" was used to refer to a time when Yahweh would defeat Israel's oppressors and restore the nation to its former glory. For Malachi and Zephaniah, the "day of the Lord" meant a day of final judgment for the entire world. On this day, the good would be rewarded and the evil would be punished. God's wrath would come down upon the wicked:

"Near is the great day of the Lord,
  near and very swiftly coming;
Hark, the day of the Lord!
  bitter, then, the warrior's cry.
A day of wrath is that day
  a day of anguish and distress,
A day of destruction and desolation,
  a day of darkness and gloom,
A day of thick black clouds,
  a day of trumpet blasts and battle alarm
Against fortified cities,
  against battlements on high" (Zephaniah 1:14-16).

The Book of Deuteronomy established the Mosaic law as the binding agreement for the people returning from exile.

put words on the lips of an historical figure in order to stress the importance of a message.

Deuteronomy calls Israel to return to the covenant and its laws. The name "deuteronomy" comes from two Greek words: *deutero,* which means second; and *nomos,* which means law. The author of this book wanted the Hebrew people to forsake worshiping idols and return to the true worship of Yahweh. The author also tried to reunite the ten tribes in the north with Judah by stressing the importance of a single sanctuary, a reference to the Temple in Jerusalem. With Deuteronomy, the Hebrews now followed the Law— the Torah. The Pentateuch, the first five books of the Hebrews Scriptures, now made up the Law.

The Book of Deuteronomy stresses personal obedience to the Law. The author believed that the Law should not be obeyed because it is written in stone, but because it was inscribed in one's heart: "For this command which I enjoin on you today is not too mysterious and remote for you. It is not up in the sky, that you should say, 'Who will go up in the sky to get it for us and tell us of it, that we may carry it out?' Nor is it across the sea, that you should say, 'Who will cross the sea to get it for us and tell us of it, that we may

Sanctuary: a place of worship.

carry it out?' No, it is something very near to you, already in your mouths and in your hearts; you have only to carry it out" (Deuteronomy 30:11-14).

The Rise of Babylonia

In 626 B.C.E., Babylon won its independence from Assyria. Its power was growing, while Assyria's strength was in decline. A few years later the Assyrian Empire collapsed altogether. The rival powers in the area fought to take Judah as a prize. First Egypt conquered Judah; then Nebuchadnezzar of Babylon fought both Egypt and Judah. The invasion of the Babylonians and the final destruction of Jerusalem in 587 B.C.E. ended Judah's brief period of independence. At this time the city was devastated. Solomon's Temple was destroyed and the people were led away to exile in Babylonia. Yahweh's people ceased to exist as a nation.

Under the direction of the prophets, the Exile became a productive time for the Hebrews. Israel was purged from idol worship and renewed direction was given to the Jewish faith and practice. The Israelites in Babylon were not free, but they were not prisoners, either. The exiles, numbering somewhere between fourteen and twenty thousand people, lived in settlements where they were able to build their own homes and farms, work, and form a community bound by their adherence to tradition and law.

During this time of exile the historical books of the Bible were reedited, the sayings of the prophets were preserved, and a theology of the history of the world was developed. These histories interpreted Israel's past, called the Hebrews to a new future, and offered programs to renew community life with religious fidelity. Despite this renewal, many of the exiles were justifiably bitter, hated their captors, and were homesick for Zion. They desperately longed for release from their exile.

It was during this time of doubt and confusion that a pair of prophets were to shape the future of Israel. They declared that the catastrophe of the Exile was the result of Israel's failure to keep the covenant and to obey God's

At the height of its power, Babylon was the strongest country in the Middle East.

The Hebrew Scriptures: Called by the Father

Word. Because of Jeremiah and Ezekiel, the people in exile renewed their religious conviction and grew in longing for their homeland.

---

3. *The Babylonian captivity was a time of crisis for the Hebrews. Out of this crisis they would emerge as a much stronger people than when they first went into exile. What are some other examples of how difficult times can result in positive change?*

Summary

- Manasseh forgot his father's reforms and reinstituted Canaanite worship in Israel. His grandson Josiah finally cleansed Judah of all foreign cults.

- The Book of Deuteronomy played an important part in Josiah's reform. It reminded people to return to the covenant and its commandments.

- When the Assyrian Empire collapsed, Babylon became the ruling power.

- In 587 B.C.E., the Babylonians destroyed the city of Jerusalem, including the Temple of Solomon, and exiled most of the residents of Judah.

- The Exile, however painful, also gave new direction to the Jewish faith and practice.

SECTION 1
Checkpoint!

■ Review

1. Why did Jerusalem become a vassal state of Assyria?

2. Name some of Josiah's reforms.

3. When was the Temple in Jerusalem destroyed?

4. What is the history of the "day of the Lord"?

5. Why was the Exile a significant period for the Jewish religion?

6. Words to Know: Manasseh, Amon, Josiah, Assyria, Babylon, Babylonian Chronicle, Nebuchadnezzar, the Exile.

■ In Your World

Going away to college can be an exciting adventure, but it also means that you may have to leave home temporarily. What do you think you would miss most about your hometown? Your particular neighborhood? How could you make those places present to you, even though you might be living miles away? Why do you think the Israelites remembered Zion in much the same way?

■ Scripture Search

1. In 612 B.C.E., the Babylonians and Medes destroyed the Assyrian capital of Nineveh. Go through the Book of Nahum and read the oracle that predicts Nineveh's imminent fall. Why might a Hebrew prophet be exultant over the destruction of an Assyrian capital?

2. Read 2 Chronicles 35. What ancient Jewish feast was reinstated here? How did Josiah's reign end?

The Hebrew Scriptures: Called by the Father

Jeremiah: A Man of Sorrows

Jeremiah's vocation was not at all to his liking. He was so tormented and persecuted during his ministry that he is known as "the man of sorrows." He was also unpopular because he proclaimed that the Israelites should be resigned to their Babylonian conquerors. King Zedekiah temporarily silenced Jeremiah by imprisoning him, and then formed an ill-fated alliance with Egypt against Babylon. This act led to the destruction of Jerusalem.

The "Martyr" Prophet

Jeremiah's life was dedicated to doing God's will. From the time of his calling to become a prophet at about the age of eighteen until the time of his death, he risked everything for Yahweh's cause, including personal security and happiness.

Jeremiah's message was painful because he had to foretell disaster for the people, the Temple, and the land he loved. Jeremiah suffered—he was scourged, put in stocks, and imprisoned—for the sake of the word of the Lord (much as Saint Paul was to suffer five hundred years later). Jeremiah's personal life was so involved with his prophetic role that it was repeatedly marked by tragedy and disappointment.

Much of Jeremiah's life was spent calling the Israelites to repentance. When Jeremiah exhorted the people to turn from their evil ways, they mocked him. When he advised them to submit to the Babylonians and later to settle down in exile, he was branded a defeatist and a traitor. When he

Jeremiah used symbolic language to proclaim God's message. These people are using symbolic language to protest war. What are other forms of symbolic language?

warned the Judeans not to flee to Egypt, they not only went but also forced Jeremiah to go with them against his will! Jeremiah prophesied that the end of Jerusalem was not the end of the people of Israel, but his words were ignored. According to legend, Jeremiah was stoned to death by his own people.

It was as if the world were singing in the key of C, and God told Jeremiah to sing in B flat. Nevertheless, through all the difficulties, physical suffering, and mental anguish, Jeremiah was faithful. In the Book of Jeremiah, passages known as Jeremiah's "confessions" reveal his despair as well as his belief in the need for perseverance and faith in God.

4. *Why did Jeremiah suffer? Name a modern-day prophet who suffered for his or her beliefs.*

The Hebrew Scriptures: Called by the Father

The Prophetic Concept of Social Justice

Two themes connect the classical prophets: first, that God had established a covenant with the Chosen People, Israel; and second, that this covenant required the Hebrews to live justly. Each of these themes reflects the idea that the covenant was freely given by God and freely accepted by the Hebrews. When the prophets called Israel to faithfulness, they were asking the people to remember their obligation.

> *"When Israel prospered, therefore, it could be assumed that her people had found favor in the sight of the Lord, and prophetic activity was consequently at a minimum. When, however, a difficulty arose or threatened to appear, it was a sure sign that Israel had transgressed against the Covenant and that God was punishing them. It was in such times of crisis and distress that the prophets undertook to determine and expound the reasons for God's anger and the ways in which the Covenant could be restored."*

The concept of moral and social obligation to other individuals comes from the prophetic tradition more than any other source.

> *"Even if the prophets only preached to their fellow Israelites and saw justice only in terms of their Covenant with God, their ringing words have carried from age to age their belief that justice was for the weak as well as for the strong."*

The prophets clearly said that God could not be served while another human being was being mistreated. To them, love for God was love for justice. People were obligated to denounce evil wherever it was seen and to defy a ruler who commanded disobedience to the covenant. The prophets called people "to live in the law and the love of God no matter what the cost."

(Adapted from Harry Orlinsky, *Ancient Israel, Second Edition.* Copyright © 1960 Cornell University. Used by permission of the publisher, Cornell University Press.)

The Book of Jeremiah is recorded as a collection of speeches Jeremiah dictated to Baruch, his friend and secretary. The Book of Lamentations is a collection of laments, or expressions of grief, about the sad state of Jerusalem. Lamentations is also attributed to Jeremiah.

Jeremiah introduced new ideas into Jewish theology. Among them was the concept that religion is a personal relationship between God and the individual; that the family was not to be punished for the crimes of one of its members; and that children were not cursed for the sins of their parents. Jeremiah also taught that salvation was not for the proud and powerful, but for the *anawim*, the poor and lowly who relied on God's help.

Heroes and Legends

Baruch was Jeremiah's friend and secretary. He recorded Jeremiah's oracles of destruction (Jeremiah 36). Then he took the scroll on which he had written these oracles and brought them before King Jehoiakim to read them publicly. The angry king burned the scroll piece by piece as it was read to him. (Jeremiah then asked Baruch to re-record these oracles.) The oracles themselves may have been from any number of the chapters of Jeremiah. They are not included in the story about their pronouncement in chapter 36. Many scholars think that these oracles were composed of material from other chapters of Jeremiah. The second copy of the scroll is now lost as well.

Jeremiah taught that religion was between an individual and God, as well as between the whole community and God.

The Hebrew Scriptures: Called by the Father

Jeremiah is known as the prophet of the covenant. Through his efforts to revive the spirit of the covenant in Israel he succeeded in reviving the people as well. Recognizing that the Exile destroyed people's understanding of the original covenant, he predicted a new one that would replace the broken Sinai covenant. In the new covenant, external actions were less important than the sincerity of one's heart.

Jeremiah's greatest contribution was the message of his own life. For fifty years he was God's suffering servant. The writers of the Gospel compared Jesus to this suffering servant. The Church applies to Jesus many words that Jeremiah used.

After Jeremiah's death, his stature increased. His influence is felt in the Christian Scriptures, where he is often referred to and quoted. Today he is considered a major prophet, along with Isaiah, Ezekiel, and Daniel.

5. *Who were the anawim? Why would God's salvation come to them? Who are the anawim in today's world?*

Literary Style

Jeremiah's work is composed of long sermons containing emotional drama, visions, and parables. Jeremiah enjoyed speaking more than writing. He used colorful images of war, plagues, cooking, and pottery making to deliver his message that Israel was to return to Yahweh and live justly.

The Temple Sermon

After Josiah's death, Jehoiakim took the throne and tried to undo the work of his predecessor. Jeremiah went to the Temple to warn against impending doom if the people did not return to the covenant. Quite simply, he told the people that their trust in Yahweh was in vain, because they had failed to keep the covenant agreement and had acted unfaithfully and hypocritically. He shocked the congregation by stating that God would destroy the Jerusalem Temple, just as he had demolished the sanctuary of Shiloh where the Ark of the covenant had been kept in the time of Samuel. It was after this fiery sermon that the people threatened to kill Jeremiah. His message was so powerful that it was recorded in two places: Jeremiah 7 and 26. Most scholars believe that chapter 26 comes closer to the actual words of Jeremiah. Read these two chapters and compare the message for yourself.

The Two Baskets of Figs

Jeremiah also used the imagery found in visions to communicate his message. One such example is his vision of the two baskets of figs found in Jeremiah 24:1-10. Read these verses before continuing in this text.

In this vision, Jeremiah saw two baskets placed in front of the Temple. One contained excellent figs, the other rotten figs that could not be eaten. The Lord revealed that the bad figs represented those who had been left in Judah under King Zedekiah, as well as those who had fled into Egypt and worshiped false gods. The good figs represented the faithful, who would be brought into exile and eventually return to the true worship of Yahweh. They would be purified during the Exile and would eventually return to their land.

Jeremiah used his many visions to explain what would happen to the people of Judah because of their sin.

The Hebrew Scriptures: Called by the Father

Of the good figs, God told Jeremiah, "Like these good figs, even so will I regard with favor Judah's exiles whom I sent away from this place into the land of the Chaldeans. I will look after them for their good, and bring them back to this land, to build them up, not to tear them down; to plant them, not to pluck them out. I will give them a heart with which to understand that I am the Lord. They shall be my people and I will be their God, for they shall return to me with their whole heart" (Jeremiah 24:5-7).

---

6. *How are you like clay in the hands of God, the divine potter?*

For Example

Jeremiah is famous for his parables. In Jeremiah 18:1-12, God is compared to a potter working at the wheel and Israel to clay in the hand of the potter. Like an artisan, God can destroy what has been made as well as remake it into the desired shape.

Summary

- Jeremiah was a "man of sorrows" whose life was given over to doing God's will.

- The prophets believed that loving God involved loving justice and denouncing evil.

- The Book of Jeremiah is a collection of speeches Jeremiah dictated to Baruch, his friend and secretary.

- Jeremiah used sermons, visions, and parables to communicate his message.

- Jeremiah introduced many new ideas into Jewish theology, including the belief that religion is a personal relationship between the individual and God. Each person is responsible for his or her own sins.

■ Review

1. Why did the Judeans see Jeremiah as a traitor?

2. For what reasons was Jeremiah's life marked by personal tragedy?

3. Summarize the prophetic concept of social justice.

4. What new ideas did Jeremiah introduce into Jewish theology?

5. Who was Baruch?

6. What did Jeremiah predict about the Jerusalem Temple?

7. What is the meaning of Jeremiah's vision of the two fig trees?

8. According to Jeremiah, how is God like a potter?

9. Words to Know: Jeremiah, Zedekiah, *anawim,* Baruch, Jehoiakim.

■ In Your World

1. Disaster and failure are never easy to endure. What attitudes can you develop toward suffering that will contribute to your mental health and holiness?

2. Research the life of Dorothy Day, Oscar Romero, or Steven Biko. How did the individual that you picked suffer for his or her belief? Write a brief summary of the life of one of these persons.

■ Scripture Search

1. Read these passages from Jeremiah and prepare a profile of this prophet of God: 1:1-10; 7:1-7; 8:23; 10:1-7, 10-14; 16:1-4, 14-15; 17:1-8; 20:8-15; 28:1-8; 29:4-15; 31:31; 36:20-26; 38:4-6; and 42:19-43:7. Include information on his hometown, his response to God's call, his message, his life-style, his attitude toward his role as a prophet, the reaction of the people to him, the fate of his prophecies, and the end of his life.

2. The Book of Lamentations describes Israel's national humiliation after the Fall of Jerusalem. As you read through the five chapters of this brief book, note how it reflects both great grief and great hope. How does the book show that Israel's faith in Yahweh might survive the destruction of the nation?

Ezekiel: The Prophet of Captivity

Ezekiel was called to prophesy during the Exile. The Babylonian conquest had come in two waves. First, the king of Judah and about forty-seven hundred of the leaders of the country were deported. Ten years later, Jerusalem was destroyed and the people as a whole were taken into captivity. Because he belonged to a priestly family, Ezekiel was exiled in the initial deportation.

Like Jeremiah, Ezekiel warned the people in advance of the Fall of Jerusalem. After it occurred in 587 B.C.E., Ezekiel became a source of restored hope for Judah by prophesying a new temple, a new covenant, a new king, and a new Jerusalem. Ezekiel also predicted that the Israelites would be given a "new heart" and that they would confess their faith by means of tradition and law. Because Ezekiel emphasized law and ritual, he is sometimes called the founder of Judaism.

The Mystical Prophet

There are some occurrences in everyday life that cannot be explained by known laws. Psychic powers and extrasensory perception (ESP) are mysterious, virtually unexplored fields of science. In dealings with people, God communicates through ordinary means such as events that take place in daily life or in history. However, God can also communicate through extraordinary means, such as visions and mystical trances.

Of all the prophets, Ezekiel was the most unusual. He was a person of colorful words whose imagination was continually active. He was a mystic who aimed to unite with God through deep meditation. His bizarre experiences and strange personality are still puzzling. (Modern psychologists might diagnose Ezekiel as a paranoid schizophrenic with delusions of grandeur.) No one really knows if the events recounted in his book were normal psychic experiences, supernatural experiences, or literary devices. In any case, God used this individual to make known the divine will. The spirit of God filled Ezekiel as he was, and made use of him just as a trumpet player breathes into his instrument to produce a sound. Ezekiel was God's instrument, however brassy or peculiar he may have been.

Ezekiel's Vision of God

Ezekiel the priest became Ezekiel the Prophet while in exile in Babylon. As you read the first chapter of the Book of Ezekiel, try to imagine yourself in his position.

Ezekiel's vision of God, though similar to Isaiah's was much more spectacular. In this vision he saw winged creatures with human bodies, each with the face of a man, a lion, an ox, and an eagle on different sides of its head. These creatures stood beside sparkling wheels that could turn in any direction. Above these, Ezekiel envisioned God in human form seated on a sapphire throne.

In this marvelous trance, God commissioned Ezekiel to speak to the rebellious house of Israel and warned him that pursuing the task would be like sitting on scorpions. Ezekiel showed his willingness to deliver God's Word by eating a scroll containing the words "lamentation and wailing and woe." Were these words of God nourishing? Ezekiel declared that the Word of God was "as sweet as honey in my mouth" (Ezekiel 3:3).

The Deeper Meaning of Actions and Images

Ezekiel was commanded to perform symbolic actions, foretelling the collapse of Jerusalem and the Exile. For instance, he was told to lie on his left side for 390 days to bear the kingdom of Israel's sins and on his right side for 40 days for the sins of the kingdom of Judah. In addition, Ezekiel was led by an angel through a series of visions. In

תְּפִלָּה

Praying the Hebrew Scriptures

Psalm 137 speaks of the exiles' remembrance of Zion (Jerusalem): "By the streams of Babylon we sat and wept when we remembered Zion. On the aspens of that land we hung up our harps, though there our captors asked of us the lyrics of our songs, and our despoilers urged us to be joyous: 'Sing for us the songs of Zion!' How could we sing a song of the Lord in a foreign land? If I forget you, Jerusalem, may my right hand be forgotten! May my tongue cleave to my palate if I remember you not, if I place not Jerusalem ahead of my joy" (Psalm 137:1-6).

The Hebrew Scriptures: Called by the Father

Ezekiel's vision portrayed all of the creatures on earth paying homage to God.

one of them, Ezekiel saw God leaving the Temple in Jerusalem in the same form in which he had seen God in the first vision.

Ezekiel used a variety of harsh images to condemn Israel for its infidelity: a faithless spouse, a withered tree, dry land, rust in a pot. But the prophet also predicted punishment and defeat for Israel's foes. One after another, Israel's neighbors would be doomed. The reason for God's harsh action is stated no fewer that seventy times in Ezekiel: "You shall know that I am the Lord."

Fidelity to the Law

Like Jeremiah, Ezekiel emphasized personal responsibility. Each person would be judged for his or her own offenses. Faith was to be seen as a relationship between a person and God.

Although Ezekiel spoke a message that condemned, he also offered consolation. The book of his prophecy ends with visions of a new Israel, a new law, a new temple, and a new city. The sign of the new people, according to Ezekiel, would be fidelity to the Law. More than any other prophet, Ezekiel stressed tradition and law by promoting the Sabbath, circumcision, and ritual cleanliness. But Ezekiel also

Symbolic Actions

Symbolic actions were frequently used to convey prophetic messages. Jeremiah and Ezekiel continued in this "audiovisual" tradition. The major messages and their manner of presentation are listed below.

Decay and uselessness of Judah: Jeremiah bought and wore a loincloth, the material a man might drape around his waist as the sole piece of clothing in a warm climate. Jeremiah then hid this loincloth in a cleft in a rock, where after a time it became rotten (Jeremiah 13:1-11).

Destruction of the city and the Temple: Jeremiah smashed an earthen flask on the ground to symbolize destruction (Jeremiah 19:1-11). Ezekiel drew a map of Jerusalem on a clay tablet and acted out the siege of the city (Ezekiel 4:1-3). He also cut his hair and beard with a sword. Then he burned a third of it in fire, hit a third with a sword, and tossed the last third in the air and chased it down with his sword. This signified that some people would die of hunger and disease, some would be killed directly, and others would be scattered and pursued (Ezekiel 5:1-11).

Exile: Ezekiel packed his bags and placed them outside during the day. At night he dug a hole in the wall of the city of Jerusalem and went out (Ezekiel 12:1-16).

Submission: Jeremiah made a yoke, a crossbar with two U-shaped pieces that encircled the necks of work animals, such as oxen. The yoke served as a symbol for slavery. Jeremiah wore this yoke in front of the people (Jeremiah 27:1-3).

Restoration after the Exile: Jeremiah bought real estate in Anathoth of Judah (Jeremiah 32:6-13). Ezekiel took two sticks. He marked one for Judah and related Israelites and the other for Joseph and those associated with him. Then he joined the two sticks together to make one (Ezekiel 37:15-22).

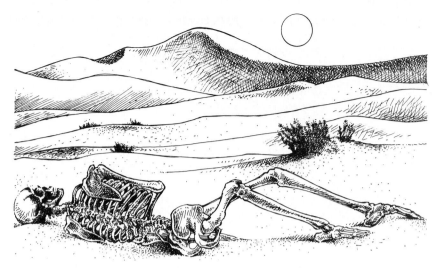

Ezekiel's vision revealed that God's power could bring life even to the dry bones—the faithless people—of Israel.

echoed Jeremiah's teaching that faith was a matter of the heart—an internal commitment to God, not a rigid, external adherence to ritual. Ezekiel had a vision of the glory of the Lord reentering the Temple. The name of the new city Ezekiel described was "The Lord is here" (Ezekiel 48:35).

Dry Bones

Like Jeremiah, Ezekiel also used visions to communicate his message. One of his most famous visions was that of dry bones (see Ezekiel 37:1-14). Here, the image of a resurrection from the dead is used to predict the restoration of Israel following the Exile. The vision's purpose is to give hope to a people who had grown weary. In it God tells Ezekiel, "O my people, I will open your graves and have you rise from them, and bring you back to the land of Israel. Then you shall know that I am the Lord, when I open your graves and have you rise from them, O my people! I will put my spirit in you that you may live, and I will settle you upon your land; thus you shall know that I am the Lord. I have promised, and I will do it" (Ezekiel 37:12-14).

---

7. *How can you be God's instrument? What kind of instrument would you be and what kind of music would you make? Explain your symbolism.*

8. *Read these three texts from Ezekiel: 34:1-6, 11-15; and 36:25-31. Each of these passages is based on a particular image. Describe the image and explain why it is appropriate.*

9. *In what ways were Jeremiah and Ezekiel alike? How were they different?*

Why Read Jeremiah and Ezekiel?

You might ask, "Why read Jeremiah and Ezekiel? They were prophets of their times. I'm not an Israelite." True, these two prophets served a distinct purpose in the history of Israel. They advised kings and rebuked citizens for their sins. During the suffering of the Exile, they also offered hope to the people.

But both Jeremiah and Ezekiel serve as examples to all as persons who put their lives at God's disposal. Merely to admire the long-suffering Jeremiah or to marvel at the strange visions of Ezekiel is not enough. Their cooperation with God in shaping the kingdom calls for emulation. We can be modern-day witnesses like Jeremiah and Ezekiel by living our lives open to the will of God.

Summary

- Because of his emphasis on law and ritual, Ezekiel is often considered the founder of Judaism.

- Ezekiel had a spectacular vision of God in human form, surrounded by fantastic winged creatures.

- Ezekiel prophesied both with words and symbolic actions.

- Ezekiel used the resurrection of the dead as an image to describe the restoration of the Hebrew people after the Exile.

- The prophet Ezekiel both chastised and consoled the people during the Exile.

■ Review

1. Why is Ezekiel considered a mystical prophet?

2. How did Ezekiel receive his call to be a prophet?

3. How is God depicted in the first chapter of the Book of Ezekiel?

4. Name some of Ezekiel's powerful images. What did they represent?

5. What aspects of Ezekiel's prophecies make them very colorful?

6. Words to Know: Ezekiel, Abijah.

■ In Your World

1. Both Jeremiah and Ezekiel criticized people's smugness, complacency, and indifference. They declared that God desired people's hearts, not their words. Often people say, "I'd rather have someone hate me than be indifferent to me." Do you think that the prophets (and even God) felt the same way? The Book of Revelation states this strongly: "Because you are lukewarm, neither hot nor cold, I will spit you out of my mouth!" (Revelation 3:16). In an essay, explain how this kind of indifference can affect a person's life. Discuss the causes, symptoms, and cures of indifference.

2. Why does God ask hard things of certain people? What examples can you share of this happening in your life?

■ Scripture Search

1. Review these four parables of Ezekiel: 16:1-43; 17; 19; and 23. Explain the message of each.

2. Draw your interpretation of Ezekiel's vision of God on the cherubim that is found in Ezekiel 1:4-28. Use crayons or colored pens.

10 Review

■ Study

1. How did Manasseh bring Canaanite practices back into Judah?

2. What nation rose up when Assyria was in decline?

3. Why is the Babylonian Chronicle important?

4. What discovery led to Josiah's reforms?

5. Where did Jeremiah get the courage to defy the tide of popular opinion?

6. How did the messages of Jeremiah and Ezekiel overlap?

7. Why was Jeremiah considered a "man of sorrows"?

8. Name some of the symbolic actions taken by Jeremiah and Ezekiel.

9. How is Ezekiel 37:15-28 a prediction of the future for the Hebrew people?

10. Read the allegory of the cypress in Ezekiel 31. How does the cypress symbolize the Hebrews?

11. How can you be a modern-day Jeremiah and Ezekiel?

■ Action

1. Some of the symbolic actions that accompanied the words of Jeremiah and Ezekiel were presented in this chapter. How would prophets today communicate their message to people? What images and symbolic actions might they use? Act out some of these in class.

2. The message of the prophets is justice. Identify and interview the people in your parish who are working for justice. Present to the class a profile of these people and why they work for justice.

3. Identify the various organizations or agencies in your neighborhood that act for justice. Find out what projects they engage in, and how you and your classmates can get involved.

■ Prayer

At times, like the Hebrew people in exile, you may experience need, danger, or trouble. Moments like these make you want to cry "Help!" Such cries for help are known as prayers of supplication or petition.

Most people are sincerely looking for ways to ease their pain and get what they desire. Because of their relationship with God, they may turn to God in prayer. Prayers of petition do not tell God what you need; God already knows that. Prayers of petition make you more conscious of your own needs and of your dependence on God. These prayers can lead you to achieve what you ask; by leading you to trust in God for what you cannot do on your own.

Prayers of petition are not selfish when they stem from a deep recognition of personal dependence on God. Jesus told his followers to say prayers of supplication: "Ask and you shall receive" (Luke 11:9). Write three prayers of petition. Using readings you've selected from Jeremiah and Ezekiel, prepare a prayer service in which you share these petitions.

The Call to Renewal

OBJECTIVES

In this Chapter you will

- Discover that, through Second Isaiah, God consoled the Chosen People and foretold a return to their homeland.

- Understand the roles of Nehemiah the governor and Ezra the priest-scribe in the restoration of Israel.

- Identify the Maccabees and their struggle for victory over severe persecution.

- Recognize that it is possible to begin again after failure or disaster, just as the Jewish people learned to do after the Exile.

O loving Creator, whose kindness and concern for us know no end, you alone can take our broken lives and make them whole. When the future looks bleak, let us find our strength and consolation in you, so that, refreshed and renewed, we can witness to your goodness.

Second Isaiah: The Innovator

Toward the end of the Exile, a prophet known to us only as Second Isaiah (because he wrote in the spirit of the original Isaiah), foretold the return of the Israelites to their homeland. He consoled the people by announcing that the time of punishment and penance had almost ended. He foretold that the one true God, Yahweh, would lead the Hebrews on a second exodus and bring them new life in a new city. This dream came true when the Persians conquered the Babylonians. The Persian king, Cyrus, allowed the Israelites to return to Jerusalem in 538 B.C.E. From this time, the Israelites anticipated an age when Yahweh would establish Jerusalem (Zion) as an universal empire.

The Suffering Servant

Second Isaiah, the unknown person who authored chapters 40-55 and who influenced chapters 56-66 of the Book of Isaiah, declared, "From now on I announce new things to you" (Isaiah 48:6). One of these new things contained in his writings is the idea of servanthood. The dominant theme of Second Isaiah, which appears in the opening line, "Comfort, give comfort to my people, says your God" (Isaiah 40:1), expresses the pain of the Hebrew people during the Exile. Second Isaiah's book is also known as the Book of Consolation. Isaiah explained that it was the meek and humble servants of the Lord—those who sacrificed without complaining—who carried out the divine plan. The idea of Israel serving God by suffering gave meaning to the trials of the people in exile.

The "suffering servant" is described in four poems in Isaiah called the Servant Songs. The Servant Songs are contained in Isaiah 42:1-9; 49:1-7; 50:4-11; and 52:13-53:12. No one knows exactly to whom they were meant to refer, or if they were meant to refer to anyone at all. At times, they seem to personify the nation of Israel. At other times, the servant appears to be the prophet himself, or a combination of the great figures in Hebrew history. The Apostles eventually saw the servant as a prophetic image of Jesus Christ, who achieved glory through death and resurrection. For instance, they recognized the crucified Christ in these lines: "I gave my back to those who beat me, my cheeks to those who plucked my beard; my face I did not shield from buffets and spitting" (Isaiah 50:6). These prophecies led to a new understanding that salvation comes through suffering.

1. *Why would it have been easy for the early Christians to see the suffering servant as an image of Jesus?*

2. *Read the Servant Songs in Isaiah. Who, from history or from the modern world, fits the image of the Suffering Servant? In what ways can you be a suffering servant?*

The image of the "suffering servant" described in Isaiah 42-53 provides encouragement for those in service to others.

The Hebrew Scriptures: Called by the Father

God's Poor

Poverty is understood in two ways in the Bible. The word *poverty* refers to being deprived of what a person needs to live. *Poverty* is also used to describe a spiritual attitude. These two meanings are illustrated in the Christian Scriptures where Luke 6:20 says in the Beatitudes, "Blessed are you who are poor, for the kingdom of God is yours," while Matthew 5 states, "Blessed are the poor in spirit, for theirs is the kingdom of heaven." What is the difference between these two meanings of the word *poverty*?

As it is first used, poverty means deprivation. It is seen as an evil against God. It is an obligation for the followers of the covenant to care for these poor people. Because poverty exists we know that God's kingdom is not yet here. The prophets, especially those of the Exile, announced the coming of the kingdom of God. When the kingdom arrives, no one will be poor. This is the interpretation spoken of in Luke's beatitudes (Luke 6:20-23).

When poverty is seen as a spiritual attitude it reveals a person who submits his or her will to God. This person has experienced his or her own impotence and poverty. These poor people Jeremiah meant by the *anawim* (plural of *anaw*, poor), and these are the ones Matthew 5 declares blessed. The idea of spiritual poverty appears clearly with the prophet Zephaniah. After the Exile, it led to the concept of a people of deep faith, far removed from political and religious quarrels. These were the people who enjoyed the simple things in life: nature, family life, peace, and friendship. All creation speaks to them a message of God's love.

The poor in spirit do not need to be rescued from their poverty. Instead, their poverty is something that all believers are called to practice. It is the highest good. It is the way that they are in communion with God.

When poverty is a spiritual attitude, all creation is seen as a message of God's love.

Second Isaiah repeats in a fresh and unique way the theme of monotheism: Yahweh is the one and only God. Yahweh is the all-powerful Creator, and no image will ever represent God. Another theme in Second Isaiah is tenderness of God. When "Zion" complained that God had forsaken it, Second Isaiah shows how God responded to their cry of affliction with a most moving passage: "Can a mother forget her infant, be without tenderness for the child of her womb? Even should she forget, I will never forget you. See, upon the palms of my hands I have written your name; your walls are ever before me" (Isaiah 49:15-16).

Second Isaiah also calls the Chosen People back to the Exodus experience to confirm that Yahweh would continue to love and save them. He foretold a new exodus. Cyrus, the conqueror of the Babylonians and the one who had freed the Jews, was a tool God would use to lead them again to the Promised Land. When their time of purification was complete, the Israelites would travel from slavery to freedom and begin a new life in their homeland. But the understanding of salvation would be expanded according to Second Isaiah. God was king not only of the Israelites but also of the Gentiles. The Lord would extend salvation to all people. It was Israel's task to be a light to all people and to all nations.

The Book of Isaiah is cited in the Christian Scriptures more than any other book of the Hebrew people. His writings helped the early Christians to interpret Jesus' life as the supreme saving act of God in Christ. Christians would experience an exodus from death to life in the dying and rising of Jesus Christ.

3. *What image does Second Isaiah use to depict God's tenderness? Discuss how this saying is pertinent to the abortion debate.*

4. *What are some concrete examples of how you have experienced the tenderness of God?*

Archaeology

On a clay cylinder discovered in Babylon, King Cyrus of Persia gave a somewhat self-centered interpretation of the capture of Babylon: "Marduk, the great Lord of Babylon, the protector of his people, beheld with pleasure the good deeds of Cyrus and ordered him to march against his city, Babylon. He made him set out on the road to Babylon, going at his side like a real friend. Without any battle, he made him enter Babylon...I am Cyrus, king of the world, great king, mighty king, king of Babylon...When I, well-disposed, entered Babylon, I set up the seat of dominion in the royal palace amidst jubilation and rejoicing."

When in love, a person will write his or her loved one's initials as a sign of affection and remembrance. How extreme is God's love for us in Isaiah 49:16 "See, upon the palms of my hands I have written your name"?

Summary

- Second Isaiah foretold the return of the Israelites to their homeland.

- The Persian king, Cyrus, allowed the Israelites to return to Jerusalem in 538 B.C.E.

- The idea of Israel serving God by suffering gave meaning to the trials of the Jews in exile.

- Second Isaiah gave new vigor to the themes of monotheism, exodus, and God's mercy and consolation.

■ Review

1. What chapters of the Book of Isaiah are attributed to Second Isaiah?

2. In what year did Cyrus allow the exiles to return to Jerusalem? How long did the Babylonian Captivity last?

3. Who is the suffering servant?

4. List and explain any two of the themes of Second Isaiah discussed in this chapter.

5. What is meant by the phrase "poverty of heart" (also called "poverty of the spirit")?

6. Words to Know: Second Isaiah, suffering servant, Cyrus of Persia.

■ In Your World

1. How does God comfort and console people today? How have you experienced this comfort?

2. Design a poster or card based on one of Second Isaiah's consoling verses. Send it to a person who needs your support.

■ Scripture Search

1. Read the following brief fragments of Second and Third Isaiah's writings. List the key ideas repeated in these verses: 40:31; 43:1; 43:3-5; 49:15-16; 60:19; 62:5; 64:7.

2. Look up the four Servant Songs (Isaiah 42:1-9; 49:1-7; 50:4-11; and 52:13-53:12). List the information that each one supplies about the characteristics of the servant of God. From these characteristics, identify the type of person who would be described by these songs.

Renovation of the Temple: A People and a Faith

Janice had set swimming records for her age group every year since she was age ten. Now that she was fifteen, she had a good chance of reaching the national championships and possibly fulfilling her dream of swimming in the Olympics. While her motivation was great, her practice times had been getting slower. Then Janice found a new coach who recognized that, while Janice was practicing long hours, she was not pushing herself to improve. Following the directions of her new coach, Janice quickly improved, and swam her best laps ever. Janice now believed that her dream could become a reality.

The Hebrew people returned from exile greatly motivated. But without strong leadership to encourage them on, their dream of a restored Judah turned into a long and difficult struggle. A hundred years passed between the time the first exiles returned to Jerusalem and the time the city walls were rebuilt. The king of Persia authorized Nehemiah, a Jew, to accomplish this task, and appointed him governor. Although beset by problems, Nehemiah fortified the province of Judah and began a reform movement that gave Judah political status and an honest administration. Nehemiah was followed by the priest-scribe Ezra who reformed the nation's spiritual life.

Four Phases of the Return from Exile

In 538 B.C.E., Cyrus of Persia decreed that the Israelites could return to Jerusalem. The Babylonian Captivity, which began in 587 B.C.E., came to a close. The return of the

When the Hebrews returned to Jerusalem, they faced many difficult years of drought, crop failures, poverty, and warring neighbors before they could rebuild the city.

For Example

Intermarriage was considered unacceptable for many reasons, but primarily because of the threat of idolatry. When a Hebrew married someone who worshiped idols, he or she would often accept the spouse's gods as well. If a Hebrew wanted to marry someone who was not a Jew, the Gentile would have to become a Jew. The story of Ruth (which will be studied in the next chapter) concerns this issue.

people to their homeland did not occur immediately, however. Not *every* exile went back to Jerusalem, since farming was actually easier in the fertile land of Babylon than it was in the rocky soil of Palestine.

The restoration of Judah seems to have occurred in four major phases. First, a small group of Judeans headed to Palestine in 538 B.C.E., shortly after Cyrus announced his decree. These people attempted to rebuild the city, including the Temple. This tiny remnant had both nature and their neighbors in conflict with them. Crop failures, poverty, and opposition from those who had not been in exile dampened their spirits. The Persian Empire, which had freed them from Babylon, was growing in power itself and threatened Israel's fragile independence. As local conditions became more difficult, the building rate slowed down and eventually ground to a halt.

A second group of Jews returned from Babylon a few years later under the governance of Zerubbabel, an Israelite in direct line of descent from King David. This second phase was encouraged by the prophets, Haggai and Zechariah. These two prophets took advantage of troubles in Persia in 522 B.C.E., spurring the Jews to quickly finish the Temple. They reminded the people of their destiny to be a light to all nations. While conditions were difficult, work on the Temple began in earnest in 520 B.C.E. Five years later the Temple was completed and dedicated, with help from the money and protection of King Darius and the Persians.

Once again, the Chosen People lost sight of their obligations and their destiny and began to engage in immoral practices. They also intermarried with their Gentile neighbors. Nehemiah's arrival in Jerusalem around 440 B.C.E. marked the beginning of the third phase of the restoration. He sponsored political and social reforms, but exercised little influence over the moral and religious life of the nation.

Moral and religious reform was the agenda of the fourth phase of the restoration, around 398 B.C.E., when a group of Jews under the direction of Ezra came to Jerusalem. Ezra and Nehemiah were both very intense, strong individuals who instilled in the people a powerful sense of national pride.

The Hebrew Scriptures: Called by the Father

5. *What difficulties did the first people who returned from exile encounter? Why would these difficulties affect the renewal of the country?*

6. *Compare how long it took to rebuild the Temple with the time it took to initially build it.*

7. *Marriage outside of one's family group, culture, race, or religion has been frowned on by society throughout history. Why is that the case? What do you think about intermarriage? Explain your answer.*

Although more common today than in the past, inter-religious, -cultural, -ethnic, or -racial marriages are still often socially unaccepted as they have been throughout history.

Nehemiah's Successes

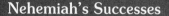

Scholars believe that Nehemiah was a high official in the Persian court, despite his claim in Nehemiah 2:1 of being a cup bearer. He was a Jew who convinced King Artaxerxes to make Judah an independent province and to name him as governor. In the work he accomplished, it is clear that Nehemiah was very competent. He began his term as governor by ordering the rebuilding of the walls of the city, which had been demolished in the war. Nehemiah organized a work force and assigned each group a specific section of the wall to rebuild. In record time—fifty-two days according to Scripture—the basic structures of the walls were finished. His first term as governor lasted for twelve years, and he was reappointed for a second term.

When Nehemiah returned to Jerusalem, he quickly realized that the people continued to neglect the Law. He used his authority as governor to stop people from working on the Sabbath, dissolve marriages with foreigners, and finance the Levite priestly assistants. Nehemiah was quick-tempered, opinionated, and extremely blunt, but he accomplished his goals. Perhaps Nehemiah's greatest achievement was giving the Israelites in Jerusalem a strong sense of identity and discipline. Read Nehemiah 1; 3:33-5:13; and 13 to better understand the story of this capable leader.

> **Gentiles:** a term used by Jews to refer to anyone who is not Jewish.

Ezra with his emphasis on the Law—Torah—is credited with establishing the framework for modern Judaism.

A Historical Overview of the Hebrew People

The following is a concise listing of the history of the Hebrew people. Go through your notes and see what other information you can add to each time period.

Time: 1900—1300 B.C.E.
    Events: Call of Abraham and the Patriarchs
    People: Abraham-Sarah, Isaac-Rebecca, Jacob-Rachel-Leah, Joseph

Time: 1300—1250 B.C.E.
    Events: Departure from Egypt, the Exodus, Covenant on Mount Sinai, Entering Canaan, Formation of the Twelve Tribes
    People: Moses, Miriam, Aaron, Joshua

Time: 1250—1030 B.C.E.
    Events: Confederation of Tribes, Rise of Military Leaders—the Judges
    People: Deborah, Jephthah, Gideon, Samson

Time: 1030—930 B.C.E.
    Events: Anointing first king, the United Kingdom—One kingdom with Jerusalem as the capital
    People: Saul, Samuel, David, Nathan, Solomon

Time: 930—722 B.C.E.
    Events: The divided kingdom, North (Israel), South (Judah), 721 B.C.E.—fall of North to Assyria
    People: *Northern kings*—Jeroboam I, Ahab; *Southern kings*—Rehoboam I, Uzziah, Ahaz

Time: 722—586 B.C.E.
    Events: 586 B.C.E.—Southern Kingdom falls
    People: Hezekiah, Josiah, Judah, Zedekiah

Time: 585—539 B.C.E.
    Events: Deportation to Babylon, Babylonian Exile, 538 B.C.E.—Edict of Cyrus
    People: Ezekiel, Second Isaiah, Cyrus of Persia

Time: 539—332 B.C.E.
    Events: Return from Exile, Post-Exilic Period, Restoration of Temple
    People: Ezra, Nehemiah

Time: 332—63 B.C.E.
    Events: Resistance by Jews, Hellenistic Period, Persecution by Antiochus IV, 63 B.C.E. Roman captivity
    People: Maccabees, Alexander the Great

The Hebrew Scriptures: Called by the Father

Nehemiah proved an exceptional administrator. According to Scripture the walls of Jerusalem were rebuilt in fifty-two days, a feat that would prove difficult even for a modern day construction manager.

8. *What changes are needed in your parish or school to make it a more Christian environment? How can these changes be put into action?*

Ezra's Reforms

In about 398 B.C.E., the priest-scribe Ezra was appointed by the Persian king to enforce the Law (Ezra 7:11-26). He launched his mission by reading the Law to the people all morning from a platform in the public square (Ezra 9, Nehemiah 8). He continued this daily during the seven days of the revived Feast of Tabernacles. The Feast of Tabernacles (Booths), or *Sukkoth* in Hebrew, is a nine-day celebration of the harvest commemorating the time when the Israelites lived in huts in the desert during the Exodus. Fasting, praying, and pleading with great emotion, Ezra prompted the men of Israel to divorce their foreign wives. The whole people then confessed their sins and sealed a

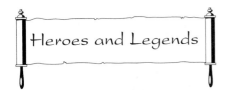

The Jewish nation after Solomon was not in control of its political future. Many stronger nations—Assyria, Babylon, Egypt, Persia, Greece, and Rome—fought it continuously. One man who greatly influenced the future of Jewish life and faith was Alexander the Great—a Greek king, military genius, and hero of the ancient world. Born in 356 B.C.E., by the age of thirty, he and his expeditionary army had conquered much of the known world. In 323 B.C.E., he died from a fever while in Babylon. In this brief time, Alexander changed the map of the world, along with its customs and language. He spread Greek culture throughout Asia Minor, Syria, Palestine, and Egypt. This process of bringing Greek culture to other areas of the world is called "hellenization." Because of the reforms of Ezra, Judaism was able to resist Greek influence.

covenant binding themselves to follow the Law. Within a year, Ezra had achieved his goal. He had succeeded in organizing the Jewish people around the Law and had given their faith a solid form. Ezra's Judaism is practiced by the Jewish people today, and it is their faithfulness to the Mosaic law that binds Jewish people together throughout the world.

Some experts call Ezra the "father of Judaism." He looked to the Pentateuch or Torah as a guidebook for the people. Ezra began a movement that emphasizes the written word. Beginning with Ezra, the Hebrew people are no longer referred to as Israelites, but as Jews. Ezra's influence was so great that the *Talmud,* a book of Jewish traditions, recognized Ezra as the person who established the canon of the Hebrew Scripture. Later, rabbis argued against including the books of Judith, Tobit, Baruch, 1 and 2 Maccabees, Ecclesiasticus, the Wisdom of Solomon, and Daniel into the canon because they had not been included in Ezra's canon. These books, however, are found in the collection known as the Dead Sea Scrolls and are considered by the Roman Catholic Church to be inspired by God.

For an idea of Ezra's reforms, read Nehemiah 8:1-9 (the reading of the Law) and Ezra 6:2-5 and 10:1-15 (Ezra's rebuke and the people's conversion).

The Role of the Priests

From early in its history, one group of Hebrew people performed priestly tasks. The books of Exodus (28-29) and Leviticus (8-10) stipulate that the high priest must come from the family of Aaron and that they are to be consecrated for their service. Priestly assistants were to be drawn from the line of Levi. Prior to the Exile, kings often offered sacrifices in place of the priest.

Before the Israelites' exile, their Temple was destroyed. During the Exile, Ezekiel insisted that the high priest be a descendant of Zadok. Following the Exile, Ezra and Nehemiah followed Ezekiel's claim and told the people that the practice of kings offering sacrifice was wrong. They helped rebuild the Temple and restored the role of

The Hebrew Scriptures: Called by the Father

Priests offer sacrifices to God. What sacrifice do Catholic priests offer during the Eucharist?

priesthood to descendants of Aaron. (Ezra claimed such descent.) They also placed great stress on studying the Law and traditions, particularly those that were in written form. It was during this time that emphasis was placed on the importance of the Torah, or the first five books of the Hebrew Bible also known as the Law.

Summary

- The return to Judah and its restoration occurred in four phases. The last two of these phases were directed by Nehemiah and Ezra, respectively.

- Nehemiah, a governor, gave the people in Jerusalem a strong sense of identity and discipline.

- In about 398 B.C.E., the priest-scribe Ezra was appointed to enforce the Law.

- Faithfulness to the Mosaic law binds Jewish people together no matter where they live.

■ Review

1. List and explain the four phases of the return from captivity in Babylon.

2. What contribution did Nehemiah make to the development of the Jewish people?

3. How did Ezra bring about moral and religious reform?

4. What is *Sukkoth?*

5. What danger might hellenization have posed to the Jews?

6. Words to Know: Darius, Zerubbabel, Haggai, Zechariah, Nehemiah, Ezra, Feast of Tabernacles *(Sukkoth)*, hellenization.

■ In Your World

1. Does the fact that couples come from different religions make a difference in a marriage? Research this question and present your findings. What does the Catholic Church require in interreligious marriages?

2. The Israelites looked to Yahweh for strength during times of distress: during the Exile, the restoration, and various later persecutions. Make a list of your worries and problems. In prayer, ask God for the strength to solve these issues. What does it mean for you to rely on God completely?

■ Scripture Search

1. Read Ezra 9-10. Why did Ezra demand the dissolution of these marriages? Was his law too harsh? Why or why not?

2. Review the ceremony of covenant renewal in Nehemiah 9-10. List the provisions made in that pact. What is the importance of this renewal for the Jews?

SECTION 3
The Maccabees

Through Alexander the Great, Greek thought became dominant in the Middle East. When the Syrian king, Antiochus IV, tried to unite his empire by decreeing a national religion, banning the practice of all other religions including Judaism, he caused a great deal of trouble for the Jews. While many Jews influenced by Greek culture complied with this ordinance, other Jews were outraged by this demand and clung to the faith of their ancestors in spite of threats of severe punishment and even death. Led by a family called the Maccabees, the Jews rebelled against this unjust persecution.

The Decree of Antiochus IV

The nation of Judah continued to exist under foreign rule until 165 B.C.E. During these "dark ages," Israel passed from the rule of the Persians to that of Alexander the Great, who considered it his mission to spread Greek culture throughout the world. Many Jews at this time emigrated to Egypt, where the city of Alexandria became a center of Jewish life.

At his death, Alexander's generals divided up the empire. Rule in Palestine transferred from the Ptolemies of Egypt to the Seleucid kings of Syria in 200 B.C.E. The Jews faced a serious crisis under the Syrian king Antiochus IV, who promoted the worship of the Greek gods and plundered the Jewish Temple. When the Jews resisted his efforts to identify Yahweh and himself with Zeus, the chief Greek god, Antiochus forbade all practice of Judaism. Many Jews were tortured and put to death for refusing to comply with Antiochus IV's decree. In 167 B.C.E., Antiochus ordered

Although he died before his fortieth birthday, Alexander influenced Western civilizations for hundreds of years after his death.

that swine be offered to Zeus, whose image had been erected on the altar of the Temple in Jerusalem. Both were deplorable acts to the Jews. The Temple was desecrated by Zeus's statue and further polluted by the swine, animals considered by the Jews to be unclean.

This religious persecution was a major crisis in Jewish history. Through it, however, the Jewish spirit was restored and some of Israel's most famous military heroes—the Maccabees—rose to face the challenge. The two books of the Maccabees contain a detailed record of the struggle against the Syrians which won the Jews not only religious freedom but also political independence.

Mattathias Hasmoneus and his five sons began a guerrilla war against the Seleucids and Jews whom they considered traitorous for accepting the Greek idol. Under the third son, Judah, nicknamed "Maccabee" (the hammer), the enemy was defeated and the Temple rededicated. This involved removing all signs of pagan worship from the Temple. Although it is Judah who was called "Maccabee," the term was extended to all the family members. It now refers to any of the Jewish heroes of that period.

The Feast of Light, or Hanukkah, which lasts for eight days in December, celebrates the defeat of the Seleucids, commemorating the rededication of the Temple by Judah Maccabee and his forces. The belief is that when Judah and his followers reclaimed the Temple, there was only enough oil in the Temple lamp to last for one day. By a miracle, the Temple lamp burned for eight days, until new oil could be made.

Today, on each night of Hanukkah, a candle is lit in the *menorah,* or nine-branched candleholder. Eight of the branches represent the eight days that the miracle occurred, and the candle in the ninth branch, called the *shammash,* is used to light the others.

---

9. *What is the miracle of Hanukkah?*

10. *The Feast of Hanukkah, which is celebrated at roughly the same time as Christmas, is an important feast for Jews. Find out about this celebration and use it in your class, your youth group, or at home.*

The Hebrew Scriptures: Called by the Father

Themes in 1 Maccabees

Many traditional Hebrew Scripture themes run through 1 Maccabees, including Israel is chosen by God and that they must worship God alone and abide by God's laws. The second book of Maccabees covers roughly the same history but gives a theological interpretation of the events, including some new ideas—the resurrection of the just, the intercession of the saints for people on earth, and the power of the living to help the dead through prayers and sacrifice. The following texts illustrate these themes:

- *"You are depriving us of this present life, but the King of the world will raise us up to live again forever. It is for his laws that we are dying" (2 Maccabees 7:9).*

- *"It is my choice to die at the hands of men with the God-given hope of being restored to life by him; but for you, there will be no resurrection to life" (2 Maccabees 7:14).*

- *"In doing this he acted in a very excellent and noble way, inasmuch as he had the resurrection of the dead in view; for if he were not expecting the fallen to rise again, it would have been...foolish to pray for them in death...Thus he made atonement for the dead that they might be freed from sin" (2 Maccabees 12:43-46).*

This is why Catholics believe in the communion of saints and the ability to pray for the dead to help them reach heaven. The Church sees itself as composed of three distinct, interdependent groups: the people in heaven (all the saints), the just who die before the Second Coming of Jesus but do not attain heaven (all souls), and those on earth (all the rest of us). Although the Roman Catholic Church considers 1 and 2 Maccabees to be inspired, many Protestant churches do not.

The important people and events during the Maccabean period are discussed below. Read the explanatory note first and then the biblical passage to which it refers.

Origin (1 Maccabees 2:1-30). The Maccabees were heroes who helped to liberate the Jews from Syrian oppression and preserve the Law. They were faithful to the Law, in direct contrast with other Jews who, during this time period, abandoned their religion to follow Syrian beliefs.

Jewish Martyrs (2 Maccabees 7:1-42). This account includes a description of Jewish heroes much like the stories of Christian martyrs and saints. Jewish law considered pigs to be unclean animals, and it was forbidden to eat of their

תְּפִלָּה

Praying the Hebrew Scriptures

The following verses based on the prophet Isaiah are often read on the fourth night of Hanukkah after the menorah is lit: ''I, the Lord, have called you for the victory of justice, I have grasped you by the hand; I formed you, and set you as a covenant of the people, a light for the nations, to open the eyes of the blind, to bring out prisoners from confinement, and from the dungeon, those who live in darkness. I will lead the blind on their journey; by paths unknown I will guide them. I will turn darkness into light before them, and make crooked ways straight. These things I do for them, and I will not forsake them.''

Hanukkah, or the Feast of Lights, celebrates the cleansing of the Temple after the Maccabees' successful rebellion.

The Hebrew Scriptures: Called by the Father

flesh. The Syrians forced some Jews to eat pork, and often killed those who refused to comply with this command. A woman and her seven sons were put to this test. They refused to obey the civil law of the Syrians (which would mean disobeying God's law), and all of them were murdered.

Rededication of the Temple (1 Maccabees 4:36-59). The height of insult and abomination occurred when Antiochus offered swine to the Greek god Zeus in the Holy Temple of Jerusalem. The Jews called this detestable act an "abomination of desolation." It was a great day when Judah purified the Temple and rededicated it to Yahweh. The Feast of Hanukkah commemorates this event.

The Hasmoneans: Judah Maccabee's Successors (1 Maccabees, Chapters 9-16). When Judah was killed in battle, his brother Jonathan assumed the role of leadership. Jonathan also acted as the high priest, although he was not of the ancestral line of Zadok. This angered some Jews, but the practice of combining the role of the high priest with the king continued throughout the Hasmonean dynasty. (The actual family name of Mattathias and his sons was Hasmoneus.) When Jonathan was killed, his brother Simon became ruler. Simon was assassinated, but his descendants ruled as priest-kings until the Roman conquest of Palestine put an end to Israel's independence in 63 B.C.E.

Both the religions of Islam and Judaism consider the pig to be an unclean animal. People are forbidden to eat pork or use any product made from swine.

Trials and Triumph

The Exile of the Jewish people before their restoration was like the modern period of Lent, the period of preparation that precedes the celebration of Easter. It was a time of turning back to God, for repentance for failings, and for renewing faith. The resurrection of the Jews was promised by Second Isaiah in beautiful imagery. Through the heroic efforts of Nehemiah, Ezra, and the Maccabees, this promise of restoration became a reality when the Jewish nation was brought back to life. In the process, the Jewish people arrived at new insights and gained a deeper understanding of their role in salvation. Through their suffering, servanthood, and loyalty to the Law, all people

How can the exile of the Jewish people be compared to our celebration of Lent?

would come to know God. The faith of the Jews withstood even bloody persecution. It was the Jewish people who gave birth to the Messiah, himself a suffering servant. Because of Jesus' death and resurrection, you, too, can hope for resurrection.

Summary

- Antiochus IV, a Syrian king, forbade the practice of Judaism, desecrated the Temple, and tortured and killed many Jews who would not follow his anti-Jewish decrees.

- The Maccabees defeated the Syrians and gained religious freedom and political independence for the Jews.

- The Jewish Feast of Hanukkah commemorates the rededication of the Temple by Judah Maccabee and his forces.

The Hebrew Scriptures: Called by the Father

▪ Review

1. In what ways were the Maccabees heroic?

2. Name some of Antiochus IV's cruelties.

3. Why was the rededication of the Temple the climax of the Maccabean revolution?

4. What is the *menorah?* The *shammash?*

5. What are some of the new themes in 2 Maccabees?

6. Words to Know: Antiochus IV, Alexander the Great, Seleucids, Mattathias, Judah Maccabee, Hanukkah, *Menorah, Shammash,* Zeus, Hasmonean Dynasty, Jonathan.

▪ In Your World

1. To what extent are you willing to fight for what you think is right? What ''battles'' are you currently fighting in your life? What role does God play in your battles?

2. The Maccabees disobeyed government laws. Do you know any other group that had done this in good conscience? When might you be obliged by your conscience to break government laws?

▪ Scripture Search

1. How do 1 and 2 Maccabees recall the Exodus and the Book of Judges?

2. Read the story of Eleazar in 2 Maccabees 6:18-31. How was this Jewish martyr a model of courage?

CHAPTER
11 Review

■ Study

1. Why were Second Isaiah's words consoling?

2. How does this quote of Jesus in Mark 10:45 reflect the "suffering servant" passages in Second Isaiah: "The Son of Man has not come to be served but to serve"?

3. What goal did Haggai, Zechariah, and Zerubbabel accomplish?

4. What reforms were instituted by Nehemiah and Ezra?

5. What physical and spiritual obstacles had to be overcome before the Jews attained the stage of restoration the prophets had predicted?

6. Who was Alexander the Great? What role does he play in the story of the Hebrew people?

7. Who were Mattathias and his sons? Why are they remembered?

8. What has preserved the Jews through the centuries despite bitter persecution?

9. How did the Maccabees live out the role of the suffering servant?

10. Name some of the Hebrew Scripture themes found in 1 and 2 Maccabees.

11. What was the importance of the Hasmonean Dynasty?

■ Action

1. Do research on the history of the Jews during the Maccabean period.

2. Research and make a report on *Sukkoth* (the Feast of Tabernacles) or *Hanukkah* (the Feast of Lights).

3. Consider the meaning and purpose of the sacrament of Confirmation. How does the grace from that sacrament help you to be a prophet like Isaiah, Ezra, and Nehemiah, or a person of conviction like a Maccabee?

■ Prayer

Formal prayer is a good way to learn the traditions of a community, but it can easily become a routine. You hear the same words so often that eventually you disregard their function as prayer, allowing your mind to wander. However, meditating on each phrase can help you pray better.

For example, the "Lord's Prayer" is a formal prayer, probably one of the first ones that you learned, along with the "Hail Mary." This prayer, which begins "Our Father," is a prayer for the kingdom. Each time Christians pray it, we ask God to establish the kingdom of justice and love as foretold by the prophets and that is prayed for daily. As you pray it slowly and reflectively, include the last line that Protestants pray regularly as part of the prayer and that Catholics add during the Eucharistic Liturgy: "For yours is the kingdom, the power, and the glory now and forever." Notice also the lines that deal with the kingdom and suggest how you can help bring it about.

Saints of the Hebrew Scriptures

OBJECTIVES

In this Chapter you will

- Meet Ruth, whose faithful love is a model for all people.

- Read the comic but heroic story of Jonah, the runaway prophet.

- Examine the story of Job, whose trust in God was tested.

- Learn about Daniel, whose obedience to God's Law was unyielding and whose faith in God was courageous.

Everything written before our time was written for our instruction, that we might derive hope from the lessons of patience and words of encouragement in the Scriptures. —Romans 15:4

The Hebrew Scriptures: Called by the Father

SECTION 1
Vehicles of God's Revelation

Several books of the Hebrew Bible center around individuals who are role models for God's people. Each of these persons excelled in a quality that should characterize anyone involved in a covenant relationship with God. In the following pages, you will meet four important figures from the Hebrew Bible: Ruth, Jonah, Job, and Daniel.

The stories of Ruth, Jonah, Job, and Daniel are significant to the story of the Hebrew people and are the result of years of reflection on the relationship between God and human beings. These texts deal with the difficult questions of life. God inspired the Jewish authors to write about outstanding Jewish men and women who were vehicles of God's revelation. By means of a good story, the unchanging truths of the Jewish faith—truths that inform our Christian heritage—are presented simply and clearly for transmission from generation to generation.

Ruth: The Devoted Daughter

The story told in the Book of Ruth begins with the saga of an Israelite family consisting of Elimelech, his wife Naomi, and their two sons, Mahlon and Chilion. In order to escape famine in the land of Judah, Elimelech and his family went to Moab (Ruth 1:1-4:22). After Elimelech died, his two sons married Moabite women named Ruth and Orpah. When the two sons died, the three women were left alone.

A number of years passed, and the famine in Judah had passed. Naomi decided to return to her home and in-structed her daughters-in-law to stay with their families in

Moab. Orpah went back to her relatives, but Ruth decided to go with Naomi, even though this meant that she would have to leave her own people. Ruth said to Naomi: "Do not ask me to abandon or forsake you! For wherever you go, I shall go, wherever you lodge, I will lodge, your people shall be my people, and your God my God" (Ruth 1:16). This passage is often used at wedding liturgies because of its profound expression of unconditional love and loyalty.

Ruth and Naomi returned to Judah just in time for that year's barley harvest. They worked in the fields with the other poor people, gleaning the remains of the barley after the reapers had passed through. Ruth attracted the eye of Boaz, a wealthy landowner and a distant relative of Elimelech. According to Jewish law, the closest relative of a dead man had the right and duty to marry the widow and buy back the family land if it had been sold to pay debts. Their first male child would then be the legal son of the deceased husband. Although Boaz was not Ruth's closest

Archaeology

Ruth was a Moabite, not an Israelite. According to Genesis 19:30-38, the ancestor of the Moabites was Moab, the son of Lot and the older of Lot's daughters. Geographically, Moab was located east of the Dead Sea, situated between the Arnon River and the brook of Zered. This area was of frequent concern to the nation of Israel from the time of the Exodus to the Fall of Jerusalem. In the time of the judges, the Moabites controlled some of the land settled by Israelite tribes. Skirmishes were often fought between the two groups. However, friendly relations between the Israelites and the Moabites existed from time to time. In the Book of Ruth, travel between Moab and Israel is depicted as relatively safe.

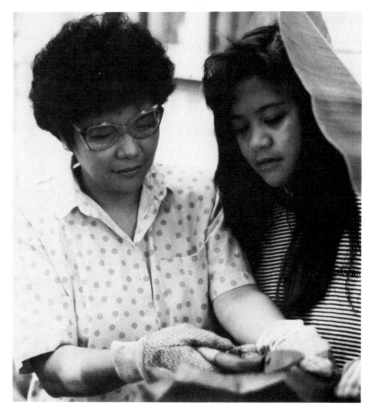

The story of Ruth is a story of faithfulness. What does it mean to be a faithful person?

The Hebrew Scriptures: Called by the Father

relative, he wanted to marry her. This union, called a "levirate marriage," was permitted, but a correct procedure had to be followed.

First, Boaz had to strike a deal with one of his kinsmen who was a closer relative to Ruth, and therefore had the first responsibility to marry her. Boaz approached the man with his request to marry Ruth. His kinsman replied that he could not exercise his claim in this matter, allowing Boaz to proceed with his plans. The kinsman then removed one of his sandals and gave it to Boaz as a means of sealing their agreement. This ritual was like the practice of shaking hands on a deal. Boaz was then free to marry Ruth and buy back Elimelech's estate. In time Ruth gave birth to a son, Obed. Obed was the father of Jesse, who in turn would be the father of David, Israel's greatest king.

---

1. *What message does the author hope to deliver in the Book of Ruth?*

2. *Why would Naomi want Orpah and Ruth to remain in Moab?*

3. *Describe a time when, like Ruth, you chose to be loyal to someone. How did this decision affect your life? Your other relationships?*

Ruth's Connection to Jesus

Pleasure. Self-fulfillment. Identity. These words are a part of our egocentric vocabulary. The story of Ruth, however, offers a different view of the world. Rather than concentrating on herself, Ruth lived for others and in this way achieved true fulfillment, freedom, and joy.

Ruth was a Moabite, not one of the Chosen People, but God still rewarded her goodness. She is seen as an ancestor of King David, and through David, of Jesus Christ. The Book of Ruth describes how, out of loyalty to her mother-in-law Naomi, Ruth gave up her home, country, and religion. Ruth's courage in going with Naomi to the Jewish region of Bethlehem is evident: as a foreigner, she

Glean: to collect food left in the field by the harvesters.

Grandparents are special people. Ruth is recognized as the great-grandmother of King David. Why is that important?

was regarded with suspicion, if not outright hostility. Her decision was an act of love.

Although the story of Ruth is set in the period of the judges, it must have been written much later because the closing verses trace Ruth's descendants down to David (Ruth 4:18-22). Scholars think that the story originated during the time of Ezra and Nehemiah, approximately five hundred years later than the story suggests. The Book of Ruth was probably written to counteract rabid nationalism and the belief that salvation was only for the Jews. Under Ezra, the Jews divorced their foreign wives. In the person of Ruth, however, God found a foreigner who was pleasing because of her loyalty, self-sacrifice, and faith. Later, through Ruth's ancestral line, God granted the greatest favor to humanity: Jesus, the Son of God. The introduction of Ruth, a Gentile, into the family tree of the Messiah indicated that Jesus was to be the Savior of the whole world, Jew and Gentile alike.

4. *How was Ruth related to King David? Since scholars believe this story to have been written almost six hundred years after David, why do you think this story establishes that relationship?*

5. *Look at your family tree. Are there people in your family whom you consider special? Who are they, and what makes them unique?*

Jonah: The Runaway Prophet

An antihero, Jonah demonstrates what witnessing for God is not supposed to be. After running away from his mission, Jonah grudgingly preached in Nineveh, the Assyrian capital. Then, when his audience repented, Jonah complained bitterly because he would rather have seen them destroyed. As you read through the brief Book of Jonah, think about how he seems to act differently than prophets that you have studied so far.

When God commanded Jonah to march into Nineveh to preach, Jonah boarded a ship headed in the opposite

The Hebrew Scriptures: Called by the Father

direction. This was a cowardly, but very understandable, human reaction because Assyria was a powerful enemy of Israel. Jonah did not follow the tradition of the other great Hebrew prophets. He did not argue with God; he simply refused this dangerous mission. But God just as firmly rejected Jonah's refusal.

Jonah fell asleep during a great storm. The sailors, ignorant of Jonah's identity, prayed to their gods for help. When this failed, the sailors blamed Jonah. He, in turn, agreed to be thrown overboard to calm his angry God. After he was miraculously transported by God to the wicked city of Nineveh, Jonah foretold its destruction. The people repented, and God repealed the sentence against them. Instead of rejoicing at his success and at God's mercy, Jonah resented being deprived of seeing his foes punished. Jonah pouted as he said: "Is this not what I said?...I knew that you are a gracious and merciful God, slow to anger, rich in clemency, loathe to punish" (Jonah 4:2). Jonah's complaint here is an expression of faith in God.

Through Jonah, God used nature to teach a lesson about love. The Book of Jonah is an example of God's use of a literary form to teach human beings. Jonah is not a historical book, but rather a short story that uses irony to relate a prophetic truth. Although its colorful details and unique situations have made Jonah a famous "fish story" and the most humorous book of the Bible, it has a serious message. While laughing at Jonah's narrowmindedness, the reader of the story is reminded that God is concerned about all people, including the hated Assyrians.

6. *What strong visual images in the Book of Jonah make it interesting and funny?*

7. *Who are your country's enemies? Your own personal enemies? In what ways might you be like the reluctant Jonah?*

Irony: the use of words to express something different from the literal meaning of the words.

Jonah: A Biblical Portrait

Who was this man, Jonah?

"A strange character, he resembles no one in Scripture. No one has had his problems, or suggestions regarding their solution.

"Is he a prophet? If so, why is there no official reference to such a title? A man who argues with God not to save men but to punish them—what kind of prophet is that anyway?

"Jonah is clumsy, less than lucky. He does not feel wanted or at home anywhere. He shows up where least expected. And refuses to go where he is supposed to go...

"Jonah is a 'minor prophet,' the poor man's prophet. To be precise, he is the fifth in a series of twelve whose words we remember, but not their lives. In Jonah's case however, it is just the opposite...

"Poor prophet, he entertains rather than disturbs, he makes his readers smile rather than weep...

"It is a story about waiting—waiting for events to unfold, about things that are expected to happen but do not. We are kept breathlessly on the edge, miraculously prevented from taking the last step. Jonah runs away, but not far enough. The boat is in danger of sinking, but stays afloat. Jonah almost dies, Nineveh is almost destroyed. One might describe it as a unique suspense story—for children—with a magnificent happy ending... The reader too is happy: if the wicked people of Nineveh escape with impunity and continue to live and flourish, why not everyone else?

"As for Jonah, is he, too, pleased with the outcome? What has he gained in the test that pits him against all the other characters in the cast?"

(From *Five Biblical Portraits*, by Elie Wiesel, 1981. University of Notre Dame Press. Reprinted by permission of the publisher.)

The comic antics of Jonah offer insights into human behavior. How would you react if you were called by God to do something you'd rather not do?

Summary

■ God inspired the Jewish authors to write about outstanding Jewish men and women as vehicles of God's revelation.

■ Ruth was a model of faith, self-sacrifice, and loyalty. Rather than concentrating on herself, Ruth lived for others.

■ The introduction of Ruth, a Gentile, into the family tree of the Messiah is interpreted by Christians to reveal that Jesus is the Savior of the whole world, Jew and Gentile alike.

■ The story of Jonah is comical, yet it delivers a serious message about God's concern for all people.

■ Review

1. Why did Elimelech and his family leave Judah?

2. What words of Ruth demonstrate her loyalty to Naomi?

3. How is Jonah the opposite of other Hebrew prophets?

4. To what city did Jonah prophesy? What was the result of Jonah's preaching?

5. What is the meaning of the story of Jonah?

6. Words to Know: Elimelech, Moab, Naomi, Orpah, Ruth, Boaz, levirate marriage, Jonah, Nineveh.

■ In Your World

1. Ruth was known for her loyalty and faithful love. What two characteristics or qualities would you like people to associate with you? After you have decided on two of these, write down some suggestions for developing those characteristics in your life.

2. Why do people run from God? When do you find yourself running away from God?

■ Scripture Search

1. Deuteronomy 25:5-6 describes the institution of levirate marriage. How does the marriage described in this passage differ from the union between Ruth and Boaz?

2. How did Jesus warn against the selfishness of Jonah in the parables of the Prodigal Son (Luke 15:28) and the Laborers in the Vineyard (Matthew 20:15-16)?

Job: The Trusting Sufferer

The stories appear daily in the news: "Young person killed in drive-by shooting." "Person walking home from school hit by falling brick at construction site." "Baby dies of AIDS contracted by mother through a blood transfusion." In a world seemingly beset with innocent people suffering and dying for no good reason, it is certainly understandable to wonder about the goodness of God. The Book of Job provides insights into situations like these.

Understanding Life's Meaning

The story of Job explores the question, "What is the meaning of my life?" It views suffering and human existence from the perspective of the relationship between the Creator and the created. The mystery of the suffering of innocent people is explored in the Book of Job through the story of a good man's utter ruin. Job was prosperous and had an excellent reputation. The text states that "in the land of Uz there was a blameless and upright man named Job, who feared God and avoided evil" (Job 1:1).

God allowed Satan to try Job, and in a short time he had lost everything—his children, his home, his possessions, his health. Although he agonized over why he, a good man, had to suffer, Job's trust in God was steadfast.

During the time period that the Book of Job was written, many Jews believed that good people were rewarded and evil people were punished during their life on earth. They interpreted suffering on this earth as a punishment for wrongdoing or sin. On the other hand, if a person was healthy, had a large family, a home, and great wealth, that person was thought to be doing the will of God.

At the end of the Book of Deuteronomy, the following blessings and curses are listed: "When you hearken to the voice of the Lord, your God, all these blessings will come upon you and overwhelm you: May you be blessed in the city and blessed in the country! Blessed be the fruit of your womb, the produce of your soil and the offspring of your livestock, the issue of your herds and the young of your flocks! Blessed be your grain bin and your kneading bowl! May you be blessed in your coming in, and blessed in your going out!...But if you do not hearken to the voice of the Lord, your God, and are not careful to observe all his commandments which I enjoin on you today, all these curses shall come upon you and overwhelm you: May you be cursed in the city and cursed in the country! Cursed be your grain bin and your kneading bowl! Cursed be the fruit of your womb, the produce of your soil and the offspring of your livestock, the issue of your herds and the young of your flocks! May you be cursed in your coming in, and cursed in your going out!" (Deuteronomy 28:2-6, 15-19).

This, however, was not a completely satisfactory explanation of why innocent people suffer, or why evil people flourish in spite of their sins. If people were righteous and did no evil, why did they suffer with disease or poverty? If people broke the covenant and despised God, why did they sometimes gather great wealth and power?

This perplexing question is the subject of the Book of Job, a literary masterpiece. Written between the seventh and fifth century B.C.E., Job's story analyzes the question of the suffering of the innocent, but it does not offer a definite answer. Instead of resolving this complex issue with simple answers, the text encourages us to accept suffering as a test of fidelity and cautions us not to challenge God. We are not, however, to ignore the suffering of others.

Heroes and Legends

In chapters 1 and 2 of the Book of Job, Satan appears as a member of the heavenly court. In this context, Satan (whose name here means "accuser" or "adversary") appears not as God's enemy but as a subordinate, a figure who can only act with God's permission. Satan poses a question to God: "Is it for nothing that Job is God-fearing?" (Job 1:9). Satan claims that Job only blesses and praises God because things are going well. He states that if Job were to experience trials in his life, he would curse—rather than praise—God. God grants Satan the power to destroy Job's possessions. With his children and possessions gone, Job still refrained from cursing God. Satan proceeds to afflict Job with boils with God's permission. Even then, Job does not curse God.

Why do innocent people suffer? What can you do to relieve their suffering?

Most of the Book of Job is a record of the debate Job had with three friends (Eliphaz, Bildad, Zophar) and a young man named Elihu, who represent the wise people of Israel. The subject of the debate is the cause of Job's suffering. Job has experienced a reversal in fortunes. Everything—his family, his wealth, his health—have been taken away from him. His friends sympathized with Job, but they insisted that since God is just, Job must have done something wrong, maybe even unintentionally, to deserve such rough treatment in life.

Job affirmed his innocence but does not complain against God. Instead, he curses the day he was born and longs for death. Finally, in despair, Job uttered this challenge to God: "Let me know why you oppose me" (Job 10:2b). In the midst of a whirlwind, God stepped in and addressed Job. Amazed at the mysteriousness and grandeur of God's presence, Job finally proclaimed to God, "I know that you can do all things, and that no purpose of yours can be hindered. I have dealt with great things that I do not understand; things too wonderful for me, which I cannot know. I had heard of you by word of mouth, but now my eye has seen you. Therefore I disown what I have said, and repent in dust and ashes" (Job 42:2-6). In the end, Job's complaints were silenced, his friends stood corrected, and

Job's Comforters?

"When the three friends came to visit Job, they genuinely wanted to comfort him for his losses and his illness. But they did almost everything wrong, and ended up making him feel worse...

"What Job needed from his friends—what he was really asking for when he said 'Why is God doing this to me?' —was not theology, but sympathy ... He wanted them to tell him that he was in fact a good person, and that the things that were happening to him were terribly tragic and unfair. But the friends got so bogged down talking about God that they almost forgot about Job, except to tell him that he must have done something pretty awful to deserve this fate at the hands of a righteous God.

"Because the friends had never been in Job's position, they could not realize how unhelpful, how offensive it was for them to be judging Job, to be telling him he should not cry and complain so much. Even if they themselves had experienced similar losses, they would still have no right to sit in judgment of Job's grief.

"Under the impact of multiple tragedies, Job was trying desperately to hold on to his self-respect, his sense of himself as a good person. The last thing in the world he needed was to be told that what he was doing was wrong...

"Job needed sympathy more than he needed advice, even good and correct advice. There would be a time and place for that later. He needed compassion, the sense that others felt his pain with him, more than he needed theological explanations about God's ways. He needed physical comforting, people sharing their strength with him, holding him rather than scolding him."

(From *When Bad Things Happen to Good People*, Harold S. Kushner, 1981. Schocken Books, A Division of Random House.)

Job's comforters had answers to his problems. They were not much help. How do you comfort another person?

God rewarded Job with twice as much prosperity as he had formerly enjoyed.

The book's author is unknown. Job himself was a sheik from Edom, a region south of Palestine. From the structure of the book, it appears that an Israelite sage living near Edom used a folktale (the narrative at the opening and closing of the book) as a reflection on life and God's justice (the poetic speeches in the middle). In writing the story of Job, the author challenged Israel's traditional explanation for suffering, insisting that God cannot be manipulated by our action or omissions but is bigger than our fears and disasters. Job's suffering was a learning experience for him, and it leaves a deep impression on all who read his story.

---

8. *Suggest reasons why innocent people suffer. Discuss God's role in human suffering.*

9. *How does the Book of Job address the question of suffering?*

10. *The Book of Job falls into five acts. After you read each section, summarize its main events in a paragraph: Act I—1:1-12; Act II—1:13-2:10; Act III—2:11-3:4, 4:1-9, 6:28-30; Act IV—38:1-41; and Act V—42:1-17.*

Summary

- The Book of Job deals with the meaning of suffering, although it does not solve the problem of why innocent people suffer.

- Much of the Book of Job consists of a debate between Job and his friends about why Job is suffering.

- Job's friends were often more concerned about their own feelings than about comforting Job in his time of need.

- In the Book of Job, Satan appears as a member of the heavenly court who asks God for permission to test Job's faith.

■ Review

1. What happened to Job? Explain the reasons for these incidents.

2. Were Job's friends helpful during his time of suffering? Why or why not?

3. What role does Satan play in the Book of Job?

4. From a literary standpoint, how is the Book of Job structured?

5. Words to Know: Job, Eliphaz, Bildad, Zophar, Elihu.

■ In Your World

1. One of the spiritual Works of Mercy is to comfort the sorrowful. Consider the ways in which helping the homeless or visiting a person with AIDS or terminal cancer would be fulfilling this Work of Mercy. How can you comfort someone who is living through a time of suffering?

2. Think about the toughest obstacle that you have faced in your life. Write a few paragraphs comparing your experience to that of Job. Did you question God, like Job did? How did you resolve those questions?

■ Scripture Search

1. God challenged Job by saying, "Where were you when I founded the earth?" (Job 38:4). Genesis is not the only book of the Bible that tells the story of creation. Read Job 38-40, Ezekiel 28:11-19, and Psalm 104. What characteristics of God do they emphasize?

2. How does Ezekiel 14:13-14 depict Job?

Daniel: Devout Jew

During the Maccabean period, the Jews were persecuted for practicing their faith. They were threatened with death if they lived out the prescriptions of the Mosaic law. The Book of Daniel was written during this period of persecution (167-164 B.C.E.) to encourage and strengthen the persecuted Jews. It is a compilation of legends about Daniel, a brave and wise man whose faith and love were put to the test during the Babylonian Captivity, sometime before 538 B.C.E. The Book of Daniel stresses the need for a courageous faith that does not yield in the face of severe opposition.

Daniel's Zeal for God

Daniel's miraculous deliverance from the lion's den and his other exploits did not result from science or luck; they were the natural destiny of a person who trusted in God. Undaunted by the laws and punishments of Nebuchadnezzar, Daniel zealously followed the law of God. When Daniel faced danger, God saved him and endowed him with the power to interpret dreams, to prophesy, and to read the handwriting that miraculously appeared on the wall.

Although the evil characters in the story historically were Babylonian kings, the Israelites interpreted them as symbols of their present persecutors. Just as Daniel and his companions were able to hold out against their enemies, so the Jews, oppressed by the Syrian kings in the second century B.C.E., should also remain faithful. The visions of Daniel offered hope by foretelling the end of the persecutions and the eventual triumph of God, when those faithful to the Law would be rewarded.

The Book of Daniel was written to offer hope to people struggling to overcome injustice. What hope would Daniel offer to these demonstrators?

---

11. *How did the Book of Daniel offer hope to oppressed Jews?*

Apocalyptic Writing

The author of Daniel traced contemporary history in the symbolic language of visions. In Daniel's vision, four consecutive empires are represented by different beasts (Daniel 7:1-28). On another level, this writing refers to the end-time, the day of the Lord, and thus belongs to the type of writing called apocalyptic.

Apocalyptic writing flourished from 200 B.C.E. to C.E. 200, and its most significant theme was the imminent coming of the kingdom of God. The style of apocalyptic literature includes the use of symbolism, supernatural events, and predictions of events that had already occurred. The prophets taught that salvation would come in this world once the Messiah brought peace. Apocalyptic writing, on the other hand, encouraged reform in order to prepare for the new age that would begin with the destruction of this world and the Judgment Day.

The Hebrew Scriptures: Called by the Father

The following stories are characteristic of Daniel's style of writing and represent basic themes in this book of Scripture.

The Fiery Furnace (Daniel 3:1-97). This story might appear baffling, because it doesn't mention Daniel once. The setting is placed in Babylon during the reign of King Nebuchadnezzar. Its message, however, applies to the Jews endurance of the terrible persecution of Antiochus IV. Remember that he had set up an idol in the Jerusalem Temple and ordered the Jews to worship pagan gods. In this story, King Nebuchadnezzar did the same thing: He set up a golden statue and told the whole countryside that everyone must stop what they were doing and worship the god whenever they heard the trumpet, flute, lyre, harp, and bagpipes playing. When three Jews—Shadrach, Meshach, and Abednego—refused to comply, they were thrown into a fiery furnace, with flames so high they even burned some of the bystanders. The three men, accompanied by a fourth described as the "son of God," however, were untouched by the flames and sang the praises of God while the flames surrounded them. The purpose of the story was to show that the God of Israel protected those who remained faithful to God. The ending was the one the Jews wanted to see happen in their own situation—that the king would recognize the miracle and pass a law defending the Jewish people and their religion. The story is meant to inspire hope.

The Writing on the Wall (Daniel 5:1-6:1). This story was set in King Belshazzar's palace, where the king entertained his guests with the silver and gold plates and goblets stolen from the Jerusalem Temple. Instead of giving thanks to Yahweh, they praised their gods of gold and silver, bronze and iron, wood and stone. Their festivities were interrupted when a mysterious human hand wrote on the plaster of the wall. The frightened king could not understand the message. He sent for astrologers and enchanters to interpret it, but they were unsuccessful. The queen recommended Daniel because of his reputation for being able to interpret dreams, explain puzzles, and solve problems. Daniel was then summoned to the court and told the king, "This is the writing that was inscribed: MENE, TEKEL, and PERES. These words mean: MENE, God has numbered your kingdom and put an end to it; TEKEL, you

Imminent: ready to take place.

have been weighed on the scales and found wanting; PERES, your kingdom has been divided and given to the Medes and Persians'' (Daniel 5:25-28). When the king did not repent, he was killed that night. The moral point was that God punishes those who worship false gods.

The Lion's Den (Daniel 6: 2-29). In this story, a faithful Jew, Daniel, was spared harm because he refused to give up his religion. This story takes place under the reign of King Darius. Daniel was a supervisor who is highly respected by the king. Other men, however, were jealous of Daniel's popularity, and they sought to destroy him by attempting to find something with which to accuse him and dishonor his name. When they were unable to do so, they decided to trap him. When the king decreed that no one was to address any petition to any god or man except for himself, the jealous men informed the king that Daniel continued to pray three times a day, with his windows opened toward

Praying the Hebrew Scriptures

In the fiery furnace, Daniel's three young friends sang a hymn of praise. The following is an excerpt from that passage:

"Fire and heat, bless the Lord; praise and exalt him above all forever.
Dew and rain, bless the Lord; praise and exalt him above all forever.
Ice and snow, bless the Lord; praise and exalt him above all forever.
Light and darkness, bless the Lord; praise and exalt him above all forever.
He has freed us from the raging flame and delivered us from the fire.
Give thanks to the Lord for he is good, for his mercy endures forever" (Daniel 3:66,68,70,72,88,89).

What "fiery furnaces" must teens face today in order to practice their faith?

The Hebrew Scriptures: Called by the Father

Jerusalem. The king had no recourse but to follow through with the prescribed punishment and throw Daniel into a den of lions. When the king could not sleep that night, he rushed to the lion's den and found Daniel unharmed. The pagan king recognized the power of Daniel's God, punished the jealous men and their families, and decreed that the God of Daniel would be honored throughout the land.

12. *Daniel was able to interpret dreams. His success depended on this gift from God. Compare Daniel's story with that of Joseph. What reasons can you suggest for the similarities of these stories?*

13. *Read the following stories: the Vision of the Four Beasts (Daniel 7:1-28), Susanna (Daniel 13:1-64), and Bel and the Dragon (Daniel 14:1-42). What is the main point of each story? How is it similar to the three stories listed above? How is it different? How is each story typical of the style of the Book of Daniel?*

Jealousy often leads people to act rashly or in anger. Daniel's life was put at risk because of such jealous behavior.

Summing Up

You are a small speck on a tiny planet called earth, a planet that is part of a galaxy called the Milky Way, which is one among many other galaxies. Until a few short years ago, you did not exist. A hundred years from now, you will most likely no longer be alive. As Scripture says: "Man's days are like those of grass; like a flower of the field he blooms; the wind sweeps over him and he is gone, and his place knows him no more" (Psalm 103:15-16). Viewed from the immensity of that perspective, one individual's life, on the surface, seems to be insignificant. The lives of biblical characters like Ruth, Jonah, Job, and Daniel, however, disprove that notion.

What is the meaning of life? Almost everyone wants to know the purpose of existence. Some people claim that the universe is an accident, a chance combination of elements; others would venture that the universe is nothing but a cruel

The Dead Sea Scrolls

In 1947 on the northwest side of the Dead Sea, a shepherd boy searching for his lost goat in the Judean desert discovered an archaeological treasure. Excavations made from 1949 to 1956 revealed that the cave was one of eleven in which were housed what appeared to be the library of an ancient religious community called the Essenes.

This find yielded roughly six hundred precious manuscripts or fragments of manuscripts, including every book of the Hebrew Scriptures except the Book of Esther. The scrolls had been wrapped in linen and preserved in sealed jars. Until the Dead Sea discovery, the oldest copies of Scripture were from around C.E. 900. The Dead Sea Scrolls originated about one thousand years earlier, around 100 B.C.E.

Scholars believe that the monks who owned the scrolls were Essenes, a Jewish group opposed to the Pharisees and Sadducees (groups mentioned in the Christian Scriptures). The Essenes (John the Baptizer may have been one.) formed a religious community and moved into the desert to prepare for the kingdom of God in their own way. They were organized under a leader known as the Teacher of Righteousness. A Manual of Discipline for the Essenes was among the scrolls hidden in the caves. The scrolls were probably secreted away in the caves to keep them out of the hands of the invading Roman forces, who eventually destroyed the community in C.E. 68.

The discovery of the Dead Sea Scrolls has influenced Scripture scholarship greatly over the past fifty years.

joke with no meaning. To Jewish believers, however, life is a gift, bestowed on human beings by an almighty and loving God. All of creation is permeated with God's glory and goodness. Human beings—the crown of creation—are God's Children, put here to tend to the earth and one another, and to give thanks to God for the gift of life.

The Hebrew Scriptures: Called by the Father

Everything is centered on the relationship between people and God. In the span of a lifetime, a person either strengthens or shatters the covenant with God.

The literature of the Jewish people is built on this philosophy. Books like Ruth, Job, Jonah, and Daniel demonstrate how to live a meaningful life. Ruth is a story of the power of self-sacrificing and faithful love. Job reveals that trust in God through every trial leads to joy. Jonah witnesses to God's love for all people. Finally, Daniel shows that steadfast obedience in observing God's Law is rewarded. These same principles underlie your Christian faith.

The stories of the Hebrew people are also the stories of Christians. They continue to share with us the richness of God's revelation centuries after they were first written. As the Hebrew people struggled with the challenges offered by life, they became aware of God's presence in the struggle. Through the great gift of the Hebrew Scriptures you can benefit from their wisdom and come to know God personally. Finally, the Hebrew Scriptures lead Christians to believe in the Messiah, Jesus.

The stories of the Hebrew people are the stories of Christians as well. Christians regularly meet to pray and study the Hebrew Scriptures.

Epilogue: Jesus Christ

In the beginning was the Word;
the Word was with God
and the Word was God ...

All things came to be through him,
and without him nothing came to be ...

He came to what was his own,
but his own people did not accept him.
But to those who did accept him he gave power to become
children of God.
—John 1:1, 3, 11-12

A little more than a hundred years after the last words of the Hebrew Scriptures were written, the longed-for Messiah appeared. For believers, he brought to completion all the expectations that Abraham's faith had set in motion. He was a liberator like Moses and the judges, but he was also greater. He was the king of David's line who would bring peace and justice and whose coming had been foretold by the prophets. Jesus, the Savior of the World, was the Son of God himself.

In Jesus, Christians believe that God's revelation to the Hebrew people has been fulfilled and a new covenant has been established.

The Jews believed in God's love for them, and for centuries they safeguarded and trusted the promise of a messiah. But God's love went far beyond any Jewish hope. God came in person—as one of us—to save us, and loved us to the point of death. In Jesus, God's people—as the result of a growth process that had gone on for thousands of years—reached the peak of their development.

Jesus proclaimed a new, universal covenant, through his infinite sacrifice and the gift of his Spirit. We become a new creation—sons and daughters of the Father—alive with the life of Jesus and bonded in the love of the Spirit. In Jesus, humanity is already glorified and at the right hand of the Father.

In Jesus, humanity was opened once and for all to a relationship with God. It remains for each individual to respond to God's offer of salvation until Christ's Second Coming in majesty at the end of the world. Then God's love and life will permeate all peoples and the entire universe, so that God will be all in all. In the words of the Jesuit theologian Teilhard de Chardin, "At all costs we must renew in ourselves the desire and hope for the great Coming."

Summary

- The Book of Daniel was written during the Maccabean period (167-164 B.C.E.) to encourage and strengthen the persecuted Jews.

- The Book of Daniel stresses the need for a courageous faith that is unyielding in the face of severe opposition.

- Apocalyptic literature uses symbolism, supernatural events, and predictions of events that have already occurred to encourage people and assure them that there is hope for the future.

- Jews believe that in the span of a lifetime, a person may choose either to strengthen the covenant with God or to reject it.

■ Review

1. Why were Daniel's visions a source of hope for the Jewish people?

2. Who were Shadrach, Meshach, and Abednego?

3. What aspects of the Book of Daniel would a persecuted Jew have found particularly helpful?

4. During what time period did apocalyptic writing flourish?

5. Words to Know: Daniel, apocalyptic, Susanna, Bel, Shadrach, Meshach, Abednego, Dead Sea Scrolls, Essenes, Nebuchadnezzar.

■ In Your World

1. You can witness to your faith by suffering a martyr's death, but can you also do it by living faithfully day-to-day. What are the similarities and differences between these two different ways of witnessing? What are you willing to do to witness for your faith?

2. You constantly face opportunities to choose good or to choose evil. Which of these choices requires more courage? Give an example of choices teens must make today.

■ Scripture Search

1. Other examples of apocalyptic writing in the Bible include Joel 4:1-21; Zechariah 2:1-11; and Mark 13. Read these texts and then compare and contrast them with the visions in Daniel.

2. What do you think the dream of the tree in Daniel 4 means? Explain your answer.

12 Review

■ Study

1. List the themes of the four books studied in this chapter.

2. Ruth constantly made good decisions. What were some of her commendable actions?

3. What symbolic act sealed the bargain between Boaz and his kinsman?

4. The relationship between Ruth and Naomi was ideal. What attitudes should young people have toward their elders? How should older people regard the young?

5. God is a main character in the story of Jonah. What do God's actions reveal about the Divine Presence?

6. How does the fact that the events in the Book of Jonah are not historical change the message that the book delivers?

7. What kinds of suffering did Job endure? What was the purpose of Job's suffering?

8. How does the Book of Job answer the question of why innocent people suffer?

9. According to the Book of Daniel, what is required to belong to God's kingdom?

10. Retell the story of the Fiery Furnace in your own words.

11. How does apocalyptic writing differ from the message of the prophets?

■ Action

1. Create a presentation of a modern Job, Ruth, Jonah, or Daniel. Use whatever medium (play, song, cartoon strip, sitcom, and the like) best communicates your message.

2. In your library, find a copy of Francis Thompson's poem, "The Hound of Heaven." After you read this poem, describe in two paragraphs how God lives up to this title in the Book of Jonah.

3. Write a short story or one-act play that has an outstanding Christian teenager as its hero or heroine.

■ Prayer

Rabbi Abraham Heschel suggests that the only real solution to tension and worry is a sense of trust in God's love. He recommends prayer as a way to keep from becoming a victim of tension. Heschel's advice is deceptively simple, because people who are tense usually find it difficult to pray. Deep prayer can only be achieved when we feel free from time pressures, fear, and mental anxiety.

The first step is to follow a schedule. Set a time for prayer each day, and don't let anything interrupt it or crowd it out. Next find a place to pray. It should be a place where you will be undisturbed and where you can relax, but not fall asleep. It might be in your home, underneath a tree in your backyard, or in a church. In some way, make your chosen space a sacred place by asking God to bless it. Finally, prepare yourself by using relaxation techniques to still your mind. One way to do this is to be attentive to your body. Begin with your toes, tensing the muscles, then relaxing them, continuing until you have reached your head. Another way to relax is to imagine yourself going down ten floors in an elevator. As you pass by each floor, slowly breathe in God's love, and then breathe it out, until you have reached the bottom floor, and the door opens, leaving you in the Presence of God. After you follow these three steps, you are ready to experience deep prayer.

Jewish Update

People forget that Jesus was a Jew. His parents and grandparents were Jews. He spoke, prayed, and dressed like a Jew. His closest friends were all Jews. Jesus lived and died a Jew. Respect and love for Jesus has inspired modern Christians to take new interest in the Jewish people. Vatican II emphasized that Judaism is the root of Christianity and that Jewish and Christian relations must improve. Saint Paul taught that because God called the Jews to a close covenant with himself, and because God's gifts are never taken back, the Jews will always be God's Chosen People (Romans 11:28-29).

Although you have studied the Hebrew Scriptures, which prepared the way for Christ, you may not be familiar with modern Judaism. The history of the Chosen People in the Bible ends with the stories of Jesus and the early Church. The Jewish people, of course, have continued to grow and change to this day.

The Hebrew Scriptures: Called by the Father

Although traditionally said to be Semites (descended from a common ancestor Shem), there are about eighty-five racial and ethnic groups that share the Jewish faith. Driven out of Palestine shortly after Jesus' death, the Jews were a people without a country for two thousand years until the 1940s, when Israel became a nation.

The Great Destruction

When the Romans rolled into Judea under General Pompey in 63 B.C.E., a Galilean rebel organization called the Zealots began an underground movement that ended in an unsuccessful revolt in 6 B.C.E. This group reorganized and fought for independence again in C.E. 67. In 70, a Roman army sealed off Jerusalem, trapping thousands who had come from Palestine for the Passover. Escapees fell into the arms of waiting soldiers, who crucified them. About a thousand refugees fled to the rock fortress of Masada in the upper city. There, in C.E. 73, they committed mass suicide rather than surrender.

No food or water passed into the city for a hundred days. Then the Romans attacked the city with fire. Flaming brands tossed into the city transformed Jerusalem into a mammoth cauldron of fire. When it was all over, the once-magnificent cream-and-gold Temple of Herod was a charred and desolate landscape.

An entire way of life was devastated by the fire. It was as if a gigantic bomb had wiped out Washington, D.C., while a national convention on religious life was being held there, killing not only the president and all of Congress but also the nation's religious leaders. With the destruction of all but one wall of the Temple, the practice of daily sacrifices, which was central to Jewish worship, came to an end. Worship in the home and synagogue took its place.

Most of the Jewish people who had not been in Jerusalem during the siege fled to Babylonia, Syria, Asia Minor, and throughout the Mediterranean world. This flight is called the Great Dispersion. The Jews since then have lived in the *Diaspora,* the term describing communities outside of Palestine. After a final uprising in C.E. 165, led by

The rabbi became the principal leader of Judaism after the fall of Jerusalem.

the messiahlike figure, Bar Kochba, the Jews were forbidden to set foot in Jerusalem.

Survival in the Diaspora

Today, two thousand years later, 15 million believers witness to the remarkable power of the Jewish people to survive. United by faith, Jews have overcome their wide separation from one another, established schools for rabbis, built synagogues in every community, and faithfully followed their religious laws and festivals.

Any man or (in some branches of Judaism) woman who studies the Law can become a *rabbi,* a specially trained layperson who is neither anointed nor appointed. In some foreign countries, chief rabbis play a role similar to that of a bishop. The Pharisees—laymen educated in the Law who had grown influential after the Maccabean wars—immediately assumed leadership. They established rabbinical schools in Jamnia near Galilee. There, with scholars in the older school of Babylon, they worked for sixty years to gather the oral teachings of the rabbis, organizing and adapting Jewish law to fit the Diaspora. The book containing this rabbinical teaching is known as the *Talmud.*

Deprived of their Temple, the people of the Diaspora built the same kind of plain buildings without the altars that

The Hebrew Scriptures: Called by the Father

had served them during the Babylonian Exile. In these synagogues, or "meeting places," the people worshiped, kept in touch with their leaders, were educated in the faith of Israel, and maintained their social life apart from their neighbors. Each synagogue has an ark (a tabernacle) in which the sacred biblical scrolls are kept. Morning and evening services, the Sabbath and community feasts, and social events are held in the synagogue to this very day.

The feasts and ceremonies of Judaism also gave the people an opportunity to express, learn, and live their faith and to hand it down to their children. The Jewish people still celebrate the religious events of their history through an annual cycle of feasts. By means of specific traditional ceremonies, each individual's life is blessed from cradle to grave. (See the feature, "Jewish Life Sanctified," page 347.)

---

1. *If the Catholic Church everywhere was suddenly forced underground, what essentials would ensure its survival?*

The Holocaust

You have probably seen films and books about the Holocaust—Nazi Germany's systematic extermination of more than six million Jews in the gas chambers of European concentration camps during World War II. (It also included the annihilation or subjugation of five million members of certain other groups: Gypsies, Slavs, and the mentally and physically disabled.) Between 1939 and 1945, under the dictatorship of Adolf Hitler, one-third of the total world population of Jews were murdered and thousands of others were forced to flee. Reviving the medieval use of the yellow Star of David to mark the Jews, the Nazis shipped them in crowded boxcars to the camps, where they were starved, used in scientific experiments, forced into hard labor, and gassed at the rate of twelve thousand a day.

Some people blame Hitler alone for this incredible slaughter. Although the Nazi philosophy was rooted in fundamentally anti-Christian beliefs, anti-Semitism was nevertheless promoted in the Christian countries of Europe prior to the war. Hitler exploited the prejudice of the people. He cloaked their hatred in misguided versions of Darwin's theory of the "survival of the fittest," insisting that only fair-skinned people such as the people of northern Germany were "the fittest." Hitler also twisted the teachings of German philosopher Friedrich Nietzsche (1844-1900) to justify his claims that the "master race"—the Aryans, or Gentiles—was superior to everyone else.

Although some Christians died defending Jews, no public voice was raised in defense of the Jewish victims—to the eternal shame of the Christian Church and other world leaders. The word *holocaust* has the religious meaning of an offering made to God by complete destruction of the victim. Today, some Christians and Jews look upon Israel's sacrifice as somehow related to Isaiah's servant figure who suffered for the salvation of the world.

Living in hiding between 1943 and 1945, Jewish theologian Jules Isaac wrote: "The glow of the Auschwitz crematorium is the beacon that lights and guides all my thoughts. Oh my Jewish brothers, and you as well, my Christian brothers, do you not think it mingles with another glow, that of the Cross?"

Jews have been systematically murdered for centuries because of their faith. The most horrible example of this happened in Nazi Germany with the Holocaust.

The Hebrew Scriptures: Called by the Father

2. *What examples can you offer of prejudice against Jews?*

3. *What can we learn from the Holocaust? What can an average person do to prevent such an occurrence from happening again?*

Roots of Anti-Semitism

A quick overview of the history of anti-Semitism reveals that for centuries Christians and others have strayed far from Christ's command to love.

Non-Jews before the Time of Christ. The Jews were disliked by Israel's neighbors because they insisted on their right to religious freedom and separated themselves from nonbelievers.

Early Christians. The criticism of Jewish leaders found in the Christian Scriptures was given out of concern for the spiritual welfare of the Jews. After all, Jesus was one with the Jews. Like the prophets, his criticism was delivered to make his own people better, not to stir up hatred. The authors of these books were steeped in a Jewish tradition which stresses that people need strong words to keep them faithful. However, some of the Gentile converts who read these books also allowed their own pagan-influenced prejudices to influence their interpretation.

Early Christian Fathers. Some early Christian leaders labeled the Jews as the people who had crucified and rejected Christ. In reality, only a limited group of members of the Jewish Council condemned Jesus. Although they were members, Nicodemus and Joseph of Arimathea were sympathetic to the cause of Jesus. Today we know that the Jews neither collectively nor individually are responsible for Jesus' death.

Medieval European Christians. During the Middle Ages, Christian teaching mistakenly held that Christians who punished Jews were God's instruments. Jews were seen as resisting grace and corrupting society; accordingly, they were attacked, robbed, and even murdered in the

Anti-Semitism: hostility toward or discrimination against Jews as a religious or ethnic group.

Auschwitz: one of the Nazi concentration camps.

Crematorium: a furnace for reducing bodies to ashes.

name of Christ. When Jews withdrew to worship in seclusion, they were dragged into courts and charged with treason and conspiracy. Open massacre was followed either by expulsion (in England, France, and Germany) or relocation into disease-ridden *ghettos* surrounded by walls that were locked every night. Jews were forbidden to own land, attain higher education, or participate in government. Socially and legally prevented from working in agriculture, industry, and certain crafts, they practiced finance and small trades.

Russian Christians. Eastern non-Orientals confined the Jews to *shtetels* (rhymes with "kettles"), villages they could not leave without police approval. Periodically, the Jews were the victims of *pogroms* (pronounced peh-grum), or organized massacres.

Spanish Catholics. When Muslim armies conquered much of Spain in the early eighth century, the Jews, who share Semitic roots with the Arab Muslims, fared well under Muslim rule. However, by the thirteenth century Christian princes had driven out the Muslims. When the Spanish Inquisition, a Roman Catholic court set up in the Middle Ages to suppress heresy, hunted down *Moriscos* (Muslims who converted to Christianity), Jews were also persecuted.

Protestants. When Martin Luther, the father of Protestantism, first recognized the Jewish roots of Christ, he wrote a book in which he called Jews "the blood brothers of Jesus." But when the Jews would not convert to Christianity, Luther grew bitter toward them.

The Enlightenment. As a result of renewed struggles for the universal right of human freedom during the American and French revolutions in the eighteenth century, Napoleon abolished the ghettos and granted Jews full citizenship in France. In America, they enjoyed constitutional freedom. These reforms, however, did not stem the tide of anti-Semitism.

Catholic Liturgy. Before Vatican II (1962-1965), the solemn intercessions for the Jews recited on Good Friday prayed that God might "tear the veil from their hearts so that they also may acknowledge our Lord Jesus Christ." It was asked that Jews be "brought out of all darkness." When the Council openly denounced anti-Semitism, the

The Hebrew Scriptures: Called by the Father

prayer was updated to read, "Let us pray for the Jewish people, the first to hear the word of God, that they may continue to grow in the love of his name and in faithfulness to his covenant."

Today's Christians. Anti-Semitism isn't dead yet. In 1980, a leading American Christian minister said at a national convention, "God doesn't hear the prayers of a Jew," while in various European countries bombs are being detonated in front of synagogues and other Jewish gathering places. In this country, some synagogues are being vandalized and desecrated.

---

4. *Someone has stereotyped Catholics as fish-eaters who are always fingering their beads and have large families. What truth do you find in these images? How would you describe a Catholic? How fair do you think stereotypes are?*

From C.E. 700 to the Present

Granted freedom of education under the Moors (Muslims in Spain), Jewish scholarship enjoyed a golden age from about C.E. 700 to 1250. The great Jewish scholar Moses Maimonides reorganized, updated, and translated the Talmud and made the Hebrew Scriptures available in Arabic. Maimonides is often compared to Catholicism's Thomas Aquinas because he tried to show the reasonableness of the Faith.

A group called the "Cabbalist" explored the mysticism of the teachings of Israel. They worked out a system of theology known as "the Cabbala." Along with number symbolism and magical formulas in their main book, *The Zohar* ("bright light"), written in 1280 by Moses de Leon in Spain, Cabbalist theories about God's closeness to the world still influence contemporary Jewish and Christian thinkers.

Maimonides (1135-1203): a Spanish rabbi, philosopher, and physician.

Saint Thomas Aquinas (1255-1274): an Italian philosopher; his great work is the *Summa Theologica*.

Hasidic Jews live in strict accordance with the Torah.

Jewish Holy Ones

Although the Jews do not have a doctrine of saints, they do have high respect for persons who give evidence of special closeness to God. A group known as the *Hasidim* (the "Pious Ones") followed such a special person—Baal Shem Tov (1699-1761), known as the "Kindly Master." This humble Polish digger of clay received a divine vision in which he became convinced that God was everywhere and in everything. He taught that even the poorest, most illiterate person could grow close to the spirit of God.

The Hasidim are strict Orthodox Jews. Following the ancient traditions of Judaism, each community is formed around a holy messiah figure, the *rebbe* (rabbi). They respond to his message with ecstatic songs and dancing. For the Hasidim, holiness is a relationship with God rather than an acceptance of rules or extensive study. They also pioneered the establishment of private schools for their children.

A Great Day

Every family celebrates its own special days. May 14, 1948, is such a day for the Jews, for it was on that day that modern Israel was born. After two thousand years of alienation and persecution, the Jewish people again possessed a homeland in Israel, formerly called Palestine.

Because the revolutionary ideas of the Enlightenment failed to dispel prejudice against the Jewish faith, many Jews became convinced of the need for a Jewish nation. In 1896, *The Jewish State,* a book by Jewish statesman Theodor Herzl, gave rise to *Zionism,* a movement originally aimed to restore Palestine as the national homeland of the Jews; since the establishment of Israel, Zionists have been concerned with the development and defense of their homeland.

During World War I, Britain made an official statement known as the Balfour Declaration, encouraging Zionism. Thousands of Jews immediately flocked to Palestine. Next, the League of Nations gave Britain a mandate to administer Palestine, and the Jews laid a foundation for their state. The tragedy of the Holocaust brought the issue to a crisis. After

World War II, in a spirit of reparation to the Jews (who were already immigrating to Palestine in considerable numbers), the United Nations Assembly voted to have the British withdraw and to partition Palestine into a Jewish state, an Arab state, and a small internationally administered area that included the city of Jerusalem. The Jews accepted this arrangement, but the Arab Palestinians felt that Palestine should be granted independence with Jews allowed to live there as a protected minority. Even so, the Jewish people had at long last acquired a homeland in November 1947.

In addition to being a political achievement, the reestablishment of Israel is viewed by the Jewish people as a new development in their covenant relationship with God, and some believe it compares with the first Exodus. If Auschwitz stands as a symbol of Christian failure in this century, the State of Israel symbolizes the unexpected rescue of the Jews. It is a resurrection of the suffering servant of Isaiah, who was sacrificed so that the world might be saved.

The nation of Israel was founded May 14, 1948.

But the Arabs, who had called Palestine their home for thousands of years, felt dispossessed. Several Arab countries joined the Palestinian Arabs in a war for domination early in 1948. They were unsuccessful, and the Jews officially declared the existence of the State of Israel on May 14, 1948. Palestinian refugees fled to the Gaza Strip, Jordan, Syria, and Lebanon, forming political and military groups dedicated to regaining their homeland in Palestine (now Israel). To this day, each side struggles for possession of the land.

While recognizing the religious meaning of the Israeli state, neither Christians nor Jews can afford to glorify it. It is not in existence primarily because once, long ago, the Jews conquered the territory, or even because the Bible speaks of a promised homeland. It arose as a vehicle to protect the Jews from murderous anti-Semitism, and it was legally established by the peoples of the world represented in the League of Nations and, later, in the United Nations. Israel must be treated like any other nation. If Israel violates the rights of others, it must expect criticism and defensive action. It is also responsible for working toward peace in the Middle East. Israel has a right to self-determination, as does any other nation, but it also has an obligation to treat other people with dignity and justice.

5. *Prepare a report on these Jewish holy men: Martin Buber, Isaac Luria, Moses Chaim Luzzatto.*

6. *When Jews have had the opportunity, they have excelled in all fields. Name the contributions made by the following Jews: Sigmund Freud, Samuel Goldwyn, Adolph S. Ochs, Arthur Rubinstein, Jonas Salk, August von Wassermann, Robert Oppenheimer, Julius Rosenwald, Albert Einstein, George Gershwin.*

Short Answers to Frequently Asked Questions

As with all forms of hatred, anti-Semitism can be traced to ignorance. When someone learns the truth about a people, he or she often will have a change in attitude or feeling. The following will provide you with answers to some of the most commonly asked questions about Judaism. Hopefully, it will help to change your image of the Jewish people and religion.

Why Don't the Jews Accept Jesus?

A rabbi once said, "It's a matter of faith in Jesus. You have it. We don't." The Jews have had many ideas of a messiah. Some Jews had nothing more than vague hopes for a glorious future age, while others have looked forward to an ideal king like David. At times, the Jews expected two messiahs, one a priest like Aaron, the other a prophet. In general, messianism includes those ideas that represent the Israel of the future as identical with God's kingdom, a time of peace and justice.

When Jesus lived, the atmosphere was charged with the expectancy of a military messiah. Unlike the Zealots, Jesus usually avoided any connection with political kingship or military takeover. Jesus' main role was to be a suffering messiah, an idea even his followers could not grasp until after the resurrection.

Today, Jewish belief remains divided about a messiah. Even those who believe in resurrection cannot accept the

The Hebrew Scriptures: Called by the Father

scandal of Jesus' saving death. "The world is no better for Jesus' coming," they say, "so how could he be the Messiah?" But the Jews' most serious objection to Christianity is rooted in their idea of God's greatness; they cannot imagine a completely holy (other) God becoming a man. They blame Saint Paul, who abolished the Sabbath and circumcision, for separating Christians and Jews. They also reject his claim to having been divinely commissioned to preach that only faith in Christ (and not the Law) would bring salvation.

What Do Jews Think of Jesus?

Jews regard Jesus as one of their own—a Jew preaching the Jewish faith of love for God and neighbor, especially the poor. In his book *Basic Judaism,* rabbi Milton Steinberg wrote:

"To Jews...Jesus appears as an extraordinarily beautiful and noble spirit, aglow with love and pity for men, especially for the unfortunate and lost, deep in piety, of keen insight into human nature, endowed with a brilliant gift of parable and epigram, an ardent Jew, moreover, a firm believer in the faith of his people: all in all, a dedicated teacher of principles, religious and ethical, of Judaism....and always there is his own personality, a superb achievement in its own right."

Jews do not see Jesus as a prophet because they say he preached more about the "other world" than about this world, and in the Jewish view it is through this life that God is glorified. They see Jesus as being indifferent to social affairs, such as the tyranny of the Roman Empire. They do not regard Jesus as the ideal human being because they say he showed no interest at all in the human concerns of philosophy, science, government, or art. They feel that his outbursts of temper in the Temple, over the unfruitful fig tree, and toward the scribes and Pharisees, and his prejudice against such non-Jews as the Syro-Phoenician woman reveal a flawed character (Mark 7:24-30). Still, they criticize him for accepting evil too patiently and passively.

Jews find the four diverse portraits of Christ in the Gospel and the different images of him in the various branches of Christianity confusing. For instance, there is the severe

> **Parable and Epigram:** two techniques of teaching.

Christ of the Calvinists; the mystical, divine Christ of the Eastern Orthodox; and the Christ of Catholics who becomes present to his people in the sacraments. They ask which of these is the true Christ.

Jews feel obliged neither to pronounce a judgment on Jesus nor to convert the world to Judaism. They feel their mission is to make known the God who spoke on Sinai. They regard it as a mystery that billions have come to know the true God through Christians who have spread the Jewish Scriptures throughout the world.

Are There Different Branches of Judaism?

Perhaps on Saturday you have seen Jewish families walking to their synagogues, the boys wearing skullcaps known as *yarmulkes* (pronounced yarh-mul-keh), the bearded men looking dignified in their somber long coats, the women in dark-colored dresses. These are Orthodox Jews, traditional Jews who strictly follow the six hundred and thirteen laws of Judaism.

You may have heard the expression, "That isn't kosher." The word *kosher,* which means "fit to eat," originates with the Orthodox Jews' obligation to kill and prepare animals in the exact way prescribed by Mosaic law. Other dietary rules prohibit the eating of pork, taking milk and meat together, and mixing dishes used in preparation of milk and meat. Because of this law, some Jewish families have two separate sets of dishes. While the original reasons for these practices are lost, these and other dietary laws transform every family meal in the Orthodox Jewish home into a religious practice.

When the men pray, they don a prayer shawl *(tallith).* At morning prayer, except on the Sabbath and on festivals, males strap to their forehead and to the arm nearest their heart two small boxes *(tefillin* or *phylacteries);* each contains a part of Scripture. Like all observing Jews, Orthodox Jews celebrate the Jewish festivals and kindle the Sabbath lights. In addition, they practice ritual washing and other prescribed actions, and they regard written revelation as their sole guide.

Orthodox Jews firmly believe in a coming messiah, but they do not expect him to be divine. For thousands of years, all Jews were Orthodox. The novel *The Chosen,* by Chaim

It is possible to identify some people as Jewish by the clothes they wear.

The Hebrew Scriptures: Called by the Father

(pronounced *hi-ehm*) Potok, presents the struggles a young person has in trying to remain faithful to strict Judaism in the modern world. With the recent freedom of Western and American Jews to mingle with people of other faiths, Judaism has divided into two other branches. One, called Conservative, is modified traditional; the other, called Reform, is much more open to change.

In the last century, a movement called Reform Judaism was organized to modernize Jewish laws and customs. This most liberal branch of Judaism abbreviated the Sabbath services. Although recently there has been a trend to reinstate the use of Hebrew, Reform Jews hold services mainly in the vernacular. They have introduced the use of the organ during worship even though, out of mourning for the destruction of the Temple, musical instruments had been forbidden since the Exile. They have also abolished many other traditional practices. Some have even considered giving up the Sabbath as a holy day!

In 1845, under the leadership of German-born Abraham Geiger, Reform Judaism shocked the Jewish world by rejecting not only the Talmud but also the belief in a messiah who would lead the Jews back to Palestine. The European Jewish community reacted so strongly that the Reform movement was transplanted to America. Today it has swung away from the principles of Geiger and reintroduced many ceremonies and customs that were abandoned earlier.

To answer a need for a middle position between the two extremes, a third form of Judaism appeared—Conservative Judaism. This form retains maximal observance of ritual law and custom despite a more liberal theology. In America, the congregations of Conservative Judaism were organized by Solomon Schecter into the United Synagogue of America. Conservative Jews place high priority on the mission of Judaism to bear witness to the true God. "Tradition, with change" is their motto. Schecter (1850-1915) became world-famous with his discovery of the last original Hebrew version of Ecclesiasticus (Sirach) in a Cairo synagogue.

Despite these divisions, all Jews experienced a profound sense of unity in the sorrow of the Holocaust and the joy of their own homeland. These three religious positions reveal Judaism's great flexibility.

Vernacular: the language native to a country or region.

Which Branch of Judaism Does Someone Profess?

The use of the yarmulke identifies the religious position of a Jew. In the West, raising the hat is a sign of reverence. Jews show reverence, especially to God, by covering the head. Orthodox males wear the skullcap at all times to remind them of God's constant presence and to honor God's name when it comes up in conversation. Other religious males wear it in the synagogue, while studying sacred texts, and while engaged in religious ritual at home. Reform Jews do not wear the yarmulke because they feel that its meaning has disappeared in modern Western society.

Why Do the Jews Observe the Sabbath on Saturday?

Six days God created; on the seventh, according to the Jewish scribes, he rested. The third commandment required Jews to rest from work on every seventh day. The Sabbath was reckoned from sundown on Friday to sundown on Saturday. It became a time for reading the Scriptures, especially with the family.

The first followers of Jesus observed the Jewish Sabbath faithfully, and then gathered in a believer's home on the following day to celebrate the Lord's Supper. The first day of the week (Sunday) was the anniversary of Jesus' resurrection, so it became known as the Lord's Day. When Christians no longer went to the synagogue, they transferred the readings, psalms, hymns, and prayers from that service to the Sunday celebration of the Lord's Supper.

Does Judaism Have Sacraments?

Like Christians, the Jews consecrate life's greatest moments, but their ceremonies are not sacraments in the Christian sense—that is, of visible signs that bring about an inward change. Rather, their ceremonies represent a remembering of God's saving events of the past for the purpose of experiencing his presence and power at the time of the celebration. The festival then becomes a pledge of God's fidelity in the future. (See the Feature "Jewish Life Sanctified" for the more important rituals.)

The Hebrew Scriptures: Called by the Father

Is the Jewish Bible Different from the Christian Bible?

Before Jesus, the Jews did not have a canon, or official list, of books they regarded as inspired, but they did have a collection of sacred writings. The Greek version, called the *Septuagint,* had been translated between 250 and 100 B.C.E. With the early Christians using this version and proclaiming the twenty-seven books canonical, the Jews settled on their own canon in Jamnia in C.E. 90. This list excluded from the Septuagint six books and some other passages that had not always been held as inspired in the Jewish tradition. (The Council of Florence in 1441 and the Council of Trent in 1545 confirmed the present Catholic canon.)

Has Anything Been Added to the Hebrew Scriptures?

Christians added their own books to the Hebrew Scriptures, but the Jews have not added any books to those they share in common with Christians. By C.E. 550, however, they had completed an additional collection of oral tradition called the Talmud. The Talmud ("to learn") is a two-part encyclopedic book of rabbinical teachings and interpretations of the Torah. It was worked on in the rabbinical schools after the destruction of Jerusalem to preserve Jewish learning.

The first part is known as *Hallakah* ("which way to walk") and consists of Israel's oral law, codified and arranged into a system between C.E. 70 and 200. The second part, called *Mishnah,* is a collection of stories *(haggadah),* sayings, and discussions commenting on the oral law. They were gathered over a period of one thousand years (400 B.C.E.-C.E. 500). When the *haggadah* stories interpret the spiritual meaning of the Scriptures, they are known as *midrash* ("to speak out"). Although Jews differ in their belief concerning divine revelation, Orthodox and Conservative Jews are bound by both the oral Talmudic tradition and the written Torah. The most widely used commentary is that of Rashi, an eleventh-century French scholar. The name Rashi (1040-1105) was made up of the Hebrew initials for Rabbi Solomon, son of Isaac.

Although burned in the marketplace and strewn page by page on the waters during times of persecution, the Talmud

The Talmud consists of Jewish laws and commentary on those laws.

Sabbath: from the Hebrew "shab-bath," meaning "rest."

Septuagint ("seventy"): this version of the Hebrew Scriptures received its name because tradition holds that it was translated by seventy Jewish scholars in Alexandria, Egypt.

still exists today and serves to protect the observance of the Torah and to preserve the high religious and moral character of the Jewish people from the corruption of worldly morality. The holy and learned rabbis who study and teach it still lead Judaism.

Do All Jews Speak Hebrew?

Just as Latin is the official language of the Catholic Church, Hebrew is still the holy language of worship for Orthodox and Conservative Jews. Although in daily affairs Jews speak the language of their country, many also learn Hebrew. Boys and, with the exception of the Orthodox, girls are expected to chant the prophetic portion of the Scriptures in Hebrew at his or her Bar/Bat Mitzvah. During the Middle Ages, the Jews developed in two geographical divisions: the Spanish Jews, called *Sephardim*; and the German-speaking Jews, called *Ashkenazim*.

The Sephardim spoke an old dialect of Spanish called Ladino. The pronunciation of the official Hebrew of modern Israel today is Sephardic. During the medieval persecutions, the Jews from Germany formed their own language, blending medieval German with Hebrew. Today it is known as *Yiddish*. Most Jews today are Ashkenazim. You may be familiar with the wonderful humor of the Ashkenazi Jews celebrated in Leo Rosen's book, *The Joys of Yiddish*.

Not all Jews read Hebrew. Hebrew is, however, the language of the nation of Israel.

Do Jews Have Creeds of Their Beliefs?

Judaism transmits its faith mainly through the study of the Torah in the home, school, and synagogue. It has no official creed or catechism besides the belief in the one living God, as expressed in the Shema. Nearest to a fully developed creed are the Thirteen Articles of Jewish Faith drawn up by the philosopher Maimonides. The Articles are summarized in the book *Judaism,* by Arthur Hertzberg, as follows:

"I believe with perfect faith that God is the creator of all things and he alone; that he is one with a unique unity; that he is without body or any form whatsoever; that he is eternal; that to him alone is it proper to pray; that all the words of the prophets are true; that Moses is the chief of the prophets; that the law will never be changed and no other

The Hebrew Scriptures: Called by the Father

will be given; that God knows all the thoughts and actions of men; that he rewards the obedient and punishes transgressors; that the Messiah will come; that there will be a resurrection of the dead."

Although not accepted by every Jew and in no way binding, these Articles appear in the Jewish Daily Prayer Book as an introduction to the morning service.

---

7. What similarities do you see between the practices of Judaism and Christianity? What major Christian feasts or rituals are not observed in Judaism?

8. Research and report any of the following ritual objects used by Jewish people in their religious practices: mezuzah, embroidered cloth to cover the bread, silver goblets, Hanukkah menorah, booths, Seder plate, matzo, yarmulke, siddur, milchig and fleishig, kosher, shehitah, wedding glass.

9. There is a growing movement called Messianic Judaism. Research these "Jews for Jesus" and make a report to the class summarizing their origin, purpose, and meaning.

10. Write a careful description of your views of Jesus as you might present it to a group of Jewish teenagers. Your purpose is to inform, not to convert.

The Sacred Round

The Christian liturgical year owes much to the Jewish "Sacred Round," as the Jews call their annual cycle of feasts. As you study the Sacred Round below, find parallels with Christian worship.

Celebration: *Sabbath*—Seventh day
Significance: The Sabbath is the most significant religious celebration besides the Day of Atonement. By setting aside a day every week exclusively for worship and reflection on the meaning of life, the Jews showed their

independence of the pagan nature-gods that demanded working *every* day to ensure material success. Instead, they honor the God of time and history who (1) is Creator and (2) enters into human history to aid and save creation.

When: From sundown on Friday to sundown on Saturday. Just before sunset every Friday, the wife and mother light the Sabbath candles. Bread and wine open the evening meal amid the scent of sweet spices. The Sabbath is spent discussing, studying, meditating, and praying over the teachings of the Torah.

Celebration: Passover *(Pesach)*—Seder Feast

Significance: The anniversary of Israel's liberation from Egypt. The Seder is the Passover Meal. No joyous festivities are permitted, including weddings, for the next forty-nine days after Passover.

When: Held at home in late March or early April during the full moon.

Celebration: *Shevout* or *Shabout* (formerly Pentecost)

Significance: The festival of the giving of the Torah, of God revealed to Moses on Sinai. It is a day of confirmation (Bar Mitzvah or Bat Mitzvah).

When: Held on the day of the new moon on the fiftieth day after the day of the Seder.

Celebration: High Holy Days (1) *Rosh Hashana*

Significance: Jewish New Year's Day, which opens a ten-day period of repentance.

When: Begins in September or October with the blowing of the ram's horn, the *shofar*.

Celebration: (2) Yom *Kippur*

Significance: Day of Atonement, or Sabbath of Sabbaths—a day of strict fasting.

When: Held ten days after Rosh Hashana.

Celebration: *Succot* or *Sukkoth*

Significance: The Feast of Booths (Tents), which commemorates God's grace and protection during the time when the Israelites lived in the desert.

When: Held in the fall around Thanksgiving. Many Jewish families and most Jewish congregations erect booths. Originally, the roofs were made of tree branches,

The Seder is celebrated yearly as part of Passover.

The Hebrew Scriptures: Called by the Father

Jewish Life Sanctified

Jews recognize the importance of various events with celebrations. The events listed below make up the major Jewish celebrations.

1. Eight days after birth: **Circumcision.** This ceremony incorporates the child into the covenant of Abraham. (A child born of a Jewish mother is automatically a Jew.)

2. Thirty-one days after birth of male firstborn: **Presentation** (redemption) of firstborn son. The Presentation releases the firstborn from service to God, to whom all firstborn were to be dedicated.

3. Puberty (age 13): **Bar Mitzvah** (boys); **Bat Mitzvah** (girls). This ritual calls the male Jew to observance of the Law and marks the individual's commitment. From this time on he may don the phylacteries *(telfillin)* at prayer. Reform and Conservative Jews have a Bat Mitzvah ceremony for girls. Bar Mitzvah means "son of the commandment" — that is, one who is obligated to observe the commandments. Bat Mitzvah means "daughter of the commandment."

4. Age 15, 16: **Confirmation.** This event marks a group commitment to the Law after graduation from nine or ten days of religious elementary training in Jewish history, law, customs, and traditions.

5. Marriage: *Kiddushin* (sanctification). Standing under a canopy, which represents the home the married couple will establish, and drinking wine, a sign of the goodness of life, the couple are married in the presence of the rabbi.

6. Death: *Viddui.* The dying person makes a faith confession (the final act of acceptance of death), prays to God to protect those left behind, and recites the Shema. After burial, there are seven days of mourning. Kaddish is the Jewish prayer recited by mourners after the death of a relative. For one year, children recite special prayers of thanks each month in the synagogue on the anniversary of the death.

When a Jewish male is able to accept the responsibilities of adulthood, he celebrates the Bar Mitzvah.

and fruits, flowers, and greenery were placed inside. Some Jews slept in these booths.

Celebration: Rejoicing over the Torah or *Simachas Torah*

Significance: This is a celebration of another complete reading of the Torah during the preceding year.

When: Held eight days after Succot. A procession, with song and dance, of the sacred scrolls from the ark in the synagogue.

Celebration: *Hanukkah* or *Chanukah*

Significance: The Feast of Lights, which commemorates the rededication of the Temple by Judas Maccabeus in 165 B.C.E.

When: Held near the time of the Christian celebration of Christmas. Like Christmas, Hannukah features gift-giving and special meals.

Celebration: *Purim*

Significance: The Feast of Lots associated with the Book of Esther, which celebrates deliverance of the Jews from persecution through Esther's courageous and patriotic action.

When: Held in late February or March. A joyous celebration with a carnival atmosphere, similar to Mardi Gras.

---

11. *Read Articles 4 and 5 of the Vatican II document, "Declaration on the Relation of the Church to Non-Christian Religions." In your own words, write a brief declaration of how Catholics and Jews should treat one another.*

12. *What insights into Christianity and modern changes in the Church did you gain from your study of Judaism? Write them in a paper to be submitted to the class. At what practical resolutions have you arrived? Note these in your paper.*

The Hebrew Scriptures: Called by the Father

Pronunciation Key

Aaron (**ehr**-on)
Abram (**ay**-bruhm)
Absalom (**ab**-seh-lehm)
Achish (eh-**keesh**)
Agag (eh-**gog**)
Ahab (**ah**-hahb)
Amalekites (eh-**mal**-eh-kights)
Ammonites (**am**-uh-nights)
Amos (**ay**-mehs)
anawim (**ah**-neh-wim)
Antiochus IV (an-tee-**ohk**-us)
Ashdod (**ash**-dod)

Barak (**bayr**-ehk)
Baruch (**bear**-uhk)
Bathsheba (bath-**shee**-beh)
Benjamin (**ben**-jeh-mehn)
Bethel (**beth**-ehl)
Boaz (**bo**-az)

Caleb (**kay**-lehb)
Canaan (**kay**-nehn)

Dagon (**day**-gon)
Decalogue (**dek**-ah-log)

Edom (**ee**-dehm)
Egypt (**ee**-jipt)
El Shaddai (ehl-shuh-**die**)
Eli (**ee**-ligh)
Elijah (i-**ligh**-jeh)
Elisha (i-**lish**-sheh)
Elkanah (ehl-**kay**-nuh)
ephod (**ef**-od)
Ephraim (**ee**-fruhm)
Epiphanes (eh-pi-**fane**-us)
Esau (**ee**-saw)
Ezekiel (ee-**zee**-kyehl)

Gath (geth)
Gibeah (**gib**-i-eh)
Gideon (**gid**-i-ehn)
Goliath (geh-**ligh**-ehth)
Gomer (**goh**-mer)
Gomorrah (geh-**mor**-eh)
Goshen (**goh**-shehn)
Gulf of Aquaba (**ahk**-eh-bah)

Hagar (**hay**-gahr)
Haman (**hay**-mehn)
Hannah (**han**-eh)
Haran (**hair**-ehn)
Hasmonean (has-**mon**-ee-un)
Hezekiah (hez-eh-**kigh**-eh)
Hiram (**high**-rehm)
Holofernes (hoe-leh-**fair**-nees)

Hophni (**hohf**-nee)
Hosea (hoh**zay**-eh)
Hyksos (**hick**-sos)

Isaac (**eye**-zak)
Isaiah (igh-**zay**-eh)
Ishbaal (ish-**bay**-el)
Ishmael (**ish**-mi-ehl)
Ishmaelites (**ish**-mi-el-lites)

Jabesh-gilead (**jay**-behsh **gil**-ee-ehd)
Jacob (**jay**-cub)
Jael (**jay**-ehl)
Jebusites (**jeb**-yeh-sights)
Jephthah (**jef**-theh)
Jeremiah (jer-eh-**migh**-eh)
Jericho (**jer**-eh-koh)
Jeroboam (jer-eh-**boh**-ehm)
Jesse (**jes**-ee)
Jethro (**jeth**-roh)
Jezebel (**jez**-eh-behl)
Joab (**joh**-ab)
Job (johb)
Jonah (**jo**-nuh)
Joshua (**josh**-uh-eh)
Josiah (jo-**zi**-eh)
Judah (**joo**-dah)

Kiriath-jearim
    (**keer**-ee-aht yeh-**har**-eem)
Kish (kihsh)

Laban (**lay**-behn)
Leah (**lee**-eh)

Maccabees (**mak**-ah-beez)
Manasseh (meh-**nas**-eh)
Melchizedek (mel-**kiz**-eh-dek)
Mesopotamia (mes-ah-peh-**tay**-mi-eh)
Michal (**migh**-kehl)
Michmash Pass (**mick**-mash)
Midianites (**mid**-ee-eh-nightz)
Mordecai (**mohr**-deh-kigh)
Moses (**moh**-ziz)
Mount Sinai (**sigh**-nigh)

Naomi (nay-**o**-mee)
Nebuchadnezzar (neb-eh-kehd-**nez**-ehr)
Nehemiah (nee-heh-**mi**-eh)
Nineveh (**nin**-u-vah)

Peniel (peh-**nee**-ehl)
Peninnah (pin-**een**-uh)
Pentateuch (**pen**-teh-took)
pharaoh (**fehr**-oh)

Philistia (fi-**lis**-tih-uh)
Philistines (**fil**-is-tinz)
Phinehas (**phin**-ee-uhs)
Phoenicia (fi-**nee**-sheh)
plague (playg)
Port Zion-geber (hesh-yon-**geh**-ber)

Rachel (**ray**-chehl)
Rahab (**ray**-hab)
Rehoboam (ree-eh-**boy**-ehm)

Samson (**sam**-sehn)
Sarai (**sehr**-igh)
Shechem (**shek**-ehm)
Shema (sheh-**ma**)
Shiloh (**shigh**-loh)
Sisera (**sis**-eh-ruh)
Sodom (**sod**-ehm)

Terah (**tare**-eh)
theocracy (the-**ock**-reh-ce)
Torah (**tohr**-ah)

Ur (er)
Uriah the Hittite (you-**rye**-eh)
Uzziah (eh-**zigh**-eh)

vizier (**vichz**-i-ehr)

Yahweh (**yah**-weh)

Zedekiah (zed-eh-**ki**-eh)
Zerubbabel (zer-**u**-bub-el)
Ziklag (**zik**-lag)
Zion (**zigh**-ehn)

Index

People and Places

Index